TRANSITIONS

A WOMAN'S GUIDE
TO SUCCESSFUL
RETIREMENT

TRANSITIONS

A WOMAN'S GUIDE TO SUCCESSFUL RETIREMENT

Diana Cort-Van Arsdale
and Phyllis Newman

HarperCollinsPublishers

TRANSITIONS: A WOMAN'S GUIDE TO SUCCESSFUL RETIREMENT. Copyright © 1991 by Diana Cort-Van Arsdale and Phyllis Newman. All rights reserved. Printed in the United States of America. No part of this book may be used or reproduced in any manner whatsoever without written permission except in the case of brief quotations embodied in critical articles and reviews. For information, address HarperCollins*Publishers*, 10 East 53rd Street, New York, N.Y. 10022.

ISBN 0-06-016278-3
Library of Congress 90-55929

91 92 93 94 95 DT/RRD 10 9 8 7 6 5 4 3 2 1

To our parents,
Arthur and Augusta (Gus) Deutsch,
who brought us together and taught us
that doing the impossible was not extraordinary.

Contents

Acknowledgments

From Diana Cort-Van Arsdale

To my husband Leonard, who promised me bright sunny days and brought them to me.

To my children Hayley and Daniel on whom I shine and who give me so much back.

To my nephew Allen, who helped me conquer the computer with many wise words, the ones I like best are, "think of it like a telephone."

To the Big Six Towers Bench women, circa 1965, Chris Fliesler, Adele Hahn, Hannah Kates, Naomi Mark, Marcia Menasse, and Elaine Salzman. Their friendship which began when we were all young mothers has helped move me undaunted into my retirement.

To all of my patients who taught me while I listened.

From Phyllis Newman

To my husband Stan for his endless patience and fortitude.

To my son Allen who always believed in me. He alone knew I could not only write a book but also master the computer.

To the women of Green Valley, Arizona, particularly Virginia Gardner, Claudia Hall, Rose Mikesell, Shirley Purviance, who allowed me to share their thoughts and experiences.

Both of us want to thank Connie Clausen, our agent for recognizing a book hidden in our early efforts, and Susan Randol, our editor at HarperCollins for her enthusiasm and encouragement.

Above all, we want to thank the many women who spoke to us with candor about their lives.

Writing this book has been a true partnership/collaboration. We talked, laughed and encouraged each other. This book is a tribute to our sisterhood in the truest sense of the word.

Introduction

How in the world did* I get to be fifty? How did it happen that several months later I was fifty-five? How did this happen when I had just finished saying good-bye to my children as they boarded the bus for their first day of school? That I had become fifty-five was one of my life's biggest surprises. The fact that I am now beginning to consider my own retirement seriously is an even bigger surprise. My sister Phyllis and I began to develop the material for this book because of the shock we felt when retirement seemed thrust upon us.

I went to college right after high school, finished college, went to graduate school for a master's degree in social work, married, worked for four years, and then had my children. I stayed home to be a wife and mother when my children were young and I returned to my career in social work when my children started school. I worked with great satisfaction as a clinical social worker and administrator of a mental health clinic for twenty-five years. About five years ago my husband began talking about reducing his working hours, which started us thinking rather abstractly about retiring. And then I got the shocking news that my sister Phyllis and her husband had decided to retire and relocate at the end of the year. Several years

* D.C.-V.A.

before they had bought a vacation home in Arizona with the vague plan of moving there some day. Now this was fast becoming a reality. Phyllis was leaving her profession, her city, her friends, and her family, but, most important, me!

She too had had a successful professional career while she managed house and family. She had worked for more than twenty years as a teacher and psychologist. We had been close friends since we were teenagers and we had shared the intimacies of our lives, our feelings about our marriages, our children, our friends, and our jobs. Now, we suddenly found ourselves talking about Phyllis's decision to retire. We spoke about her hopes, dreams, and aspirations for the next part of her life. How odd! We'd never spoken about this before. The retirement issues brought up many complicated feelings involving autonomy, separation, and aging. We began to realize that when we were talking about Phyllis's retirement situation, we were talking not only about her unique problems, but also about special and specific problems facing the women of today.

We began to examine the available literature on retirement. Many studies on preretired and retired persons have been done. Most note the importance of emotional adjustment, and several strongly suggest working on emotional adjustment in preretirement courses and workshops. However, there is little practical information in the retirement literature, and the professionals working in the field of retirement have only begun to follow through on this suggestion.

We discovered that most of the books available on retirement were for men only, or for women as part of a couple. The advice given to women in these books basically came down to keeping communication with your husband open, keeping your husband out of the kitchen, and finding a hobby. Many pamphlets and books included lists of hobbies. The remainder of the literature gave financial advice as well as information on where to retire.

With no maps to chart her way, Phyllis began to think of herself as a pioneer who was about to travel into unknown territory. She had to be ready for problems she could not anticipate.

As each new problem and emotional reaction arose we began to look for some framework in which to explore her feelings. What were the similarities with other stressful times of her life? How had she coped with other transitions through which she had lived? Was she unique in her anxieties? Had she planned sufficiently? How had this retirement decision been made? Was there actually an ideal plan for retirement?

What does retirement mean to those of us who are contemplating retirement today? We are the first generation of liberated women, whether or not we took a direct part in the women's movement, whether or not we felt the impact in a personal way. As a result we have feelings and ideas about our identity that differ from those of previous generations of women. This means we need to redefine retirement. The previous conceptions of this time of life have little meaning within the current structure of women's lives.

Many of the women who are facing retirement today fought for equal pay and equal status. Many were involved in initiating the concept of an identity separate from that of wife and mother. Many moved into a life of emotional and financial independence never dreamed of by women of their mothers' generation. What does retirement mean to them?

Many women were less directly involved, but no woman has been unaffected by the women's movement. As a result of the change in attitudes, most married women of this generation have had two careers: first, wife, wife and mother; second, a job outside the home. Think of the unique problems that arise for them as the retirement years come into view. While men's careers are reaching their peak after more than twenty-five years, many women who entered the work force after their children were grown are still thinking of making their mark. These women do not want to retire in the traditional sense. What do the retirement years mean to them?

Retirement issues have not yet been addressed by the women's movement. To many women retirement means a step backward to the preliberation days. Many of this liberated generation say, "Not me, I'll never retire." But why not? Why should women not have the same benefits as men at this time of life? Why not a change? Why not a more relaxed life? Many women are curious about retirement, but don't know what to expect. For several years prior to the writing of this book Phyllis and I conducted discussion groups for women. It was apparent that many of these women who were over forty had specific and vital concerns about their retirement. When we decided to write this book, we realized we had a natural resource in the women who were in our groups as well as the women we saw in our individual practices of psychotherapy. When we traveled and conducted workshops we enlarged our network of women who were concerned with this new time of transition. Being at that time of life ourselves, we know many women in the pre-retirement and retirement time of their lives.

When we initially began our research we conducted open-ended interviews. These inquiries and the concomitant responses helped us to devise our questionnaires. We then had most of the women answer our questionnaires at their leisure, and we interviewed them for follow up assessment and discussion. All of the women in our research finished high school and many had finished college. They all were interested in self-awareness and in improving the quality of their lives. The women were all financially secure, albeit with some financial concerns. (At the time of our interviews, most were not focused on the economic considerations necessary for a successful retirement.) Although most of the women were from large cities, we were fortunate to be able to interview women from all over the United States, including women from various retirement communities. We have changed most of the names of the women we interviewed and have made composites of several of the women.

Through our research, Phyllis and I came to the conclusion that a woman's retirement years are a unique time and must be planned for in a particular way. Some women may choose to work forever in their job or career, just as some women chose not to work outside the home. The operative word is *choose* and the important word is *plan*. The fact is that, for most, the time comes when retirement has to be addressed. Friends, relatives, or colleagues will be considering what to do when they retire. Husbands may begin to plan for their day of retirement. The interests common to the people in the workplace change as you become the older worker. No matter what your physical condition, the pace and the hours take more of a toll. Ready or not, like it or not, retirement becomes an issue. What you choose to do and what you plan are up to you.

As Phyllis and I continued our dialogue and our research, we discovered many issues that shaped the decisions women made about their retirement years. The impact of the early years, the youthful fantasies of what life should and would be, the realities of marriage and motherhood all have a place in the decision-making process. The significant relationships a woman develops over a lifetime play an important part in her decisions. Most important for many is the issue surrounding the meaning of the work itself, and whether it had been in or outside the home.

We considered the possibility of putting all women together as having the same retirement issues. Are there common denominators in retirement for women regardless of whether they are single, married, widowed, or divorced? What is each woman retiring from? What is she retiring to?

Confounding any discussion of this time of life is a new social phenomenon, "the sandwich generation." This concerns the women who find themselves caring for children and parents simultaneously. Children come home from college or perhaps from a failed marriage at the same time many elderly parents need more time and attention. What are the priorities and options here?

We are in many ways the first generation confronting these situations and our pioneering experience will be a model for future generations.

In the last third of our life we will need new attitudes and new courage. We are not being fair to ourselves if we sit in one place and watch our arteries harden. In our fifties we find for the first time that we are talking about how much time is left, rather than how much time has passed. For the first time in our lives we know we are no longer young. We cannot quite believe it, but we are faced with the fact that other people can. What are the best ways to handle our new feelings of mortality? What is the impact of these feelings on the retirement years? How are these feelings coloring *your* decisions at this time?

Life expectancy for women is now more than eighty years, and the quality of life is expected to be good. With what conflicts do we need to make emotional peace so that we can enjoy the next twenty-five or more years of our lives? What can we do now to prepare ourselves for the future? Whether single, widowed, married, or divorced, we will live longer and healthier lives. We will continue to cope with life's demands, our own expectations, and our need for emotional security. If we plan well, we can use this next block of time with energy, satisfaction, and joy.

This book will help women plan, before retirement, for a fulfilling life accompanied by emotional security. It will also help women in the early years of retirement enhance their lives. We have anecdotes, discussions, and questionnaires designed to help you begin a journey toward self-knowledge. We give you a framework within which you can examine the many roles you have played throughout your life, and the changes you have gone through as you matured. We give you a structure in which to assess your current attitudes toward your life situation. We define the problems you may encounter as you make your decision and begin this next phase of your life. We guide you through the process of making successful choices. The self-knowledge you acquire will allow you to develop new abilities, new ways of coping and enjoying the future so you will have more power and control over the next important years of your life. We will help each of you realize your options and use your unique strengths to develop new abilities and ways of coping with the future.

I

Women's Lives Are Different Now

To be nobody but myself—in a world which is doing its best, night and day, to make you everybody else—means to fight the hardest battle.

E. E. CUMMINGS (1894–1962)

So Larry and Susan retired. They waved good-bye to their friends and family and moved from Minnesota to New Mexico. Financially secure, both in good health, young in heart, happily married for thirty-two years, a dream come true. Two years later, Larry was delighted, Susan was bored, disillusioned, vaguely depressed, deeply dissatisfied, and unable to figure out what had gone wrong.

A woman's retirement gone awry. Certainly not the first.

Avoidable? Absolutely!

What had gone wrong?

Susan had always been thoughtful about her life. She finished college in the 1950's when women were expected to find a husband while in college or at least a year or two after graduation. Susan met Larry in her senior year of college and they got married one year later. She worked for two years, became pregnant, and left her job in her eighth month of pregnancy to stay at home to be a wife and mother. Three years later another child was born. Although Susan enjoyed staying home, she looked forward to going back to work. When her children were twelve and nine years old and Susan was thirty-five, she and Larry decided that it would be a good idea for her to go back to work.

She found a job as an administrator in a small growing business in downtown Minneapolis. The money was helpful, for Susan and Larry anticipated that both their children would be going to college. The family also began to rely on her income for extras. Susan's organizational and administrative talents enabled her to grow with the company. She became a part of upper management.

Twenty-two years later, both children had finished college and moved into their own apartments. Larry was sixty-two, Susan was fifty-seven, and Larry was ready to retire to New Mexico where he felt the quality of their life would be better and where he could enjoy the easier winters.

Susan and Larry had planned their retirement for at least two years. With his profit sharing, her pension, and careful planning and spending until Social Security cut in when he was sixty-five and she was sixty-two, they could manage. In fact, they agreed they could travel and have most of the things they wanted.

Susan knew that her job had been an important part of life, but she figured she'd find "something to do" in New Mexico. She didn't think it was necessary to probe this situation any further. After all, she was looking forward to spending carefree time with Larry. Didn't they both deserve the good life?

What Susan had neglected to assess were her own needs, separate from Larry's. She did not have a sense of how different she had become from the Susan who came of age in the 1950's. She had been raised by a mother whose life centered on her home and family. She had expected to follow her mother's path. Although she was aware that her life had gone in a different direction, she did not realize that she had become a woman who needed identification and involvement aside from her marriage.

She changed her lifestyle and even some of her priorities as society's values changed, but she had not thought to examine some of her basic assumptions regarding marriage and personal needs. She embarked upon retirement without recognizing how profoundly different her life would be. She needed to know her inner self better if she and Larry were going to have the good life.

This would not have been necessary if Susan had been living in her mother's generation. Although she may have had some ambitions beyond her home, she would not have had the opportunity to be as successful at her career—indeed, if she had had a career at all. She would not have experienced the same job satisfaction or the sense of personal achievement. More important, she would now be seeing herself first and foremost as Larry's wife. Retirement would not have been her decision. If she had had any sense of dissatisfaction or unrest it would have been denied or passed off as "women's problems." Her husband's happiness would be primary.

If Susan is to cope successfully with retirement, she needs to find the many ways in which she is different from her mother. She also needs to discover some of the ways in which she is similar. She needs to find how her values have changed since she came of age in the 1950's . . . and the ways in which they have not changed. The retirement model of the cottage for two, shopping, cooking, golf, travel, this is not enough for Susan as she is today.

Anita has been a teacher for thirty years. She began teaching as soon as she finished college and always enjoyed it. She lived with her parents until they died eight years ago when she was fifty. She never married and has remained close to her brother and sister-in-law and to her nephews and nieces. She has several friendly relationships but has always been at ease in her own company. Anita has especially enjoyed working with the children, and she has taken pleasure in camaraderie with other teachers. With several of her friends she was active in the teachers' union.

In the past six years, Anita's life has slowly started to change. Her nieces and nephews have finished high school and started college out of town. Her brother and sister-in-law are more involved with each other as they are experiencing the pleasures of the empty nest. She finds she is spending less time with them. Although Anita still likes her work, she finds fewer challenges. Perhaps of more significance to her, many of her married friends have retired or have set dates to retire. As her friends leave, she has less in common with her new colleagues.

Anita doesn't want to retire yet. During the past few years, however, early in the morning, she has begun to feel that perhaps there are other things she could do with her life. She is frightened at the thought of retirement, although work has lost much of its luster. She questions what her job means to her, and wonders what she wants to do. Although she had never thought of herself as an unhappy person, she has begun to feel much less energetic and just a little sad. She needs some help in finding answers.

Had Anita been living in her mother's generation, her life as the dedicated and devoted teacher might have sustained her. She might never have begun to question the way she was feeling. She would have felt fortunate as a "spinster" to have been able to support herself and would have been content with whatever family involvement was available.

The changing role of women has changed Anita's view of herself and her options just as it has changed her life in the past twenty-five years. Single women now expect to be independent and mobile. They look for and find fulfilling lives. The future no longer has to be merely a continuation of the present. Life is waiting to be lived. What Anita has to do is decide what she wants it to be. The answer is within her, but she must do some self-assessment to find it.

Too often we unconsciously hold on to an ideal of conduct different from the way we actually live our lives. We grow up internalizing a set of values, mores, and expectations. We change our actions and adjust our behavior, but the values set in our unconscious still motivate us. As we move from one place in life to another, we still tote some of the old baggage. The old values and expectations become burdens that must be shrugged off so that we can choose new behaviors to suit our needs.

What happened to Susan as she went off to have fun with Larry? They had a good marriage, they cared about each other, but because of Susan's early orientation, she was not prepared for the empty space in her life left by an aborted career.

Anita, too, despite her independence, her travel to far-off places, and her financial freedom, could not envision life outside teaching. She could not emotionally open her horizons despite her intellectual awareness of the opportunities. She is fearful and still carries the myth of the "spinster's lot" around in her head.

The questionnaire "You and the Women's Movement" which follows is more open-ended than the others will be. It will help you assess just how much you have changed your values and expectations over the years. These questions are designed to help you understand the extent to which the women's movement has affected you. It is important for you at this time of transition to discover your unique relationship to the societal changes you have lived through. There are two aspects to your understanding. One is connected to your age and time of life when this revolution began, and the other is a function of your early conditioning. This questionnaire will enable you to consider both these aspects and will facilitate your understanding of yourself. Although you may now feel that the effect of the women's movement was minimal, when your assessment is completed you may be in for a surprise.

As you go through the questionnaire, try to keep in mind myths concerning femininity that you may have stored away. Try to balance the old values with the way you actually live your life. How do you respond to the opportunities around you? If you have utilized the opportunities, do you know what effects they have had on your life? If you've been aware of the opportunities but afraid to take advantage of them, perhaps this questionnaire will help you to feel more free to pursue them.

Find a quiet time to reflect on yourself. Driving alone is a good opportunity for this. Standing at the sink and washing dishes is a good time to dream along. (The advent of the dishwasher should not discourage you if you need time to reflect.) You know what times will work for you.

Perhaps one question will strike you as more interesting than another. That's fine; stay with that. Being drawn to one sentence, one idea, one question instead of another is an important landmark for your meanderings.

Don't think of this as a questionnaire that demands specific answers. Have fun. Take your time. Relish the opportunity to explore some inner secrets. Your life is changing, you are entering a new phase and it is time to prepare!

You and the Women's Movement: Questionnaire

Question 1. What were you doing between 1950 and 1960—High school, college, married, children, working, other? Were you just beginning your adult life or were you already established?

Question 2. Did you feel that your mother's life was one you wanted to emulate? Was there any other woman you admired?

Question 3. How did you feel about the women's movement when you first became aware of it?

- Did you respond, "Right on! Tell me more!"?
- Were you fearful of it?
- Did you feel it was nonsense or not important?

Question 4. Many women were caught up in the excitement and pressure of the women's movement before they had sufficient time to assess their individual needs and priorities.

- Did you discover that the women's movement did not fulfill its promise to you?
- If so, in what way would you have things different?

Question 5. You may have ambivalent feelings about the lifestyle and the opportunities of the young women of today, both socially and in terms of career.

- Do you envy them?
- Do you feel sorry for them?
- Are you sympathetic to their goals?

Question 6. Do you have a daughter? If yes, describe her life. Does she have a career? Is she married? Does she have both a husband and a career?

Questions 7 and 8 are for married women only.
Question 7. Do you have friendships with women that are separate from your marriage?

Question 8. Do you spend some leisure time involved in activities without your husband?

Question 9. Many women feel that they would have lived their lives differently if they had had the opportunities available to the young women of today. What would you do differently in terms of:

- Job or career?
- Marriage?
- Children?

You and the Women's Movement: Assessment

1. What were you doing between 1950 and 1960? Was adulthood just beginning for you? If so, you were just leaving school, in the early days of marriage, or in the early days of a first job. You were on the fringe of the change in women's lives. Now you may be in the most confused group of women in transition. You spent the first twenty years of your life believing that home, family, and marriage assured you a "happy ever after," and you spent the next twenty years watching the beliefs in these institutions undergo great alterations. You expected to work until you married, became pregnant, and began your life as wife and mother. You probably saw your job as just that—a job—rather than as the first step in a career as the young women today regard it.

Marriage and family were the only goals for women—college-educated or not. College was often the way to get a husband first and then get enough education to keep up with him, as his career advanced. (How many young women of the 1950s aspired to marry a doctor or lawyer? Young women today go on to become the doctors and lawyers themselves.) Long-term goals probably did not seem important because women did not like to look beyond motherhood to menopause and what was considered the pain of the empty nest. It was not really spoken of —just dreaded.

If you belong in this transitional group there is much for you to sort out, but it will be worth the effort. Concentrate on your early perceptions and expectations. See if you are able to assess their influence on your current outlook and status. Life changed considerably in the 1960's and 1970's but the internal standards of many women did not. There are many myths dating back to the 1950's that are not yet ancient history.

For example, consider the belief that men do not cherish women who are smart and capable. Many women, particularly of this age group, are wary of speaking their minds in social situations that include men. Women, married or single, who matured during this period never dared to voice an opinion or make a strong statement in mixed company.

Tradition dictates that a husband's needs are primary and that his wife's needs are secondary. That this is not yet a dead issue is exemplified by the married woman who is still reluctant to ask her husband to be on his own for dinner even though she has something on her schedule. It is extremely difficult to shed your early conditioning.

Are any of the above ideas still lurking in your unconscious mind as part of your inner standards? Do you still have a sense that life after the childbearing years is only half a life? If you are unmarried, do you feel you are a failure and that you can never be fulfilled as a single person? If you were entering adulthood in the 1950's your perceptions and expectations were influenced by many of these current attitudes. True, women's lives are different now, but the older notions may still exert a strong pull.

As you evaluate your readiness to enter the next phase of your life, see if you are still subscribing to any of these old ideals. If you are, examine them closely and decide how valid they are for your life today.

Susan was surprised at what she discovered about herself as she reflected on these earlier times. She had almost forgotten her original goal, which was to be the devoted housewife and mother. She thought she had given this up when she went into the business world and set new goals for herself.

She had successfully managed her house and children with help from Larry while she was working. No one complained, and in fact the family was supportive of her outside responsibilities. She was, however, aware that she was still in charge of the household. At the time this did not seem significant to her.

As she evaluated her circumstances, Susan began to understand what had happened to her when she and Larry retired. She no longer had the responsibility of her job, so by an unspoken agreement from their earlier conditioning, Larry and Susan assumed that Susan would resume all the household chores. Larry liked to have three meals a day and Susan returned to her former conditioning to prepare breakfast, lunch, and dinner. Susan planned her daily activities around Larry's needs. Despite a successful career and "liberated" lifestyle, Susan had not changed her values. At this time of her life she did not question the concept of women's responsibilities. She became the devoted housewife and was very unhappy.

As Susan began to understand her dilemma, she began to see options. She saw that the situation had as much to do with her expectations as with Larry's. She knew she would be able to speak with him once she understood what the problem was and what changes she might make. She knew that she needed a more independent life and that she would have to plan for this.

Susan is now thinking of training to work as a docent in the local science museum. She has negotiated the household chores with Larry, and he is responsible for making his own lunch in addition to doing the grocery shopping. Susan is on her way to an accommodation between her conditioning as a young woman and her changed needs as a retired woman of the 1990s.

If you were well into the life of an adult by the decade between 1950 and 1960, you were of the group of women who entered adulthood during the years of World War II. Your perceptions and experiences are different from those of your friends who are ten to fifteen years younger. Women in this older age group had less conflict about the female role than did the women in the younger age group. These older women were already set in the traditional mold when the changes in society began.

They were nurtured with the same myths as their younger sisters, and most of them did not think to question the validity of the life they were leading. For most, the women's movement was more of a curiosity rather than a pertinent issue at that time. If they were unmarried they were set in a suitable job or career and much less liable to think about a different life. If married they were already on the track that included house, suburbs, and children and were unable to think seriously about changes. They did not question their values until later on.

If you fall into this category, Betty Friedan was writing about you in *The Feminine Mystique*, the *Uncle Tom's Cabin* of the women's movement. She expressed the dissatisfaction and feeling of suffocation felt but not understood by many women. She expressed the feelings of helplessness and tried to explain them. She was writing about you but many of you did not take heed until much later.

You probably continued the traditional path and did not modify your direction for many years. Married women eventually may have returned to school or entered the work force when their children were older. If you were not married, you took advantage of new opportunities and mobility in living arrangements and leisure time, although often you were not able to do the same in your job or career. If you followed the traditional route, you were certainly aware of the choices available to your younger friends and, eventually, to your children.

Have you ever examined your feelings about your life in relation to the changes in society's attitudes toward women? Have you explored the issue of self-fulfillment? If you expanded your life in some way, either with school, job, or outside interests, and if you achieved a sense of satisfaction, did you measure its importance in terms of your marriage? Did you ever explore the reason why you opted for more than marriage?

As we spoke with the women in this age category we discovered that most of them had not given much thought to the changes that their lives had undergone. When they did begin to consider their choices along the way, each had a time when she would have gone a different path if she had lived in today's society. This was not an occasion for regrets or recriminations but the occasion for a reassessment of values now that a time of decision was at hand.

You may accept yourself and your lifestyle today and expect to continue along the same way in retirement. If you are comfortable with this, there is no reason to explore further. If, now that you have explored your inner attitudes, you would like to make some modifications, this is a time to do so. These retirement years are a bonus and by reflecting on your choices in relation to your current values you can better determine your future options.

The women of today who were still preteens or young teens in the 1950s have less excess baggage. If this is you, you grew up in the age of self-realization heralded by *The Feminine Mystique*. You probably more comfortably reconciled your femininity with your need for self-fulfillment. You may in retirement have less difficulty than your older friends considering the importance of your needs in relationship to the others in your life. Other expectations and mores of our society, however, may still be a part of your feminine heritage. Be aware, that the feminine myths that shaped your perceptions and expectations can suddenly become unwanted, unexpected obstacles. Look, especially, for your true feelings concerning yourself as a woman in the labor market.

Examine your status in your marriage. Are you still the primary homemaker and caretaker? Are you content with this? If you have no conflict with your situation then you needn't examine further. If you are aware of a certain sense of dissatisfaction, determine your expectations of yourself before you try to make changes. You may be the one who is holding on to an image that does not fit your current situation.

No matter what your age group, if you are contemplating retirement the information you get about yourself in answer to *question 1* will help you put the girl you were in historical perspective. This information will help you to understand the pressures of society which molded the differences as well as the similarities between the woman you are now and the young woman of yesterday who did not aspire beyond a husband and children. To successfully move on to the next phase, you must know the influences that shaped you.

2. *Do you admire your mother (or some other woman) and wish to emulate her life?* If you can remember your feelings about the way your mother lived her life it will help you reflect on your own life. Try not to evaluate from today's perspective but try to recapture the child's viewpoint. This may take some new ways of thinking. Perhaps you remember how easy it seemed for your mother to care for her house, cook meals, and be available for you and your brothers and sisters. Did you grow up thinking this was what your life was to be like when you grew up? Did this seem okay for you? Or did your mother's life seem like a good deal of drudgery? Did you say you would never do what your mother was doing? Was your father the one you envied because he was in charge? Was that an issue with you even then? Is it still?

If your mother was the major force in the family perhaps your life as a woman in the modern world has less conflict. The feeling that women are powerful gave you the hope that you too could have power. If you saw your mother as subservient and powerless, the struggle to identify yourself as powerful has been a more difficult task.

Mothers are the first and most important models and their influence always makes an impact. You probably have not given thought to the way your mother might be influencing you at this time of your life, but this is a good time to start to think about your mother in a special context.

Most of the women who grew up in the fifties and sixties remember their mothers as housewives. Although some women worked outside of the home, this was not the norm. It was not unusual for a woman to devote her life to her children and to consider her children's lives as an extension of her life. Many women enjoyed their lives as housewives and mothers. They were on their own schedules, did their work as they pleased, and enjoyed their independence. What could be bad about this?

Most little girls grew up thinking this would be their life. You probably did too. You probably never questioned as a child or even as an adolescent that you too would care for a home and family. The women's movement changed your direction, but unconsciously many women still cling to the fantasy that staying home and keeping house is the most comfortable life. After all, the biggest influence on the present is the past, and fantasies and expectations from an early time do not easily vanish.

Jane is a fifty-six-year-old woman who grew up during World War II. Her mother was a housewife who loved her home, enjoyed the domestic life, and felt fulfilled by shopping, cooking, and cleaning. During the war years she involved herself in the war effort. She became an air-raid warden, planted a victory garden, and kept house creatively in spite of the various shortages. She had a happy marriage and was involved in her children's lives and in her daily routine. Although Jane experienced her mother as a contented person, she knew that her father, who worked outside the home and "brought home the bacon," was the powerful person. Jane wanted to be like her mother but she envied her father's power.

Jane went to college and became a librarian. This offered her the opportunity to have an interesting career and be financially independent. Today Jane has a successful career and a successful marriage. Now that she is considering retirement she is concerned about staying home during the day and having more time for household responsibilities. She really wants to try the life her mother enjoyed, but she is afraid that she will lose her power and position if she follows her preference. She still believes that housewives are subservient. Jane needs to reassess the reality of the power in her life today in relation to her early perceptions so she does not remain shackled to the ghosts of her past.

If this is your conflict, you should remember the operative word *choose*. Women of yesterday had few choices, but today the choices are many. This is not the time to consider whether you would have taken a different path; rather, it is time to consider what part of your mother's life you might enjoy now that you have come to retirement. It is important to remember that giving up a job outside of the home is not the same as giving up power. Power is where you are. If you think you will enjoy the shopping, cooking, and cleaning part of your life, you can choose to do as much of it as you want and stop when you want. Control over your choices gives you power and you can be in control when you retire. Why devalue the things you enjoy? This is the time of your life when you can set the standards and make the rules.

Some children who grew up in the 1950s and 1960s saw their mothers' lives as unfulfilled and knew they did not want to emulate them. The thought of being subservient to men and living through their children's lives was antithetical to them. They became the generation of liberated women who embraced the ideals of the women's movement and looked for fulfillment outside the home. These women were determined they would not sacrifice their needs, values, and desires.

Camille is a fifty-eight-year-old woman who worked most of her life as a bookkeeper. She remembers her mother as being totally under the influence of her father. She experienced her mother's life as circumscribed and limited and saw her mother as unfulfilled and powerless. She vowed she would never have her mother's life. She knew that a career would be her ticket to independence and knew she would not be a housewife when she married. This was an unusual stance in the 1950's and Camille felt vaguely guilty about it. Her marriage had some difficult times because her husband wanted her to be a more traditional wife. Although she loved being a mother, she went back to work as soon as her children could be left with baby-sitters.

Camille has worked for the past thirty years and is now on the brink of retirement. She is thinking it might be fun to stay home for a while after she retires. She has made one of her children's rooms into a study for herself, has redecorated her living room, and is even enjoying the cooking. She can't help but feel that something is wrong when she finds pleasure in these activities. A voice from the past is telling her that imitating her mother's domestic activities will leave her powerless. Camille is troubled by this feeling. This is the time for her to assess her pleasures and her priorities. She can expand her life's pleasures if she understands the ghosts from her past.

Were you one of those women who grew up thinking that self-fulfillment could only take place outside the home? If so, you may need to reassess aspects of your mother's life in order to move comfortably into your future.

OTHER FEMALE ROLE MODELS

Was there some other woman in your life who influenced you? Was this person someone you would not characterize as "wife and mother"? Many women had ambitions outside of marriage and motherhood. With few exceptions these ambitions were secondary to the marriage. Even Eleanor Roosevelt was a wife and mother first. If the person you admired had goals in addition to or instead of home and family, you probably had dreams beyond the traditional. Perhaps you felt unconsciously that women's lives should have other dimensions. For many reasons, you may not have pursued these goals but the idea was there.

Elaine remembered her mother as a traditional housewife. All the women neighbors had similar lives except her mother's friend Dorothy. Dorothy kept house but she also did clay sculpture. In her spare time, Dorothy went to her basement to sculpt, and she encouraged her own children as well as their friends to join her. She had wonderful paintings, sculptures, magazines, and books in her home, where there was a feeling of freedom and a sense of joy and love. Elaine sensed that Dorothy's ambitions and interests were different from her mother's. Dorothy spoke of art exhibitions and museums and interesting places away from the neighborhood. She told the children that someday her sculptures might be shown in a museum. Elaine learned from Dorothy that women could be creative, that they could have a passion and hopes and dreams that had little to do with their lives as homemakers.

Marilyn's mother was also a traditional wife and mother. Marilyn remembers her Aunt Sophie, her mother's sister, as the person who made a difference in her life. Sophie never married and lived alone. She had many friends and an occasional boyfriend who would come to visit. She had a job she loved, she took exciting trips to unusual places, and she owned her own car. (None of the women on Marilyn's block even drove a car.) Marilyn was fascinated by Sophie's freedom and independence. All the other women she knew were housewives and mothers. She dreamed that maybe one day she could be like Aunt Sophie.

The women who touched your life will never have the same impact as your mother, but it is likely these women showed you possibilities in life that you otherwise would not have known existed. Think back to the women who influenced your life, the women you wanted to emulate. They will have something to tell you once again. For Elaine, it is time to revisit Dorothy, the person who showed her a different way to be, the first woman Elaine knew who had a passion for creating and an ability to be original in her daily life. As Elaine admires and remembers this passion and originality, she may be able to use this knowledge as she begins to develop the next phase of her life.

3. *How did you first respond to the news of the women's movement?* Ah—the women's movement. We do not remember the day we became aware of it for the first time—not as we do Pearl Harbor (if you are old enough) or the assassination of President Kennedy —and yet it has changed and shaped everyone's life with equal force.

If you were captivated by the ideas, immediately joined a consciousness-raising group, and demonstrated in marches and parades (*statement a*), you know the impact it had. Most of you probably went to work or asserted your independence through some activity outside the home. You consider yourself and are considered by others to be a liberated woman. You will carry these ideas and ideals about yourself into retirement and there is every reason to believe that you will have a liberated retirement.

If this person is you, it is important to remember that the autonomy you enjoy may be the consequence of your work or activity; if this is the case, be certain that you look carefully at the impact of your *early* conditioning. Retirement from this part of your life makes it necessary to examine the feelings you have about yourself as a woman, feelings that are based on your early experiences. If you are not an introspective person and have not given some of these issues much thought, what you discover may surprise you.

Wendy had embraced the ideals of the women's movement almost as soon as it became a public issue. She went to college in 1960 when she was thirty-seven and a married woman with a ten-year-old son. She graduated from law school when she was forty-five in 1968. She is now considering retiring from her job as an attorney in a small law firm in a midwestern city. She finds herself with many questions, the important one being, Will she be forced to give up her independence when she leaves her job? What about her identity as a lawyer, which she has savored for the past twenty years?

Wendy sees her decision to join the women who strove for independence as rooted in her experiences during World War II. Although she was married then—her husband was in the service and away most of the time—she worked as a secretary to a congressman in Washington, D.C. She loved everything about her job and was an efficient and effective worker. She knew how to handle people and had good political instincts.

Over the four years she worked she received several promotions and earned a good salary. She was well on her way to a significant administrative job when the war ended. Forever after, she referred to the World War II era as the "best years of my life." Despite this, she never questioned the move back to her hometown with Herb when he returned from war. She never questioned her decision to be a housewife and mother. Indeed, she never really saw it as a decision.

Fifteen years later the women's movement exploded on the American scene, and Wendy became a part of it. She sees now that it was not an accident that she made her decision to begin a career when the opportunity presented itself; her early taste of individuality and independence had not been forgotten. She has a strong need for autonomy. Her ambivalence about her retirement is directly involved with her concerns about this. She would like to stop working but sees her career as the basis of her independence, and she is now becoming aware of how easily some of her earlier perceptions concerning the roles of women could interfere with this need.

If you as a liberated woman find yourself involved in this conflict, you must become aware of your true feelings concerning yourself as an independent woman even without your work.

If you were fearful of the women's movement (*statement b*), particularly in its early years, you are not alone. Several of the women we spoke with could remember worrying about compulsory government service or, even worse, coed public bathrooms. It is almost hard to believe, but the idea of women functioning on their own was new and different.

The fear that we are concerned with is more subtle and not always as consciously realized. Early conditioning had made many women feel uncertain about their abilities outside the home situation. Early conditioning had caused them to suppress their ambitions. Early conditioning had women dependent on the men in society, and many women enjoyed that status. Independence was a scary idea.

If you were or perhaps still are frightened by independence, you are a person who depends on others. If this style has worked for you and you are comfortable with your life and yourself, you needn't change. As you move into retirement, however, you may want to address some of these feelings and perhaps modify how you handle these needs. Statistically, a married woman can expect to live the last fifteen years of her life alone. Independence may be thrust upon you. As you continue this questionnaire and respond to the other questionnaires in the book, particularly focusing on transitions, the subject of Chapter II, you will gain insight into your feelings about independence and dependence and will find practical steps that you can take to modify the way you handle these feelings.

If you answered that you originally saw the women's movement as unimportant (*statement c*), you probably have taken a second look by now. It may have seemed like a passing fad at the beginning, but it has gone far beyond that. You do not have to do much reading or venture too far to recognize that a woman's life is different now.

Life is different for women of retirement age as well as for the younger women in society. A woman can expect to be physically and emotionally healthy into her eighth and even her ninth decade. If she is young in outlook and energetic in spirit there are many possibilities for her to enrich and fulfill herself as an individual.

Women are taken quite seriously in modern society: Businesses consider their needs as consumers, and politicians consider their wishes as voters. The medical profession, which now includes many women, has changed its attitude about women's illnesses. "Female complaint" is no longer a viable medical diagnosis. Physical ailments of menopause get serious consideration and treatment with hormones or medication if needed. So do emotional problems such as anxiety and depression. You are taken seriously and you must seriously consider yourself. The women's movement has given us this opportunity.

Anita remembered that when she first began hearing about Betty Friedan and the problems of women in society she thought the whole idea was pretty silly. She did not see that it had any direct relationship with her situation, since she was single, was teaching, and felt herself to be free and independent. As the years went on and she did not marry she never experienced the "bored, disillusioned, and unfulfilled" syndrome suffered by many of her friends. She went on with her life as a teacher and expanded her horizons with the many opportunities available to single women. But she never particularly credited the women's movement for her lifestyle.

As she looks back she is beginning to recognize how different her life might have been if she had listened to the early messages of the women's movement, which were not only for the unhappy housewife. She taught because that was what women did after they went to college, and she took care of her parents because single women were expected to perform and sacrifice in this way.

Anita has looked to the past not to feel regrets for what might have been but to free herself of her long-held myths and to consider possibilities ahead.

She has many trepidations but is beginning to see that she can reach beyond teaching; she is considering returning to school for a master's degree in chemistry or physics. It may be too late for medical school, but Anita feels that she may still be able to contribute in the area of research. Just contemplating the possibility has given her a sense of power and pleasure that she has not felt for years.

4. *Has the women's movement fulfilled its promise to you?* Josephine, who is fifty-five, earned her MBA in 1957 when not many women were considering business as a career. She went to work part-time for a small employment agency when her children were young. When she felt that her children were old enough she continued there on a full-time basis. She was responsible, capable, and creative and became an integral part of a company that eventually grew to be a large corporate business.

Although the director and owner of the agency acknowledged Josephine's abilities, the promotions went to men. He was a man who believed men should be in authority. He was willing to pay Josephine the salary she deserved but could never bring himself to make her a vice-president of the company. When she confronted the director with this he insisted that although she was capable the men he promoted were more so. There was little Josephine could do about her situation since the owner ran his company as he pleased. The work was challenging and rewarding and the money was good, but with no hope of promotion, the job had become a dead end.

For Josephine, the liberation movement's promise of equality in the workplace was not fulfilled. Equality between the sexes was supposed to follow if women worked hard and struggled for it. Many women have been able to negotiate changes in their marriages so that equality can prevail, but equality in the workplace has been a more difficult task. Most of the women of the 1950's and 1960's will have to make peace with the fact that equality in the workplace will not take place in their time.

Many women such as Josephine felt cheated. Their expectations had been high because of the promises made by the women's movement. They had done their best, and wanted to enjoy some of the power that had been promised. One of the results of this disappointment, for women who are working in what they consider to be dead-end jobs, is that their retirement decision is easier to make.

There are many other illustrations of the backlash to the women's movement. Did you get carried away in the excitement of self-fulfillment—only to find yourself wondering later what it was all about? "Is that all there is?" Do you think longingly of baking bread, redecorating the bedroom, or refinishing the bookcases instead of running the world?

If you can identify with some of these feelings of disappointment, if you have found the world of work not all you hoped for despite the fact that you have navigated a successful life, you might want to think about living a less pressured lifestyle in retirement. Perhaps this is the time to allow yourself to move at your own speed. You can begin again right now if you choose. And if your place is in the home, you have earned the chance to enjoy it. If you felt thwarted in your pursuit of power or authority in the workplace and like Josephine feel you are retiring from a dead end job, you may want to consider taking your talents to a community organization or a political party. If you choose well you will find yourself fulfilling your needs at the same time you perform a service.

You may want to consider utilizing your skills in a business of your own or perhaps on a consultant basis. The women's movement has made definite inroads in the community as a whole, whether or not it did so in your particular business or industry. You can find a welcome if you search realistically. You should refer to Chapter III—The Many Meanings of Work for more information on how to proceed in this area.

5. *How do you feel about the lifestyle of women today?* Discussions with older women concerning the lifestyle and opportunities available to the young women of today evoke very diverse feelings and opinions. Many women felt that the conflict between being feminine and being professionally competitive was insurmountable. They did not envy these young women their increased power and authority in industry and business because they felt the price was too high. The women who particularly did not envy the battle were those who had daughters or daughters-in-law involved with the issues and conflicts surrounding marriage-versus-career or motherhood-versus-career. They had seen it at close range and did not see young women having easy lives. Most of the older women did, however, envy the career alternatives available today and some regretted that they would never have a similar opportunity for power and control in their professional lives.

If you are envious of the young women of today in terms of career, or even in terms of available options, perhaps it is time for you to start pursuing some options of your own now that you are entering a new phase of your life. It is true that women facing retirement lack many opportunities available to women beginning adulthood, but there are many more options than your mothers would ever have dreamed possible. If you are searching, we can help you find these options.

In discussions with women fifty years old or older about the social aspects of the lives of the young women of today, we discovered that most look with dismay, envy, or at least great interest at the premarital living arrangements and the delaying of marriage. There were many opinions on the difficulties of younger people to commit themselves to a relationship. Examine your feelings carefully. Are they simply compassion for the many complications a young woman has to deal with today? Are you dismayed? Or do you pity them? A strong feeling of contempt may mask a feeling of envy. Are these attitudes tinged with your own regrets? Try to answer honestly. You will find out even more about your changing attitudes as you move into retirement in this different world.

This is hardly the time, nor are we even subtly suggesting that you change your commitment or your lifestyle, but it is not too late to have some independence and some freedom within the framework of your life. This is the time when you can look forward and evaluate your needs and assess priorities. A new phase of your life is beginning.

The older women of today are learning many lessons from the young, who are demonstrating the possibilities of a wide range of alternative lifestyles. As a result, all women are experiencing more options in their lives. The idea of a divorced or widowed woman living alone and enjoying her independence has become an important theme. These older women, widowed or divorced, who are having relationships with men to whom they are not married, discover options about the kind of living arrangements they want for the next phase of their lives.

Maureen was widowed at the age of fifty-seven. A year after her husband's death she joined a bereavement group. She met a man in the group whose wife had died several months before. They began seeing each other outside the group. They saw each other for about a year without telling their respective grown children, who were married with families, very much about their relationship. They are now at a crossroads. They want to continue to be with each other; they also want to travel together and to bring their extended families into their relationship. They do not, however, want to live together, since each wants to keep her or his home. They do want to be together when they choose. This way of life would have been antithetical to Maureen earlier in her life, but now it is an option. Although she feels conflicted about her plans, she thanks the young women of today for showing her the alternative.

6. *If you have a daughter, how would you describe her life?* Just as

you reflect your mother, your daughter reflects you. The two of you may be very good friends or you may feel you are totally separate. She has, nevertheless, internalized many of your values and your capabilities. See if you can figure out which of her attitudes toward her life reflect your values. It will help you. Maybe you can find the rebel in yourself or the achiever—or the traditionalist. Discover yourself in your daughter.

In what way is your daughter's life different from yours? One difference many women expressed was that their daughters married later in life and had their children later. One woman told us how she would compare herself with her daughter by thinking, "I was married when I was her age," or "I had a child when I was her age."

Young women of today often put off marriage and children because they have important practical and emotional work to do before they commit themselves to a relationship. These young women want to experience the world and their lives in a way women of the 1950's and 1960's never could. Young women want to be established, and they pursue their goals with a tenacity that surprises their mothers. For them, marriage and a family can wait until they have gained their independence.

Women of the 1950's and 1960's were taught to compromise their goals and defer to the needs of other people. Do you still want to do this with the same generosity? Can you take some lessons from your daughters and put yourselves first, particularly if you are doing something that is truly important to you? Retirement can be a time of great fulfillment and may be the time for you to be tenacious about your own needs.

Many other women spoke with incredulity of their daughters' independence compared with their timidity when they were of the same age. Gloria remembered a love affair she had had when she was nineteen that ended when her boyfriend went to Europe to study medicine. She didn't follow him because her family would not allow her to go to Europe unmarried and "alone." At the time she agreed. When her twenty-year-old daughter found herself in a similar situation, her daughter used a small inheritance from her grandfather and packed up and went to Europe to see where life took her. Although she asked Gloria's advice she was not in any way looking for permission. She had achieved a degree of autonomy and independence unknown to her mother. Gloria looks at her daughter's life with some envy, but more with admiration for her ability to challenge herself and meet the unknown.

What does Gloria's daughter's independence mean? To most women of Gloria's generation the possibilities and opportunities in life were always blocked by the expectations of others. The daughter navigates these with finesse because she doesn't see them as obstacles. Just keep in mind that your daughter did not become a woman of independence without some modeling or approval from her mother. Especially if you have a daughter like Gloria's, look for the opportunities for independence that will come your way during this next phase of your life. You may be surprised to find the way no longer blocked. You do not have to stay with your legacy from your past. If you are married and your husband doesn't like to travel, perhaps you can plan a trip by yourself or with a friend. Remember Jimmy Carter's mother, who joined the Peace Corps when she was in her sixties.

Many women we spoke with were aware of the ease with which their daughters decided to go to college. It was as if college was their destiny.

For many young women of today education is a perquisite of life. Perhaps this was not true for you, as marriage and the family were the goal. Can you make education a perquisite of your future? Have you yearned to take that course in ancient history, poetry, or painting? Retirement can be the time to obtain an education with the same ease and expectation you have given your daughters.

Most women we spoke with felt their daughters' lives were quite different from theirs until their daughters married and had children. Then the young women who originally decided to juggle parenting and a career often ended up as their mothers did—sacrificing their careers (at least for a time) and becoming the major caretaker. This is an interesting if not welcome phenomenon.

The women's movement created many opportunities for

changes in the woman's role, but it appears the struggle is still on and the revolution is temporarily stalled. The work to change the role of women in society is obviously more than the task of one lifetime. Some gains have been solidified, however, and in retirement you can use what will give you the most comfort and joy.

Married women, especially, will benefit from self-assessment in response to questions 7 and 8.

7. Do you have friendships with women separate from your marriage? Although never explicitly stated, it was understood by married women of the 1950's and 1960's that they were part of a relationship at the expense of some of their independence. One of the manifestations of this understanding was that the female friendships of a married woman were often considered to be within the province of the husband. Since his needs came first, his time had to be considered when an outside friendship was involved. Your response to this question will give you some insight into your independence within your marriage.

Friendships after marriage often became a problem for women. If the husband did not enjoy the company of the wife's close friends, or if the husbands involved did not get along, relationships of long duration suffered or completely atrophied. Budding friendships from the park bench, the office, or the PTA never flowered because the husband of one woman or the other had a problem with it. It was difficult to maintain a friendship with a friend if the husband was not a part of it. Social life was negotiated as a couple.

Most of the women we spoke with could remember at least one instance when they either gave up a relationship of long standing or did not follow through on a relationship because of their husbands. Although they expressed dissatisfaction, they never questioned the eventual dissolution of the relationship.

If you have one or more friendships of your own, you have an element of independence in your life. You value independence. It is important that you know this as you contemplate your retirement. You may be content as half of a couple, but be cognizant of the self who has friends of her own.

Dana is twenty-nine years old and has been married to Susan's son Arthur for three years. Susan recalled a recent conversation about Dana's leisure time that had left her feeling troubled. It seems that Dana has remained close to three of her women friends from college (all now married) who get together on a weekly basis for dinner. They see each other after work and often stay out until midnight. Susan was shocked at the fact that the young women saw each other so regularly without their husbands and during time that Susan had always considered to belong to a woman's husband. She even went so far as to wonder about the strength of her son's marriage and to feel sorry for her son, who was obviously being passed over for Dana's friends. When Susan asked Dana why the husbands didn't join them, Dana looked surprised and simply dismissed the idea.

Susan started thinking about the many times she would have enjoyed spending an evening in the company of a friend from work but did not follow through because she had to be home for dinner. She remembered several times when her college roommate was in town on business; Susan had invited her to the house for dinner, although she would have much preferred a visit with just the two of them. It had never occurred to her that she might have done just that.

As she evaluated these thoughts and feelings, Susan's needs in terms of autonomy and independence became quite clear to her. Her job had been supplying the means with which she fulfilled these needs. Besides allowing her an independent identity, her job had enabled her to have independent friendships as well. Retirement meant much more of a change for Susan than she had realized.

If you recognize some of Susan in yourself, be aware of how different you have become, and recognize that the world has changed enough to allow you to continue to fulfill your needs.

8. *Do you spend some leisure time in activities without your husband?* A *yes* answer to this question has similar implications to a *yes* to

question 7. If you have leisure time activities that do not involve your husband, then you are a person who needs independence and autonomy in your life. Do not overlook this facet of yourself as you plan your retirement. You may feel that the activity itself is not really so important to you, but the fact that you pursue this on your own denotes a need to be separate.

Several retired women told us that it was too easy to give up an activity such as a bridge game or an art class when it did not fit into the new retirement schedule. Women who married in the 1940's, '50's, and '60's more often than not expected to arrange their lives around the lives of their husbands. They had never thought to assess the significance of independent activity in their lives.

If the activity is of great significance to you, you will quickly recognize that you need to carry it into retirement. Janine had spent at least two to three days a month for the last five years working on various ceramics projects and was looking forward to spending her retirement involved in this. Ethel was very involved with her bridge club and had played once a week since the early days of her marriage. She planned on entering various tournaments when she retired. These women had worked out their need for independent time for their activities over the years.

Virginia, who was a career housewife and mother, had a different problem. She noted that she spent independent leisure time and had friendships that were separate from her marriage. She had been involved with community activities and through these had developed some close friendships. As she contemplated her husband's retirement, she realized that both she and her husband were expecting that she would give up the community work so that they could spend more time together. She has begun to give this some serious thought in terms of possibly continuing her involvement on a less intense basis or perhaps simply planning ways to continue the meaningful friendships.

We have only scratched the surface of the issue of independence and autonomy within marriage in these questions 7 and 8. The questionnaire and discussion in Chapter VI—For Couples Only will give you the opportunity to gain greater insight into your desires and needs in this area of your life as you continue planning for the future.

It is a new concept for some women to think about their lives in terms of their personal needs, but these needs must be considered for a successful next phase of life.

9. *What would you do differently?* If you have never speculated on this question before, think about it now. Did you fantasize at one time about writing a newspaper column, or running for political office? Did you think of owning a small book and gift shop? Did you think of designing jewelry or painting in watercolor? Many women put away "young dreams" when the realities of husband, children, and earning a living become paramount. Those yearnings of your youth can have a special meaning as you enter retirement. You may not be able to do exactly what you dreamed of doing, but retirement can offer you the opportunity to pursue buried or forgotten dreams.

CAREER

In the 1950's and 1960's the reality of women's lives meant planning for a future at home with husband and children. It was the unusual woman who was able to put her needs and desires for a job or career first during these years. Many women who had the same drive and ambition as men channeled their ambitions into wifely duties or into the stereotypical jobs available to women. Even the women who remained single did not for the most part venture into the world of power and influence.

Many of the women we spoke with felt that, although diminished by time, the drive and ambition of their youth remained. Many women felt that if they had it to do over they would have gone for corporate jobs and sacrificed home and family for the success of a Lee Iacocca.

Others we spoke with said they would have gone to college after high school and still regret that they did not avail themselves of an advanced education. It is difficult to think back to that mentality today, but education was not considered important for women; they would be staying at home to raise a family.

Myra knew she would have gone to college and become a math teacher if she had taken the opportunity. She had been a talented mathematics student in high school and had been encouraged to continue her studies by her teachers. When Myra finished high school she became engaged to her high school sweetheart. They planned to be married within a year, and Myra quickly gave up her dream of being a mathematician to become a secretary. It was more important to put money away for her future with her husband then to think about her own individual future.

She married, had children, and almost forgot her dream. When her children were grown she took various secretarial jobs, since money for her family was always her primary goal. This may finally be the time for Myra to follow her dream. Many women go back to school in their fifties or sixties. Maybe it is finally her turn. Maybe it is yours.

Another woman told us, "I went to college after high school to become a nurse. I thought helping people would be an interesting career and at that time there were so few professions open for women. Now that I think back to the time I made my decision, I remember that what I really wanted was to take time off from school and be aimless for a while. I thought I might travel, not just running from country to country but renting a villa and living alone in a foreign city."

The woman who said this has had a successful and interesting career in nursing. She realizes she still has this dream of foreign travel but she never considered it important or possible. But why not? When she plans her retirement, she should consider taking time off to be aimless. She may find there are no obstacles to spending a season on the Costa del Sol, now that a new phase of life is beginning.

Grace knew she was a woman with great energy and drive. She had been a teacher for most of her life, but teaching did not come close to satisfying her needs. Grace knew that had she been a young woman growing up in today's world she would have been a lawyer and gone into politics. She had given up on law school many years before but knew she still needed some challenge in her life. Several years before retiring she volunteered her services at a center for abused women. As she worked there she saw the complex needs of battered women and decided to become actively involved in their struggle. She joined the center's board of directors and is now in charge of the center's lobbying group which seeks funding from the state legislature. Her new role, which she carried into retirement, satisfied her need for power.

MARRIAGE

If they had had the opportunities available to young women of today, many of the women we spoke with would have waited to marry until they were older. They would have used their early twenties to establish their independence and thus would have had an earlier opportunity to experience themselves as capable and self-directing.

Many of them felt that they would have negotiated a different kind of marriage. They spoke of the desire they had felt over the years to be more independent within their marriage and the difficulty they had becoming comfortable with this feeling. They felt they had established a pattern early, made a contract that was difficult to alter as the years went by.

All of the women remembered society's pressure to get married and the stigma attached to becoming an old maid. Some of the women felt they might not have married at all if there had been other opportunities available to them. Women whose marriages had ended in divorce felt they might have dated more and been more selective about their choice of a husband. Some of the married women felt that they would have liked more social and sexual experience.

Reflecting on your marriage will give you more insight into who you are and how your needs have changed over the years. As you enter a new phase of life you will be making changes in your lifestyle. The more self-awareness you have the more power you will have over the changes you are making.

CHILDREN

There was little question that if you were married in the 1950's and 1960's you were going to have children. That's what women did, like it or not. You probably have no regrets about having had your children, particularly now that they are grown and for the most part involved in their own lives.

What might you have done differently about your children? Many women remembered that they timed their children to please their parents, not themselves. You may be one of the many women who do things to make people happy, even if the timing doesn't fit your life. Do you choose to continue this pattern?

A few women spoke of the sacrifices they had made for their children, usually in the financial area of life. They had given up many things such as vacations and leisure time so that their children could have special lessons or go to the college of their choice. Many of them questioned the importance of doing all of this now that they have the luxury of hindsight. Women of the fifties and sixties were not aware of self-fulfillment and they never questioned that their children's needs came first.

They note with some envy that young mothers are more open about taking time for themselves and their own needs; the younger women allow themselves more because they live in a world where issues have shades of gray, not just black and white.

We hope at this point that you are gaining insight into your expectations, dreams, and strengths. Are you a closet feminist? Or do you secretly yearn to stay home and bake bread? Have you always wanted to write a book, or study archeology and participate in a dig? Now is the chance to indulge yourself. We do not expect you to have sudden insights. This is the beginning of an ongoing process of self-discovery.

You have the opportunity to discover what myths of being female you still live by. Which are working for you and which are limiting you? For long, women's lives have been structured by society's expectations. Women entering the retirement years today have few guidelines and few expectations. It is a time to make new beginnings.

II

A Lifetime of Transitions

When our parents were driven out of Paradise,
Adam is believed to have remarked to Eve: "My
dear we live in an age of transition."

DEAN WILLIAM R. INGE (1860–1954)

Claudia finished college in 1951. She returned home to Ohio after college to live with her family. At first things went well, but after a year she found that she was slipping back into the role of her parents' little girl. The relationship with her parents and the living arrangement became more and more of a problem for her. Two years later with much trepidation she left Ohio with a friend to live in New York City. They found an apartment and Claudia got a job as a secretary. She was happy on her own but she always felt underemployed and unappreciated at her job. She dated irregularly and wanted very much to be married. This was the 1950s and the women's movement had not yet entered Claudia's life.

In 1959, when she was twenty-eight, somewhat older than many of her friends and fearful of being the proverbial "old maid," Claudia married. She married a man she loved very much although she knew he did not share the same passion for her.

She put her doubts aside and fervently hoped she would live happily ever after.

What actually did happen was rather short of perfect. Claudia and her husband had two children in the first five years of marriage. Instead of the relationship growing closer during this period, Claudia had every reason to suspect that her husband was "fooling around" with other women. She had no proof for many years, but she lived with a vague feeling that his irregular hours and preoccupations were more than the ordinary stress of making a living. She had her house in the suburbs, however, and her two little boys with whom she was fully involved. She taught Sunday school, had friends, gave parties, went to parties, and enjoyed summers with her children and weekends with her family.

Always feeling inadequate and frightened of being alone, Claudia rationalized that her marriage was acceptable and decided to stay married. But the situation eventually became untenable and the humiliation more than she could bear. When she was forty-four years old and had been married sixteen years, Claudia asked her husband to leave and she filed for divorce. Her children were in high school and needed less of her attention. With the help of the women's movement and a consciousness-raising group, Claudia went out to find a job. Believing she had an artistic flair, she took a job in a newly formed company that was designing and marketing greeting cards. Her talents developed and she has been having a successful career.

She is now 59 and has been with the company for eleven years. Recently, a newly hired young woman who has many years' less experience than Claudia has been given an assignment for which Claudia thought she would have been more appropriate. In fact, the whole office is starting to be full of young people, many of them about the same age as her children. Claudia doesn't want to retire, but she is starting to think she may slow down. She is beginning to feel unsettled about the future.

Claudia is at a crossroads. She doesn't want to leave her job, but she is feeling older, particularly when she looks around at her co-workers. Retirement is an event she had not planned for, although she had been putting money in an IRA for the past ten years.

Another transition is looming in Claudia's future. The way in which she copes with this transition will be pivotal to the rest of her life.

Jean was an only child who grew up during the 1940's. She was fourteen in 1941 when the Japanese bombed Pearl Harbor and the United States entered World War II. She met her husband when she was sixteen. He was home on a furlough from the army. They corresponded, fell deeply in love, and married in 1946 when she was nineteen.

Jean had never imagined a life other than being a wife and mother and eagerly anticipated becoming pregnant and caring for her baby. Her husband was pleased to have her stay home and she loved being home. She was born into the tradition of being wife, mother, and homemaker. She was deeply involved with her children. She went to Open School Nights, became active in the PTA of her children's school, and became co-president of the PTA when nobody else wanted the responsibility.

When Jean was forty-four her mother had a stroke. Her father could not cope and Jean found herself in the position of caretaker for both her mother and her father. Her parents' illnesses necessitated arranging for medical appointments, household help, visiting nurse service, and a senior citizen day facility for her father. Fortunately, her children were able to take care of themselves after school when Jean could not be home. She found herself commuting between two households and juggling everybody's affairs.

After a seven-year illness, Jean's mother died. Jean took her father to her home to live with her family. This arrangement worked out poorly. Her father's health declined. Never a resourceful person, he became more and more clinging and dependent.

Jean's husband and children tried hard to understand, but

after a few years they felt drained and realized that Jean needed some life for herself. Jean and her husband decided to place her father in a nursing home.

At the time of this writing, Jean visits her father regularly. Now, however, Jean's husband is ready for retirement. The children are on their own. Jean is ready to start a new life. She says that this one is to be for herself, but she is concerned about handling this new phase. How can she cope with this transition?

People live through many transitions. Transitions are markers. They are often upon us ready or not, like it or not. The first big transition is from home to school—leaving mother or father and making that independent step. Each of us made that transition in a unique way.

Each transition from then on is a reflection of the first, modified greatly by the acquisition of knowledge and experience. If on the first day of school you waved a cheerful goodbye to mother and made three friends, you have probably negotiated other transitions in your life in the same easy fashion. If, on the other hand, you clung to mother and warily considered the classroom scene in front of you, your style of handling transitions is more deliberate.

Life's transitions's fall into two distinct categories. The first involves the transitions over which adults have had some measure of control—pivotal junctures where choices had to be made. The choices we are talking about involve families, careers, and individual environments.

The second transitional category involves sudden death, illness, or accidents; war or other catastrophes; or career or job changes that come about because of external factors beyond the individual's control. This part of life involves the unexpected. Most people do what is necessary in their lives to get through, unaware that they have successfully negotiated a transitional period.

People are not accustomed to conceptualizing life as a series of transitions. For most of us it is a matter of simply living. For some, life is what is happening while plans are being made for the future. As you look back, you will begin to be aware of the many transitions you have lived through in the past thirty years.

Each of your life's transitions can be evaluated to enable you to understand your coping style. Once you understand your coping style, you will have the power to modify it as necessary. The awareness of your style will help negotiate your next important transition even more successfully.

HOW DID YOU COPE
WITH CHANGES YOU COULD CONTROL?

Transitions by choice (Category I) concerns the changes in life over which humans have some measure of control. Most of these times are universally applicable, although some may have little significance for you. Deal with all that apply to your life.

Each question in List A involves a specific transitional period. Each question asks how you determined the decision or choice you made at that time. It does not ask you to evaluate the event. We are concerned with your motivations at that time.

List B gives you a selection of motivations that may have been behind the way you coped with each transitional event.

Consider each question in List A separately. For each question, evaluate which item or items from List B best explains how you made the decision that you made. Sometimes more than one choice will apply to a particular transition. Life is never simple, and decisions are rarely of one dimension.

We are not asking that you evaluate *what* you did; rather, you should try to focus oh *how* the decision to do it was made. For example: In answering *question 2*, Claudia said that she had left her parent's home to be on her own three years after her return from college. She chose three items from List B to explain how she decided to make the move. She made her decision to leave on economic terms, as she had waited until she felt able to afford the move (c); she asked advice of several relatives and friends (f); and she had examined other alternatives (b). She felt that all of these answers explained how she made her decision to leave her parents' home.

Transitions by Choice: Questionnaire

LIST A

1. When you graduated from or left high school, how was the next step of your life determined?
2. When you left your parents' home to be on your own for the first time, how was the decision made?
3. How did your decision to marry or not to marry come about?
4. How was the choice made to be or not to be a parent?
5. If you ever seriously considered it, how did you make the decision to divorce or not to divorce?
6. If you remarried, how was that decided?
7. If you are currently single (not widowed), how did this come about?
8. Consider each time you changed your residence in your adult independent life. How was each move determined?
9. How was your career or job choice made?
10. If your current work is not your original career, how did this come about?

LIST B

a) I followed the path I thought was expected of me.
b) Things just happened that way.
c) My choice was in economic terms—what I could afford.
d) I did what everyone else was doing.
e) Somebody of importance to me (for example, parent, husband, sibling) knew what I wanted to do and told me.
f) I asked advice of others and took it.
g) The choice was clear to me at the time.
h) I examined alternatives before I made a decision.

Transitions by Choice: Assessment

As you reflect on your responses, become aware of any pattern you may have been following as you faced each transitional period. You may see that you are repeating the same pattern now that you are contemplating retirement. If this pattern has worked for you and you are using it to make your retirement decisions, you are doing well for yourself. There may be pieces of this pattern which did not work well for you and an awareness of these pieces now may enable you to make better choices in the future.

In your evaluation you may become aware of certain coping patterns with which you are dissatisfied. You may wish to think about making some modifications. This new transitional time of retirement is a fine time to begin.

Reflecting upon and evaluating life's events in a particular framework will illuminate and facilitate your current decision-making.

QUESTION 1—*High school graduation*. The decision-making process for women in the 1950s involved expectations that society had for them. Women were expected to be passive, so young women followed the expected passive path or took the advice of somebody important in their life. Therefore, any of the first five choices (*a, b, c, d,* and *e*) are not unusual responses to this question for women who were coming of age in the 1950s and early 1960s.

There are differences among these five choices, and your choices can give you insight into yourself and your decision-making style. If you chose, "I followed the path that was expected of me" (*a*), you've found a need for social and familial conformity that was hardly unusual for the men and women who grew up at the time. Perhaps you never questioned your need for conformity. Claudia always knew she would go to college and had looked forward to this during her senior of high school. The decision was right for her.

Other women knew they were expected to work after high school and had looked forward to having secretarial positions and money of their own. They readily stated that they have not regretted the decision for a minute. Following an expected path is a way of handling transitions that works effectively and happily for many.

Perhaps you are like Dorothy, who came from a family of educators and had been expected to continue her education in college. She did just this despite the fact that she had wanted to train as a nurse. She never felt she was a scholar, and did not particularly like school, but she did what was expected of her, never even contemplating that she might have had a choice. She did not come to the realization of her power to make choices until later in her life. Dorothy still finds that she must force herself to focus on her needs when she is making a decision. She has a strong tendency to do what is expected.

A choice of "things just happened that way" (b) implies that you had little control over the circumstances surrounding this transitional period. This too was hardly unusual for the time. Teenagers seldom felt much control over their destiny. Girls settled on the available jobs, colleges, or secretarial schools, or on marriage. Life seemed to happen, rather than being sought after. The feeling that you could "go for it" was still in the future.

If this was one of your responses, examine it carefully. You may have been more in charge than you believe. Even if you did drift into college, you may at some point have taken control of the direction of your college career. It was not common, but some women, even then, chose engineering over teaching.

The answer "my choice was in economic terms" (c) is a seemingly straightforward process at any time. In the 1950's and early 1960's there were fewer ways and means to get a higher education, and if no money was available the young person, particularly a woman, went to work after high school. In order to understand if this choice has particular significance to you, you should look at your feelings about your decision.

Do you have regrets or resentments about the choice you felt forced to make? Did you take any job because you couldn't afford to have the education you wanted? Have you always felt deprived because of the economic disadvantage? Have you felt that your career was always second best?

Anita, whom you met in Chapter I, became a teacher for economic reasons. She wanted to go to medical school but her family could not afford it. She always felt, with some element of resentment, that she had missed out. As we spoke with her, she began to see that she had had opportunities to have a career in medicine. Anita used economic realities as a cover for other insecurities, particularly her fear of the unknown. This insight into her fears will be helpful as Anita plans for her retirement. The financial considerations are not always as clear-cut as they seem at a casual glance. Watch for this as you evaluate your pattern.

Many of the women we interviewed simply accepted their economic circumstances and moved on with their lives. They went to work, enjoyed it or did not, married, had families, and did not look back. This ability to accept a situation and live with it is a good insight to have about yourself.

Some women found a way to continue their education. They went to night college or saved money and went to school at a later time. Some searched out a job with a career path that could fulfill their educational and economic needs. Many of these women had never given themselves credit for the courage and perseverance it took to overcome their financial problems.

In these modern times of independence and initiative it is difficult to admit to following the crowd, but the response "I did what everybody else was doing" (d) is a common one. The power of peer pressure is always strong and in the teen years probably at its strongest: If everyone is getting married, why bother with college? If everyone is taking jobs with the telephone company, isn't it fun to be where your friends are? If all the kids are comparing college choices, who wants to be different?

Here is the important point worth examining: If this was one of your choices, to what extent were your needs and desires the same as those of your peers? As a corollary, consider whether you did indeed examine your needs and desires. Were you thinking about yourself at all when you made your choice at this time of transition?

The choice of "somebody of importance knew what I wanted to do" (e) indicates the power of authority figures during your times of transition. Many women who grew up in the 1950's and the 1960's relied on a parent and then on a husband to make decisions for them. Women of this era were not encouraged to be independent, and they did not consider themselves capable of handling their own lives. As a result of this, many woman waited to be told whether college, marriage, or work should be the next step after high school.

Who was the authority figure in your life at that time? Is that person still around for you now? Often instinctively a woman will give decision-making power to someone in her life who knows what is best for her. She will not take advice randomly. The reliance on authority can be a productive decision-making technique. Was this decision in your best interests?

A response of "asking advice of others" (f), or "a seemingly clear choice" (g), or "examining alternatives" (h) indicates less involvement in society's expectations for women, and more independence and self-awareness. If the response stands alone without any of statements a through e, you've found an element of nonconformity in your decision-making process.

The seeking of advice (f) implies an awareness of the power to make an independent decision. It is distinct from "somebody of importance knowing what I wanted to do" (e), since the decision was not in the hands of others. Your ability to use good judgment is an important issue here, and must be considered carefully.

Who were the people from whom advice was sought? Were they people from whom you needed approval? If this was so, did you let their ideas and ideals supersede your own? Did you seek advice in terms of your needs? If you did ask advice about the direction your life would take after high school, you were aware early that you have a right to look for help.

If you felt that "the decision was clear at the time" (g) and made your decision accordingly, you've again found the implication of individual choice.

The third choice in this group, "examining alternatives before making a decision" (*b*), implies a great deal of maturity, which many teenagers were unable to achieve. If you were acting with this degree of independence, you were and probably still are an unusually autonomous person.

If you were an independent decision-maker at that time of your life, you may want to look at how this came about. It is possible that you were encouraged to be this way by your family. You may have learned this difficult lesson early in your life. It may be a pattern you have followed all along. Have you been satisfied with your choices?

If you have not been satisfied with your choices, you may discover that what appeared to be an autonomous decision was actually rebelliousness. Rebelliousness is the other side of conformity and can be equally restrictive. It does not give one a free choice, because the action taken is in response to someone else. Often this is a product of adolescence and fortunately is left by the wayside when the later transitional periods occur.

Question 2—*Leaving Home. Questions* 1, 2, and 3 may overlap in terms of your early life. For young women of the 1950's and the 1960's, leaving home before marriage was not common. Claudia came home after college and made her decision to leave with much difficulty. Anita never left her parents' home. Jean graduated from high school, left her parents' home, and married —all within a few months; all three transitions for Jean occurred simultaneously.

For purposes of the discussion, *questions* 1, 2, and 3 will be considered as separate transitional times. In light of the close relationship of these events you will see a strong similarity as we discuss the significance of several of the responses as they apply to each of these three questions. Observing patterns will expand your insight and is the reason for what may seem like duplication.

If your response to *question* 1 (how you decided the next step after high school) was "I followed the expected path," ask yourself to whom the standards belonged? Was it a consistent person or persons? Did you follow your family and their expectations? Did you follow in terms of a changing society? Did you follow

in terms of a changing peer group? Is this comfortable and successful for you?

If "I followed the expected path" (a) was also one of your
choices in response to *question* 2 (on leaving home for the first
time), you've discovered a need to conform, not uncommon at
the time. You may want to identify who it was that expected
you to be independent. Were you following the expectations of
your family or the peer group with which you were involved at
the time? How comfortable were you with the decision at the
time? How successful was your decision as you look back?

Did the move "just seem to happen" (b)? This response still
carries the implication of a lack of control over the events of
your life. If you were young, it was not unusual for the time.

Sometimes events really do fall into place, and often we are
not as passive as we seem. The friend who offered to share an
apartment at the right time, or the ad you saw one Sunday as
you browsed through the paper may not have been as casual a
happening as you thought. There was a time when a young
woman did not go out on her own, and admitting the desire for
a home of one's own had difficult connotations. It was easier and
more comfortable to believe that it "just happened."

It is also possible that the decision was just that straightforward. In any event, was it right for you, both at the time and in
retrospect? Was it this one time that things just happened or
does this occur often? Patterns again.

Decisions based on "economic considerations" (c) are a fact
of life. Young women and men stay at home because their
money is needed to support their family. Or they come home to
stay because they do not have the funds necessary to live on
their own. Or they leave home so there'll be one less mouth to
feed.

Watch for "economic considerations" (c) if this occurs as a
pattern in your life. It is too easy to use financial concerns as a
mask for other problems that are the real obstacles in transitional
planning.

Did you leave home because "everyone else" (d) was moving
out? As you evaluate this response, think of your age at the time

the move was made. The reliance on everyone else is often a product of being young and loses its significance in decision-making as one matures.

On the other hand, what everyone else is doing can be support for your needs and may make a transitional decision less difficult. If you look for this form of help it will be important for you to know this about yourself as you face this preretirement period. One of the difficulties faced by the pre-retiree is that the peer group, the family, and even society provide few guidelines for decision-making for this time. Everyone is doing something else.

Was it "somebody of importance" (e) who was involved in your leaving home for the first time? Often a sibling or an older friend was the person who knew what was best for you. If your response to *question 1* (next step after high school) included "somebody of importance" (e) as well, was it the same authority to whom you turn in pivotal times? Do you look for someone to turn to when you are faced with an important decision? If this is part of your style, you should acknowledge this fact as you make decisions about this time of your life.

If you went from parental home to independent living rather than to marriage; if you came of age in the 1950's or early 1960's; and if you made this decision based on "advice of others" (f) or on what seemed to be a "clear choice" (g), or if you made it after "examining alternatives" (h) you have demonstrated qualities of autonomy and independence unusual for young women of the time.

There are just a few words of caution. Many women were quite willing to admit that the decision to marry or to leave home immediately after high school graduation was a form of rebellion. Although they asked advice at the time, the advisor was one of their best friends who they knew would concur with their decision. They believed they had examined alternatives, but in retrospect they know better. What seemed a clear choice then was not always a wise one.

Look to the timing of the event and the circumstances that went with it for any special insights. Tina had finished at a local college, taken a job, and continued to live at home for over five years. When she began to suspect that marriage was not imminent she started to think about living in her own apartment. This was in 1958, when she was twenty-eight. At the time young women were still expected to live at home if they were of marriageable age. Tina was used to following the flow and living within the expectations of others. She was aware of certain family obligations. She knew what was right for her, however, and despite her natural inclination toward conformity, she arranged to move into an apartment with a friend.

As we talked with Tina, she began to have a sense of the courage it took for her to make this step. She had never considered leaving her parents' home before she did it, and she had never considered herself to be an independent person when it came to making decisions. Indeed, autonomous decision-making is not her strong point, but the courage to act in her own best interests has served her well and will continue to do so. The awareness of this attribute and the fact that she has never regretted making this difficult decision has helped Tina in planning her retirement.

Question 3—*To marry or not.* It may be difficult to be objective about your answer to this question. Love, physical attraction, and sexual preference are all part of the decision to marry. Despite their importance, the extent to which these have motivated you in making this transitional decision is not relevant for these purposes. Try to separate these factors as you respond to this part of the questionnaire.

It is relevant to think about whether or not your decision to marry was based on the same factors you considered when you left high school and when you left your parents' home. Go over these answers. Note if there is a consistent pattern.

Is there any point in your answers when you see a significant change in your pattern of decision making? This major decision may be that point. The decision to marry frequently changes the way a woman views herself. She may at that time of her life become either more or less autonomous. An independent decision-maker may find herself making decisions based on her husband's needs. A young woman who consistently conformed to her parents' expectations may get a taste of her own power as she moves into a new phase of life.

Sometimes the economic factor changes in importance. A woman who has been economically secure may find that marriage makes her more responsible and more cognizant of financial obligations.

If "somebody of importance" (e) has been prominent as a response, did the "somebody" change from one person to another? Did the authority become your husband rather than your father or mother?

The decision not to marry was less clearly understood by the women we spoke with and may be more difficult for many of you to evaluate. Unmarried women often responded that "things just happened that way" (b).

More insight can be gained if the question is conceptualized within the context of a situation. Evaluate a particular time or times when marriage was a distinct possibility. For each of these situations choose one of the responses in List B. You may see yourself following your usual pattern after all.

You may find that there was more choice involved in being single than you previously believed. The clue for Anita was when she said, "I never met anyone whom I wanted to marry." She had had several opportunities and each time she stated that the choice was clear to her.

Tina saw the impact that her family had on her style of coping with transitional times. She had summoned the courage to leave her parents' home but she had never found anyone her mother liked well enough for Tina to marry.

Neither Tina nor Anita regretted not marrying. This was true for many of the women. If there was a regret it was in terms of the loss of a particular man with whom the woman had been deeply in love.

Question 4—*Parenting.* In the view of many women, particularly those who grew up in the 1950's and 1960's, children come as a part of marriage. The scenario consisting of two children, a dog, and a home in the suburbs may not be as attractive today, but it was most popular for many decades. If you are of this time and you followed this plan as though it were prearranged, you were not alone. Statements about the decision to have children before the women's movement altered some of society's standards are of particular significance. Although most women we spoke with believed the decision to have children to be theirs, when they examined their decision further they concluded that there had never been much personal choice involved. Parents, husbands, and peers expected children to follow shortly after marriage, (a), (d), and any career plans or travel plans were secondary to these expectations. Even the women who said the choice was clear (g) agreed that there was a strong element of expectations of others involved as well.

For most women, parenting was not a matter of choice as it is in today's world. It was difficult in the 1950's and 1960's to postpone having a family, even if economic circumstances were not optimal. The women who felt that financial considerations (c) were involved in the decision to have children stated that they always thought about how soon they could afford to have a family, not about when it would be comfortable for them in terms of their relationship and their individual needs.

It may be difficult to look at this decision with detachment, but what you discover will tell you a lot about how much society has changed in a very few decades. Transitional times, during the 1950's and 1960's, particularly from high school graduation through to parenthood, did not appear to many women to be events that included the element of choice. Too often alternatives did not seem to be available. For the women of today, alternatives and alternate life styles are the norm.

If you feel that you made a clear and independent choice concerning parenthood during those early years, you are probably still handling many decisions autonomously. Many of the retirement decisions you have to make may not be as difficult for you as for the majority of women who were more influenced by yesterday's society.

The retirement issue is in part difficult because there is no traditional path to follow, many authority figures are gone, and economics are no longer clearly restrictive. The decisions to be made involve your own needs and your expectations of yourself. In order to negotiate this next transition successfully, you may have to modify your coping and decision-making styles. Women's lives are different now.

Question 5—*Divorce.* It is important not to lose sight of the information you are seeking from this questionnaire. You should focus on the decision-making process, not on the emotional aspects of the event. It is easy to get off the track, because the transitional periods we discuss are difficult to think about.

The decision about divorce is usually more complex than the decision to marry. There are many determining factors (*a–b*) that operate during the period of transition. Try to list them all using chronological order as a structure. Then attempt to discover the most compelling reason.

Are you beginning to see a pattern of behavior during critical junctures of your life? Is this a point at which you changed or modified your style? For many women this was the time when they first became aware of their own control over their lives.

Dorothy, the woman who had wanted to be a nurse, had handled the transitional periods in her life by following the expected path (*a*); going along with the authority figures in her life—her father and her husband (*e*); and feeling that things just happened (*b*). Divorce became a reality when she discovered that her husband was having an affair. As we spoke with her it became apparent that this discovery triggered a period of transition for her. Her usual coping methods were unavailable to her. She could not confide in her father who had made previous decisions for her. There were no guidelines available concerning divorce either from her religion or from her family or friends. She was on her own.

Dorothy looked at her situation from an economic stance and considered what life would be for her and her two children. She asked advice of a friend who had been divorced for several years. She actively examined alternatives for herself. She finally made the decision to confront her husband with his affair. After months of agony she decided to stay in the marriage.

When Dorothy evaluated the way in which she had handled this transition she increased her knowledge about herself and about the resources she has for coping with difficult times. (Mistakenly, she had always felt that she had been too passive in handling that time in her life.) Now that she is facing retirement it is important for her to be aware of her capabilities so that she can make intelligent choices.

If you were divorced (whether or not the ultimate decision was yours), you need to evaluate how (not why) it happened. Were you a passive participant? (a, b or e?). Like Dorothy, did you take a more active stance? How did your reaction to divorce compare with your coping style during your other transitional times?

As you continue to evaluate your responses to the questionnaire, focus on your consistencies. Carefully examine your responses for inconsistencies, if you find any. These can be meaningful, particularly if you view them in the context of your comfort or discomfort with the outcome. The questions target life's passages, and the responses enable you to look at yourself within a structure. Each transition you evaluate gives you further insight, as each response adds more to your understanding of your behavior and its implications.

Questions 6 and 7—*Remarriage.* In responding to these questions, we must ask you, as we did in *question 3* (concerning your decision to marry initially), to be as objective as you can. Separate the inherent feelings of sex and love from the motivations we are concerned with here. If you remarried after being divorced or widowed, see if your responses to *question 6* (how you decided to remarry) are the same as they were to *question 3*. Was your approach to marriage completely different after the first time?

Paula saw the decision-making process for her second marriage as very different from the one involved in her first marriage. She had married at the age of twenty-five because everyone expected her to marry Bill (a). At the time, she felt that she had been left behind because all of her friends had married before her (d). Bill was a good man and a good provider. Everyone liked him and thought that he was good for her (e).

The marriage did not turn out well, and after eight years Paula and Bill were divorced. They had been in marriage counseling and Paula continued with the counselor for three more years. During that time she met David and they married.

Her decision to marry David involved a different decision-making process. This time she considered her life as a single woman, considered the option of a steady relationship without marriage, and weighed these against marriage (*h*).

She did not ask advice of anyone, although she did spend a lot of time in counseling evaluating her feelings. As time went on, "the choice," she said, "became clear" (*g*).

If you have married more than once, evaluate each marriage as a separate transition. The more transitional times you have negotiated, the more information you will have about your style.

If you are currently single and are finding it difficult to determine how this came about, it will be helpful for you to evaluate each opportunity you may have had to marry. You will gain more insight if you handle it in this fashion.

Are you satisfied with the way you've made your decisions? Would you like to modify your style to some degree? Do you feel that you are able to do so? Sometimes it is a matter of accepting what we do and who we are. Don't judge! Accumulate information and evaluate it.

Question 8—*Change of residence.* This matter may have little or no significance for you as you consider life's transitions. Your geographical location may be the consequence of where you were born and where your family located. Think carefully, however, before you dismiss this question of how your moves have been decided. If you ever moved your place of residence, how was the decision made? Was a decision made not to move? How did this come about? The more transitional times you evaluate, the more you can discover about yourself.

Theresa discovered a quality of independence in herself as she evaluated the decisions to move to the various places she had lived in her lifetime.

She had married during World War II and, unlike many of her friends who waited at home, she chose to follow her husband as he fulfilled his army obligations. She was fortunate, since he spent the war in the United States, but he was stationed in the West and their home was in the East. They left home, family, and friends. Theresa found a job in the town near the base and she and her husband Bob enjoyed themselves despite the war.

The courage of this decision may not be as apparent today in our mobile society. Those of you who lived through this time will remember the way it was. During wartime, travel and communication were limited, and the decision to make the separation from the familiar was not reached casually.

At another juncture in their lives, after their children were born, Theresa and Bob began to need more living space. Again, despite the example of their friends and family, they chose to move to an undeveloped suburb quite a distance from where their lives had been secure.

There was no question that the decisions on where to move had been Theresa's, although she and Bob had discussed the alternatives. There is also no question that these decisions reveal Theresa to be an independent decision-maker who has the courage to make choices that are not always conventional.

Were you a corporate wife and married to your husband's job as much as he was? Were you forced to relocate each time he got a promotion? Perhaps you enjoyed this. One of the women we spoke with loved having a new home to decorate each time they moved.

If you feel that any moves were not within your control, how much control did you take after you settled in? Did you make a good life for yourself in each place you lived? Did you take a job? Did you make friends? Did you join in community activities? Were you content, at least after a while?

Examine each move. Could you have had more impact and changed the direction, geographical or otherwise?

If relocation is a consideration for you in retirement, examine your participation in earlier decisions concerning change of residence. Examine it in the light of your eventual satisfaction or dissatisfaction. Do you wish to repeat the pattern or would you like to see it altered in some way?

Question 9—*Original job choice.* It is possible that your decision about your career or job was a part of the direction you followed after high school (*question 1*). If this is so, you are not alone. In the 1950's and 1960's, many teachers, nurses, and social workers prepared for careers from the first year of college. Many female high school graduates of the 1950's and 1960's became secretaries or bookkeepers. They either used the skills of typing, shorthand, and bookkeeping they had learned in high school or they went to a business school after graduation. For the women who remained unmarried, the job often became a career and a life. The others worked until they married and had families. When they decided to return to work they simply resumed their former careers.

Most women of this generation never questioned their career decision even if it was made originally because of earlier expectations (*a*), economic reasons (*c*), or to please someone in authority (*e*).

This is not the time to question your decision, just the time to look at how much the world has changed since you made your decision. There are many more opportunities and options for women today. If the choice fulfilled your needs at the time, do you still have the same needs? This is the time to look forward and perhaps make some changes.

Jane is fifty-eight, and has been an English teacher for what she says seems to be hundreds of years. She had stayed home with her two children for only three years because her husband's income was never quite adequate enough for them to live the way they wanted to. Her salary always seemed necessary.

She liked her job well enough, and although she would rather have been at home, teaching was a good compromise. She was there for her children not too long after they got home from school each day and on holidays and during summers. It worked out well for her. She never thought to question her career choice despite the fact that she had over the years become increasingly bored with the work.

Her children are grown and have been living on their own for several years now. She is eligible for a retirement pension and does not want to continue teaching, but she does not like an unstructured day and would like to feel productive. The original decision-making basis, which involved economic necessity (c) and following the path expected of her by her family and peers (a), has not been a factor in her life for years. Her needs have changed and fortunately for her the world has changed.

Jane has always loved to read. She reads quickly and after years of correcting themes and papers from her students she is an efficient proofreader. She has fantasized a career in publishing as an editor and recently came across an ad for an editor of children's books. She did not apply for it but it did start her thinking. She is currently researching the job possibilities and the necessary training for this other career. She has discovered that it is a field where freelancing is possible. She also has discovered that her background as a teacher could be a natural entry into this aspect of publishing. Jane is beginning to broaden her horizons.

Your responses to this question will give you more insight into how you handle transitions. Did you make a decision to have your career at home as a homemaker, wife, and mother? Carefully assess the reasons for your career or job choice, whether it was made directly after your high school graduation or later in your life. Evaluate your decision on whether you would work in or out of the home. Was this decision a result of needs that are no longer operating? Was this a result of the needs of others in your life? Do they still have the same need of you? The needs may no longer be the same but perhaps the job is as satisfying as ever. You are fortunate.

If you are not happy in your work at this time you might want to use this information about yourself to start thinking about some specific changes as you move into retirement. There is a lot of life still ahead. It is possible to use the retirement years to go in a new direction.

Question 10—*Second or third career?* If your current work is not your original career, what different reasons motivated you in each career choice? Did you choose in response to your needs both times? Did you choose in response to the needs of others? Did you change your focus as you changed careers?

If your first career or job choice was made because it was expected (*a*) or because it was what everyone else was doing (*d*) or because someone of importance told you to do it (*e*), was the second career more within your control (*f,g,h*)? Or did you follow the same pattern as the first time? Is your current work fulfilling your current needs? This is an important aspect for you to consider. If you are comfortable with what you are doing now, then your most recent decision-making process has worked for you.

Did you perhaps originally begin a career that you gave up because of economic needs and outside pressures? Was your second career a second choice because of this (*c* and *e*)? Perhaps it is not too late.

Ellen gave up on her desire to go to law school because she married right after college and decided to become a homemaker. When she entered the work force years later she took an administrative job. She and her husband are now considering retirement and she is thinking of retiring to law school. She says that she may never work as a lawyer but she believes that she will enjoy the learning experience.

What is important is self-knowledge. The transition ahead—retirement—can be negotiated more easily if you know the patterns you have used previously to cope with change. As you plan ahead you can be prepared to stay with a style if it has worked for you, or you can modify what may have been less successful.

You may cope in an active way by facing transitional situations head on. You prepared to marry and planned for your career with a strong sense of what was right for you. You may have found that at the same time you depend on others for help in making the decisions; perhaps a relative or your best friend has always been there for you to consult.

You may have found that while you have a tendency to let others lead the way, they cannot lead you beyond the destination you have decided on. However you cope, however you make your decisions, it is your pattern and part of who you are.

It has been successful for you or you would not now be at this point in your life.

Make your self-assessment by evaluating your total picture. Look at your pattern of behavior rather than how you acted at one particular time of your life. Look for differences and try to understand why they occurred. Appreciate your style if it has been successful. Look for ways to change what may need altering.

Let's return to Claudia, whose divorce process we described at the beginning of this chapter. Claudia found interesting patterns as she looked at the transitional times of her life. She had always believed herself to be a realistic person. She saw herself as making decisions based on practical considerations. She felt rather proud that she did not let emotions color her choices. She views herself as an active decision-maker. She asks advice and examines alternatives. Often, she says, the choice just seems clear to her.

She stayed at home with her parents after college until she felt that she had enough money to move away. She asked advice of everyone before she finally made the decision to move to New York City.

She examined all of her options, explored all of the financial possibilities, and consulted several friends and a marriage counselor before she left her unhappy marriage. She spent at least three unhappy years before she felt ready to make the move. Finances figured prominently while she made her decisions.

As she made her self-assessment she began to be aware of how she used economic considerations each time that she faced the need for a change in her life. What she had viewed as a practical sensibility had also provided her with a rationale for immobility. She had great difficulty with change and separation. Rather than face these anxieties as she contemplated leaving her parents' home and leaving her husband, she focused on the financial problems. Although she finally made her decisions her pattern was to live far too long in uncomfortable situations.

She also became aware of how many friends, as well as

experts, she consulted before she could make a move. Despite the respect that she has for her decision-making abilities, and although she knew early on what she needed to do in each situation, Claudia continued to consult with others. As we evaluated she began to see this strategy as another way she put off making decisions that involved change and separation.

These insights are especially helpful to Claudia at this time in her life. She is in the process of repeating her pattern. She is in a job situation that is becoming increasingly uncomfortable. She is consulting everyone and examining the economics. She understands that she is on her way to remaining on the job and spending a few unhappy years waiting for the situation to become *too* uncomfortable or *too* humiliating. She is taking a close look at her pattern and at her options.

Retirement is an option but true economic realities must be faced at this time. Claudia does not, however, have to allow these factors to trap her as they have done previously. She can set her own timetable and have control over her decision rather than allowing severe discomfort to determine her fate.

At this writing, Claudia is exploring ways to free-lance her talents so that she can continue to have an income, be more autonomous, and have free time for travel. She foresees that if she plans wisely, she will soon be free to leave a job situation that may no longer be filling her personal needs.

Consider another example. Carol, who exemplifies a totally different style of handling transitions. She found a far less active pattern as she evaluated her responses. She followed what was expected (*a*), did what everyone else was doing (*d*), and consistently took the advice of others as to what her choice should be (*e*). Each life transition was handled this way.

Her parents expected her to go to college and she went. Her father introduced her to her husband and was much in favor of the marriage. Her friends were having babies, her husband wanted children, and her father wanted grandchildren, so Carol and her husband Ted had three daughters. Ted worked for a large corporation and each promotion meant a geographical move, so Carol could not even decide where she would live.

Carol went back to school and became a social worker at the urging of her husband, and started work when her children were in school full-time. Her friends were all entering the work force.

This pattern has worked for Carol. She had not regretted her decisions, whatever they were based on. They were right for her. She is now sixty-two years old and has been working in a civil service job as a social work supervisor for twenty-three years. Her daughters are on their own and are reasonably successful. She has enjoyed her career and is only now beginning to feel that she would like to retire. However, she is quite uncertain and finds herself mildly anxious when she contemplates making a decision. This is in part because her coping mechanisms for transitional periods, successful though they have been, are not available to her this time around.

Her father has been dead for several years and she relied heavily on him when decisions were to be made. There are no real guidelines for women who want to retire from their job. Does she go back to homemaking? Should she join organizations? Should she do volunteer work? Travel? What is the expected path for Carol to follow? Everyone else is doing something else. Many of Carol's colleagues cannot envision life without the daily routine. Many are retiring and relocating. One good friend has begun volunteer work in a hospital, but the friend had always expressed interest in doing this.

Just as Carol relied on her father, so had she relied on her husband to help her to make decisions. She knows that she will still do that now. They have had many discussions on the subject of retirement. Ted has many conflicts about his own retirement date and in addition has been giving serious thought to moving to a warmer climate. Carol is aware that this decision will be Ted's and that he will make it with her needs in mind as well as his. This is not a problem for her. She is having trouble, however, with what to do with her life wherever they may live.

Her daughters, who are very much daughters of the women's movement as well as of Carol and Ted, are busy giving her advice as to what she should do. "No way," they say, "should you give up involvement in your career. It has meant too much."

They insist that she will not be happy unless she has a part-time job in her field of work.

Carol's response to their advice is interesting. She is not, as she thought she might be, accepting it wholeheartedly. They may indeed be right, but she questions if their values apply completely to her and her life. She has relied on other people to help her make decisions but she instinctively selects those who best reflect her basic nature. She is not at this time accepting her children's evaluation of her situation and moving with it. She is completing her own evaluation of what she needs to do.

This is another instance where things are not quite as they seem. Carol's less active coping style is tempered with an instinctive knowledge of her own needs. It is important for Carol to know this about herself, particularly now. She wants to make a decision about her retirement. Knowing that she can trust her instincts has given her a feeling of her own power.

Like Claudia and Carol, you too have the opportunity to take a good look at how you have coped with those transitional periods of life that were within your control. You can become aware of your style of decision-making, for many of these times involved junctures where choices were to be made. You can assess how satisfied you are with your style and with your choices.

You have the chance to gain a greater appreciation of how far you have come and how much you have done. Perhaps there are changes you wish to make within yourself. Perhaps you wish to make some alterations in your immediate environment. Insights into your coping pattern can give you the power to program your retirement years for success.

HOW DID YOU COPE
WITH CHANGES YOU COULDN'T CONTROL?

Imposed transitions (Category II) are life changes that involve unexpected and undesirable situations over which you have had no control. You may be one of the fortunate to whom this section does not apply. You may find that more than one transition applies to you.

Each of the four questions concerns a specific transitional period. Each is followed by several choices that focus on the actions you took at a particular time of your life. Choose the statements that best describe how you coped with that period of your life. Several choices may fit each picture. Do not try to evaluate the event or your feelings; stay with the specific actions you took.

You may have had a catastrophic event that differs from the ones listed; even so, the statements below may help you gain insight into your coping style.

You may find that you have had to deal with more than one event in a particular category. If so, evaluate each event separately. The more transitions you handled the more information you will have about yourself.

Imposed Transitions: Questionnaire

Question 1. Did World War II, the Korean conflict, or the Vietnam war necessitate a prolonged separation from a loved one? How did you cope with this change?
  a) I went back to my usual routine as soon as I could.
  b) I saw to it that the necessary daily routines continued for the others in my life who depended on me.
  c) I accepted the help offered to me by others.
  d) I sought help from a support group or a counselor.

Question 2. Were you faced with a career or job change because of circumstances beyond your control? How did you cope with this?
  a) I took the first job I could find as soon as possible.
  b) I pursued all jobs for which I was qualified by means of networking, registering with employment agencies, sending out résumés, or answering want ads.
  c) I used this as an opportunity to change the direction of my life either by training for another line of work, going into my own business, or changing my career goals.

d) I was out of work for a few months without actively job-hunting.

e) I went to a career counselor.

Question 3. Have you had to deal with the serious illness or injury of a loved one? How did you deal with this?

a) I contacted the necessary people (medical personnel, hospital administrators, care givers, others).

b) I rearranged my schedule so that it would include the time necessary for caretaking.

c) I saw to it that the necessary daily routines continued for the others in my life who depended on me.

d) I arranged personal time for myself.

e) I accepted the help offered to me by others.

f) I sought help from a counselor or a support group.

Question 4. Have you experienced the unexpected death of a loved one? How did you cope?

a) I contacted the necessary people (relatives, friends, lawyer, bank manager, others).

b) I made the funeral arrangements.

c) I saw to it that the daily routines continued for the people in my life who depended on me.

d) I went back to my usual routine as soon as I could.

e) I accepted the help offered to me by others.

f) I sought help from a counselor or a bereavement group.

Contemplation of your behavior during the above events can highlight unrecognized capabilities. Just as catastrophic events change lives forever, they also tap previously unknown personal resources. How you coped with the situation may not seem remarkable to you, but as you evaluate your responses you may get some surprises and find some unexpected resources within yourself. As you face this new transition of retirement, be aware of the strength and courage you displayed over your lifetime.

Imposed Transitions: Assessment

Question 1. Wartime separation. Being forced to cope with a separation that is beyond your control presents difficult and special problems. This is true no matter the cause. If you were faced with this transitional period and you coped successfully you displayed a measure of strength you know will always be there. We found many women who had never thought to give themselves credit for the way they had managed difficult transitions.

These particular transitions have characteristically left vestiges of mixed emotions. They were often so incapacitating that many women couldn't recollect the entire story. Try to look at the strengths you used for survival and allow yourself the credit you deserve.

If you quickly went back to your regular routine (*statement a*), you utilized a most practical way to cope. This strategy makes your life as comfortable and familiar as it can be during a difficult period. As you continued your usual activities you provided yourself with a structure that made it easier to handle the unfamiliar and difficult aspects of your life. This coping strategy can be important to remember and utilize as you move into retirement. You may have misgivings about the change, yet it can be minimized if the structure of your life remains intact.

If you saw to it that the daily routines continued for the others in your life (*statement b*), you again chose a practical way by continuing with what was comfortable and familiar. Tending to the needs of others is a constructive way to cope when life is difficult.

Did you, however, choose this without continuing your own routine (*statement a*)? You may want to look at the meaning this has in terms of your coping style. Some people rise to the occasion when the needs of others are involved but have difficulty when the need is just for themselves. You may want to use this information about yourself as you assess your retirement options.

Elaine married her husband in 1945 when he returned from World War II. She was eighteen and just out of high school.

She did not work outside the home and their only child was born within the first year of the marriage. She described herself as devastated when her husband was recalled to active duty and sent to Korea late in 1951.

Elaine was able to continue the daily routines for her daughter, who was in nursery school. She said, however, that she had great trouble continuing with her own life, which had involved many social and charitable obligations. She did what she could but was far less active during this time of her life. She feels she coped as well as she did because of her child's needs, but she never saw coping as an accomplishment. She never felt she had done anything special.

Elaine recognizes herself as a woman who has always put the needs of others first. She is not alone in this category. Women often expect themselves to be this way. Elaine's husband will soon be retiring from his job and she knows this will be an important transition for them. As she reshapes her life once again, she would like to feel that she is responding in terms of her own needs, not just reacting to meet the wishes and needs of her husband. She would like to try to use some of her coping abilities and her inner strength to serve herself as well as others.

If you were able to accept help offered to you by friends or relatives (statement c), you demonstrated that you were aware of your limitations and needs and were willing to look for outside support. Many women told us of the help they received at this time from other women: friends in similar circumstances who supported each other emotionally, mothers or sisters who helped with child care, and often mothers-in-law who made themselves available. If you were able to take advantage of this help, you reach out to others as a part of your coping style. You recognize that finding support is a productive way to cope with problems. This will serve you well.

Support groups and counselors (statement d) were not readily available during the years of World War II and the Korean conflict. It is not likely that many of you who were trying to deal with these transitions took advantage of this kind of help. Be aware that you can call on these services during the transitions still to come. Those of you who did use this outside help have the self-awareness to know when you cannot deal effectively alone. You also know where to go to get the aid you need. This coping strategy will be important to you as you face the retirement years.

If you negotiated this transitional period with any degree of success it is important that you appreciate the courage and strength it took. This is particularly true if you are a woman who came of age in the 1940's. You were of the generation who expected your husbands, fathers, or brothers to make decisions or in some way shape your lives. You expected to be dependent on men and instead you found yourself faced with a world in which you had to make decisions on your own, a world that forced you to be independent as well as lonely. Your lives were altered by this transitional time because, no matter what your expectations about life after the war, you were never the same again. You called up resources you never knew you had, or at least had never tested. Think back to that time and reflect on what you accomplished.

Shirley was eighteen years old on December 7, 1941, when the United States was drawn into World War II. Although she had just married she was not surprised when her husband, Walter, enlisted in the Marines almost immediately. She continued working at her job when her husband left for the service and remained alone in their small apartment in Brooklyn, New York. She had some financial problems and after a few months took in a roommate to cover the rent.

The roommate had a job in the Brooklyn Navy Yard working on the assembly line making three times the salary that Shirley was. It took some time and soul-searching but Shirley decided to change jobs and became a line worker at the Navy Yard. She enjoyed the work, discovered she was competent, and enjoyed the extra money. When she was asked to become a leader of her department she realized she had a talent for managing people.

Despite the pleasure of the job, she missed Walter and was pleased to have him home on leave. When the war was over she left her job at the Navy Yard. Walter soon returned to work and Shirley stayed home to raise her family.

Shirley and Walter had three children. Shirley was always rather restless as a housewife and became involved in many community activities. She went back to college and got her degree in 1966. She has been working since then doing various freelance jobs that involve political and community projects. Walter, who has serious health problems, is now eligible for his pension and Social Security. Shirley is willing to consider the possibility of retirement.

In evaluating her feelings and her options at this time. Shirley was pleased to discover qualities of strength of which she had not been clearly aware. She never recognized how successfully she had negotiated the period when Walter was in the service. She had made financial and career decisions on her own and managed the stress of having a man away at war. She made a life for herself which included friends and activities that gave her pleasure.

She knew that her return to school and to work in the 1960's made her a participant in the women's movement. She was proud of this but never connected her restlessness or her ambition with her earlier experiences during the war years. Shirley had never acknowledged her success.

Because of Walter's serious health problems, Shirley has postponed planning for her retirement, although she needs to do some important practical planning. She has begun to look at her life with greater insight and appreciation as she reflects and evaluates where she has been and what she has accomplished during her lifetime. She is beginning to acknowledge her reservoir of courage and feels better able to plan for the next transition in her life.

Question 2—*Unexpected job loss.* This can be an extremely painful transitional period. No matter what the reason for the job loss, the experience involves rejection and requires action. It is difficult to feel rejected, experience loss, and take sensible action all simultaneously. All of the women we spoke with who have had to deal with this transition felt that it was one of the worst periods of their lives, even though they eventually moved on and became successful. The pain of the experience was not diminished, although many of them were able to say it was for the best.

If you found yourself faced with this situation and if you took the first job you could find (*statement a*), you may feel that you did so for economic reasons. This may be so. No one can deny the reality of the need for an income. If you acted quickly and successfully for your financial benefit, then you coped well with a difficult time.

You were fortunate if a suitable job was available to you at the right time. You may have searched quickly and competently and located the job almost immediately. This is not usual, but it sometimes happens.

It is also possible that the rush into another job was a way of avoiding the bad feelings that are a part of this transition. Several women who had immediately taken other jobs acknowledged that this was what they had done. In each case they had settled on a new job that was inferior in some way to the one they had been forced to leave. They had been upset by the rejection and loss and had accepted the first job offered to them.

This is a strategy which indicates that you are a person of action. The ability to change an uncomfortable situation is useful when you are negotiating a transition. If you have a tendency to act precipitously in times of difficulty, you must acknowledge it as the difficult issues of retirement emerge. Do not allow the stress of this change to cause you to commit yourself to a new place or new situation before you are ready.

If you vigorously pursued the jobs for which you were qualified (*statement b*), you too displayed an active style of coping. You were able to take hold of a difficult situation and move in a practical direction. If you competently took hold during this transition you should know that you have the ability to do the same as you move toward retirement.

How did you actively pursue your goal?

If you utilized networking, you will call upon other people as you cope with your problems. You may want to have discussions with retirees about their feelings and perceptions about their situation. This is a valuable resource and being able to utilize this strategy will give you insight into how you want to negotiate this period for yourself.

If you registered with agencies and had them do a job search for you, you rely on an authority in times of difficulty. It is a sign of strength to recognize a need for help and where to find it. Calling upon community and private agencies such as the American Association of Retired Persons (AARP) for information can help you better understand what life will be like during the retirement years.

If you answered want ads and sent out résumés, you have an ability to rely on your own resources even in difficult times. This style of handling transitional times will serve you well as you begin to plan your retirement.

Marie told us that when she lost her job fifteen years ago as an administrative assistant with a publishing company she had a difficult time finding a new job and was out of work for more than six months. Most of the publishing companies had laid off people at the same time because the industry was in a slump. She nevertheless sent out résumés to the other publishing companies as the main part of her job search. She did not bother looking at want ads or going to employment agencies to seek other positions. She received replies telling her that her résumé would be kept on file. She could not find another position.

Until we talked, Marie had not questioned why she had persisted in a futile job search and saw no particular significance in her handling of the unemployment situation. She saw only that she had coped with an active, independent style and had been unsuccessful. She soon began to understand that more had been going on.

She had been upset when she realized that most of her friends at work had not lost their jobs. She felt a deep sense of rejection and the blow to her self-esteem prevented her from accepting the fact that the industry was in trouble. She had been forced to leave her job because of her lack of seniority but she couldn't look past the feeling that she had been singled out. She felt unable to face another job and she denied her painful feelings by going through the motions of a job search. She had not been coping realistically with her situation and therefore had been unable to see productive ways she could have used to find another position.

Marie was out of work longer than was needed because of various emotional issues. Unwittingly she had reinforced her feelings of being a failure with her unsuccessful job search and thus became even more depressed. She eventually pulled herself together and took another job from which she is now considering retiring.

Marie felt that her evaluation afforded unique insight into some underlying issues of importance as well as into her actions at the time. She had never recognized that she might have changed her situation if she had been able to act differently; instead, she had felt herself to be the victim of circumstances. As she faces this new transitional time she will try to recognize her own power to change and control her life.

If you used this particular transition as an opportunity to change the direction of your life (*statement c*), you must give yourself credit for the courage it took to transcend this difficult period. Know it and count on it as you move into retirement. As we stated before, no matter how impersonal the reason, no matter how much beyond your control, the loss of a job has a strong impact on one's feeling of self-worth. The ability to marshal your resources and make a new plan indicates a strong faith in yourself and your abilities.

Helen had worked in advertising in New York City since her graduation from college. She had never married and for ten years had had a successful career which culminated when she was promoted to art director of the agency. After she had worked in this position for five more years, the agency was taken over by a large corporation. Due to changes that followed the takeover, Helen found herself without a job. She was given a generous severance settlement that provided some financial security, but she was extremely disturbed at her circumstances, because she had planned to spend her career at the agency. She was forty-five years old.

She felt angry and "homeless." For a brief time she felt unable to go on with her life. She received emotional support from her many friends in advertising agencies and other areas of her life and although the job market in advertising was soft, Helen tentatively began to think about whom to call and how to go about job-hunting.

This unhappy period and the emotions engendered forced her to evaluate her needs and determine the direction she wanted her life to take. She began to think about leaving advertising altogether. She had never seriously thought about making a change, but it suddenly seemed to be a distinct possibility.

She researched and planned and a year later she bought a small business in a resort area outside of New York City. This was fifteen years ago. She now owns a shop that features paintings and crafts done by American artists. She has been successful after a slow start and has been amazed and delighted at the form her new life has taken. She often travels to buy artwork and has become friendly with people from all over the country. She has more leisure time because she makes her own schedule. Most important, she feels that she has a greater appreciation of what life has to offer.

She is now thinking of retiring on a part-time basis. She is deciding if she wants to hire a manager for her business and live for six months of the year in a warmer climate. She is handling another transition.

Helen's story is unusual but not unique. Women have demonstrated that they have the ability to recover from adversity and move on. Many women have taken similar situations and turned them to their advantage. If you were able to take stock and change direction when you lost a job, make sure you give yourself the credit that you deserve.

If you responded to your job loss by staying out of work for a few months (*statement d*), determine why you took the time and how you utilized it. If you decided that you were going to give yourself an enjoyable and productive vacation, the implications we are discussing here probably do not apply to you.

Very often the feelings experienced by the loss of a job will leave one unable to embark on a job search. This may have happened to you. However, you now know several important things about yourself that can be useful to you as you plan for the future. First, you tend to respond to difficult situations by withdrawing. Second, you are able to move on even if it is not as soon as you would like (you did not remain immobile or you would not now be in the process of considering your retirement). Third, you know how you can best recover (if you reflect on the time you will probably see what initiated your trip back).

Many women who had spent several months without actively job-hunting spoke of feeling totally uninterested in thinking about their employment situation. None of them was in financial need, although a few did mention that they had to be more careful how they spent their money during the time they were out of work. The married women, particularly, busied themselves with household chores. Few of them had seen it as a period of depression until they looked back upon it.

Each had an individual moment when the energy and the interest to continue returned. Some women found that the opportunity for a job presented itself. Some felt that others in their lives gave confidence. A small number of women went for outside professional help. Others said that they just decided it was time to go back to work.

If after losing a job you stayed out of work without making a conscious choice to do so, you may have a tendency to become reclusive during times of change. Retirement can trigger similar problems since it is one of the many transitional periods that involve loss. Be aware that you may respond in this way. Use your previous experiences to help you prevent or negotiate it.

How did you finally work it through? Did you seek help from others? Was this help from a professional or was it from supportive people in your life? Did you wait for some outside intervention? Is it realistic to think that it will come at this time as well? Or do you just need personal space and time to evaluate and assess your emotions? If retirement triggers similar problems you will be able to utilize this self-knowledge to your advantage.

The advent of the career counselor is new (statement d). It was a resource not utilized by the women we spoke with, possibly because it was not readily available to them when it was needed. Counseling was originally available only for the recent graduate or for the person with no work experience, but it is now becoming a popular avenue for anyone who is unemployed. It's often difficult to acknowledge that you need help and then to follow through. If you were able to request help, you have the self-awareness to face your needs and to try to fulfill them. Counseling can be valuable if you are thinking of a second or third career when you retire.

The transitional period that involves losing one's job has in the past been considered the province of men. Although women have flooded into the labor force over the past twenty years, and although they have lost their share of jobs, job loss for women—except for single women—was never seen as much of an event. Women, after all, were supposed to receive their identity from their homes, husbands, and children. It was the man for whom a job was all-important.

One thing came clear in our discussions with women and in light of the reality of the marketplace: The idea that women's work does not have a strong emotional component is a myth we can file away with "A woman's place is in the home." Whether it is a job or career, women are invested in what they do. They have a sense of pride in their accomplishments and their abilities as strong as any man's.

Question 3—*Illness or accident.* If you had to deal with an unexpected illness or an accident that incapacitated a loved one, you are aware of the anxiety and despair that can accompany this catastrophic time. You also know the practical problems that accompany it. The transitional period is not usually remembered as a time when a difficult challenge was met and conquered, but is remembered more with a sense of resignation.

Women have traditionally been called upon to cope with these situations. Women are expected to be available and capable. It is the unusual woman who saw herself as doing anything special when she had to deal with the many problems and complications involved in her situation. Jean, whom we met early in the chapter, is a typical example of the attitude presented by women who have coped with this transitional period.

As a mother and housewife, she never regretted her choice

to stay home, but she expressed admiration for her friends who had gone into the labor market. She admired their energy and ability to manage their two lives. Several of her friends returned to school and obtained college degrees. She admired their drive to achieve. She never considered herself a possible object of anyone's admiration for the way she had coped with her life.

As we discussed the way she handled the illnesses of her father and mother, Jean began to have a sense of her capabilities. Though it was not always easy, she dealt with doctors, health care workers, insurance companies, and hospital administrators. She saw that her parents, her husband, and children were cared for properly. She had taken hold of a situation much as a skilled executive might have done, scheduled, delegated, and coordinated her life and the lives of others. Her friends who had gone to work or back to school had accomplished no more.

As part of the evaluation, Jean began to see another aspect of her coping style. She had a need to take charge completely. She felt called upon to do everything by herself. She did not accept the aid that had been offered by her brother and sister-in-law, and as a result she never had time for herself. She never felt she did enough. She never gave herself credit for doing anything special so she just kept trying to do more.

Jean is beginning to appreciate what she has accomplished and is beginning to view herself as a more competent person. She is becoming aware of how well organized she is. As she begins to respect her abilities she is beginning to respect her needs and to make room for them in her daily routine of caring for others. She is beginning to appreciate how competent she is in the face of crises. She is gaining a greater self-esteem, which had been eluding her. Now that her husband is planning his retirement, Jean is thinking of returning to school for a college degree. She has found the courage to make some plans of her own, although she knows she will continue to be the accommodating and loving wife she has always been. A new life is upon her and she is looking forward to living it.

If you have had to deal with the illness of your husband, your parents, or perhaps your child, you should be aware of how strenuously you have been tested. If you took hold and contacted the necessary people *(statement a)*, put time in your schedule for caretaking *(statement b)*, and kept others in your life cared for *(statement c)*, you must give yourself credit for success. The stress of the situation made it difficult but you were able to cope. You must respect your ability to function despite your feelings of discomfort or despair.

All of the women we spoke with who had faced this situation had, to one degree or another, negotiated it successfully. Some had initially been overwhelmed before they could begin to cope, while others had taken hold at first and then experienced difficulty. Each woman had had a unique set of problems and a slightly different scenario, but each had overcome the problems they encountered.

What the women neglected was themselves. In particular, they did not take personal time *(statement d)*. If the accident or illness occurred more than twenty years ago, the concept of individual entitlement for women was unfamiliar. Any need they felt for some time of their own was denied or accompanied by feelings of guilt. This was particularly true of single women, who felt that since they did not have husband or children, their time and energy were expendable.

The women's movement, which spurred the emphasis on self-fulfillment, has made inroads into this attitude. Personal time and personal entitlement are now more permissible concepts. It is no longer acceptable to ignore your own needs. The women we spoke with who had to deal with this transitional time in the past ten years were often pressured by family (usually their children) and younger friends to look to their own needs. Many of them expressed their reluctance to do so because of their earlier frame of reference. Those who allowed themselves to be persuaded were able to appreciate the benefits.

If you arranged to take time for yourself, you have an advantage because you have shown the ability to recognize and fulfill your needs. This will serve you well as you plan your retirement years. Retirement is a time of more independence and autonomy. To take full advantage of this time you must know yourself.

The inability to accept help offered by others was another

way that many of the women we spoke with failed themselves at the time of crisis (*statement e*). The women's movement has contributed to a change in attitude as well as behavior. Men as well as women are now feeling they should be contributing to the caretaking of a loved one. This concept widens the available help by 50 percent. It is now more acceptable to call upon a husband, son, or brother to help with caretaking situations. Jean had been one of many who decided that it was her task, as the daughter, to care for her parents. She did not expect that her brother would help because he was busy with his work. She would not ask her sister-in-law for help because she was not "family." The single women we spoke with who had siblings of either sex found themselves in a position similar to Jean's. Each felt herself to be the caretaker of choice (everyone's choice) in the situation. Each was the one to cope on a daily basis with this difficult period in the life of the family. Whether the care was physical or perhaps just managerial, it was responsibility. Some of the women were more able to accept occasional help, particularly if the offer came from a sister.

Many people are better able to give care when they feel they are receiving support from the others. If you were able to call upon the resources of others when you were facing these difficulties you know it helped to sustain you as you went about your routine.

The caretaking woman often finds it extremely difficult to utilize the proffered help of others. She has a strong feeling that she must do it all or she is not doing enough. There is also a sense of satisfaction from the sacrifice of time and energy. You might want to consider if this attitude motivated you while you were coping with this transitional time. Was this why you found it difficult to accept the help offered to you? If this was you, you might want to consider how you feel about this attitude of sacrifice now as you move into the next phase of your life. Consider this: Retirement is a time for *you*, a person who has her own needs and entitlements.

Seeking professional help is another relatively new technique for coping (*statement f*). Most of the women we spoke with had not sought this type of help because it was not as accepted or available as it is today. Support groups and counseling are now available in almost every city for almost every situation. Support groups can make the difference in the way you handle situations and they can make the difference in the quality of your survival. Those of you who have been able to take advantage of this resource know how much it has helped. It is a reflection of your self-knowledge as well as your courage that you were able to utilize this important resource. Women have coped, caretaken, and sacrificed and they will continue to do so, but the process of sharing the experience and attempting to better understand it can be the difference in how women feel about themselves.

Question 4—*Coping with an unexpected death.* Two significant facts emerged from the assessments of women who had been involved in the unexpected death of a loved one. First, each at the time had not expected that she would recover and continue with her life, and second, each did not recognize the courage it took to cope successfully with the event and move on from it.

They saw their actions as reactions to what needed to be done. Once finished they had seldom looked back on the time because of the pain it brought to them. As they did reflect, many of the women were surprised at the distance they had traveled. Many could begin to see the event in a perspective that enhanced their understanding and respect for their coping behavior.

If you were able to cope with the necessary contacts (*statement a*) and you were able to make the funeral arrangements (*statement b*), you can understand that you initially rise to an occasion. There are many people who in the shock of the moment go through the motions and handle all the necessary details. Do not diminish this ability. You have an inner coping strength that is available when you need it.

It is important to remember, however, that you will grieve and feel distraught at some later time. Your strength and courage can mask issues that should not go untended. These issues can rise to the surface when all appears to be resolved and the delayed reaction will illuminate the presence of unfinished business.

The ability to continue the daily routines for others as well as for one's self (statements c and d) varied in style among the women. Everyone managed to get back to a life that had a purpose, but the timing as well as the quality were unique to each story.

It appeared that the women who were widowed with children found themselves back on track more quickly than women who were childless. Finances were another important variable. The woman who had to support herself and her family returned to work and to her routine almost immediately. The courage involved here does not have to be described to anyone who has suffered through this tragic loss.

Betty was thirty-five years old and had been married for eight years. She had two sons aged two and five. She worked as a senior buyer for a large department store in the Midwest. She was involved with juggling her job, her children, and her husband.

Her husband, who was forty years old, had just started working for a company that installed computer programs. The job involved extensive traveling. He was on his way home from the airport one Friday night when his car skidded off the road and turned over. He was killed instantly.

Betty did not fall apart. Although she loved her husband, she felt she had to go on because of her children and because of financial problems. Her husband had been out of work for several months before he started this new job and this had eroded their savings. In addition, she was not eligible for life insurance as the waiting period in his new job had not been met. Her job was the basic source of income. She told herself she would have to grieve in her own time and in her own way. She felt she could not afford the luxury of time out.

Several months later she was unable to sleep after extremely tiring and stressful days at work. She was subject to crying jags and temper tantrums, even on her job. She knew she needed help and she found it. She joined a bereavement group and for a short time received individual bereavement counseling as well. Betty discovered that her courage to do what was necessary and her strength to cope had caused her to neglect her own needs. It was another strength, her self-knowledge, that made her aware of her needs.

She learned about her tendency to deny her feelings and her needs. She has tried to be aware of this tendency as life presented other problems. It has helped her through the past twenty-three years, which have been spent productively and happily. Her children are now living on their own. She met with continued success on her job. She remarried twelve years ago. She is evaluating her needs now as she and her husband move into retirement. She wants to be sure that she is looking clearly at her feelings, needs, and priorities.

For many women, coping with this period was made easier because they were able to accept the help others offered to them (*statement e*). This is a time when the tendency to withdraw is strong, and it takes self-knowledge and courage to remain involved. While it is true that no one can change what has occurred, a support network can ease the pain. This is one of the reasons bereavement groups and bereavement counseling are successful (*statement f*). Several of the women who reached out for help said that although the others in their life meant well, they were unable to give the kind of support that was helpful. The women who had the advantage of meeting with a support group agreed it had served a basic need.

Gail had to cope with what some people view as the ultimate loss, the death of her son when he was sixteen. He was her special child, an excellent student and a popular young man. He developed an acute form of leukemia and died within a year.

She was devastated and unable to cope with life. She barely managed to get out of bed for the first month after he died. She barely spoke with her husband, who tried to console her, despite his own grief. Her daughter tried to help, but she had just started college and needed to return to her own life. The bank where Gail worked as a supervisor gave her a leave of absence and told her to return when she was able. She could not improve the way she was feeling. She felt physically ill much of the time. She refused the professional help available to her. Gail found it difficult to continue her relationships with her friends. She managed to resume her job on a part-time basis before a year had gone by, but she had trouble participating in ordinary conversations with anyone outside of business.

Gail is not sure when her life began to turn around or what if anything precipitated the change. She just gradually recovered. She feels that life has never been the same, though she and her husband have continued to have an enjoyable life together. She has been promoted several times in the bank and enjoys watching her three grandchildren grow up.

It was important for Gail to get a sense of the courage it took for her to endure. She had only seen the despair she suffered during the mourning period until she realized she had utilized all of her emotional resources to achieve a recovery.

It is important for those of you who have been tested by these catastrophic transitions to know that you have used emotional resources to cope. Your survival is a testimony to your capabilities and your strength. Women have neglected to give themselves credit for the resources and capabilities they displayed in times of crisis. Traditionally women are expected to be caretakers and sacrificers. When women perform in this expected way, even at times of severe emotional stress, they are not considered remarkable. Unfortunately, even with changes in recent years, this attitude—held by both men and women—has a tenacity of its own.

III

The Many Meanings of Work

No one ever asks a man how he manages to combine marriage and a career.

AUTHOR UNKNOWN

Stacy was ready to retire. She had been in a holding pattern for the past seven years. For some time she owned a house in Florida which she rented out on a seasonal basis for extra income. She was now ready to reclaim it and to leave her home in the north for a warmer, more pleasant climate. She was going to write short stories. She had taken courses in writing and believed she had talent, but she needed time to develop her style. Stacy looked forward to her pension and profit-sharing income to make her retirement possible.

Stacy married right after high school, as did many of her friends, and after her marriage she decided to stay home and be a housewife. Many of her friends also did not work outside of the home, so they visited during the day and in many ways kept the lives they had as teenagers. Most of her friends waited for their lives to begin when they had children. Neither Stacy nor her husband had strong feelings about a family and when they were unable to conceive a child they both agreed not to do anything about seeking medical intervention. Stacy continued her life as a housewife and spent her time taking care of her home and her husband. She felt a strong sense of independence about her time, since her husband spent much of his time involved with his job. She would go to lunch with friends, play Mah-Jongg one or two days a week, and generally set her own schedule. She enjoyed her life and now looks back on those days as being carefree.

She did not want to be divorced. Her husband, however, had started a relationship with a woman he met at work, and by the time Stacy became aware of the situation, his choice to leave the marriage was not negotiable. After her separation and divorce, she felt completely lost and bereft of her identity. She sees this period as the most difficult transition of her life. She went to work out of necessity, since the divorce settlement was not favorable to her and alimony was minimal. She reluctantly entered the labor market. She never clearly evaluated the kind of work she would enjoy. Feeling frightened, she took the first job offered to her. The job was as a receptionist in a small but growing personnel firm in the business area of town. After one year on her job, management told Stacy that she had the personality and aptitude for employment agency work and gave her more responsibility. Although she liked her job and enjoyed her success, she had many nagging feelings of inadequacy. She had concerns about her performance, with an ever-present feeling that she would be "found out" to be less than she appeared. In spite of her feelings of inadequacy and her fears, she did her job well and worked her way up to a middle-management position. She ultimately supervised ten young people, the one part of her job she really enjoyed. After twenty-two years she was one of the oldest workers in the company and enjoyed the esteem of the office personnel, who regarded her as a mentor and advisor. Many of the young men and women wanted her advice about their personal problems, and many of them sought her out to discuss their careers and job options. Stacy liked this status and was aware of the pleasure it gave her, but she never thought to examine how important this was to her self-image.

Despite the fact that she had been given more responsibility, as well as excellent salary increases, the feelings of inadequacy about her performance remained, and this made it difficult for her to evaluate the way she felt about the job itself. As she neared retirement, however, she was pretty sure that the job had become routine and unsatisfying to her. She had a vague notion that when she retired she would miss something about her work, but she was not quite sure what it was. She didn't think about it much, since she knew how much she yearned for relocation, a less stressful life, and more leisure to write. She appeared to be in a perfect retirement situation and was eager to begin her new life.

Stacy retired and liked her new situation at first. It was only gradually that she became aware of a vague sense of dissatisfaction. She could not understand it. Her writing was going well and she was beginning to feel that she might have a second career, having received several encouraging letters from small women's magazines. She made several friends in the community and was active in her church group, so it was not the loneliness of the creative process that was making her feel dissatisfied. She added a few more social responsibilities, becoming chairperson for a church fund-raising event. She loved Florida, but still felt that something important was missing from her life. Stacy had to sort out what it was that was making her dissatisfied with her retirement.

Lillian is sixty-one years old. She is the youngest of two children from a family that traditionally valued education. Both of her parents finished college; her mother was a teacher, her father a journalist. Her mother had taught elementary school, and Lillian remembers with great pleasure the class trips with her mother's students and the visits to her mother's classroom at the end of the school year to help her clean up. She remembers that her mother was often busy and tired during the school year, but she also remembers the summers when her mother was home as times of great pleasure for the family.

During high school Lillian prepared herself for college and

never questioned her decision to continue her education. When she finished college with honors she knew she wanted to go to law school and her family was delighted with her decision. She was accepted by a small law school in the Midwest and, with her family's encouragement, financial assistance, and love, she finished law school. When she graduated she came back east and joined a small law firm that allowed her to practice in a diversified way. She loved the law and she loved being a lawyer. She knew she was the token woman in the law firm, but she was smart and earned the respect of the other lawyers. Although she knew she wanted to be married and have children, her career came first. When she was twenty-nine and established in her career, she married a psychologist, had two children, and continued practicing law. After having her children, she often thought of herself as a lawyer who was also a mother. She remembers this in sharp contrast to many of her friends who thought of themselves as mothers who had a career. Before the phrase and concept became popular, she remembers calling the time she spent with her children "quality time," and this helped assuage her guilt about being away from home. By the time her children were grown, Lillian felt she had made a good compromise between being a mother and having her career.

Throughout the years, Lillian has practiced the kind of law she enjoys. She has had many friends and colleagues. In the past several years many of the older partners in her firm have begun to discuss their retirement. Lillian finds herself in an unusual situation. She knows she doesn't want to retire and has told several of the partners she will "die with her boots on." She enjoys her status as a seasoned attorney, but when she looks at the competitive and ambitious young lawyers, she realizes that her needs and ambitions have changed, Lillian sometimes feels she is in a strange land when she walks the halls of the firm. She sees many younger, unfamiliar faces and many more women. In fact, the lawyers graduating from law school seem to get younger every year. Many of her colleagues in her age bracket are taking longer vacations at unusual times of the year. These peers, whom she could always count on for lunch or an afternoon consultation, are no longer as available, since their work-days are shorter and their weekends longer. She feels fortunate that her psychologist husband wants to continue to practice his profession, although he does speak about "burnout" and reloca-tion. She feels she will be able to stall their decision to make changes, for a while at least. Lillian knows she still loves the law and wants to remain a lawyer, but she too is facing retirement issues.

Elsie graduated from high school, married her childhood sweetheart, and couldn't wait to have a baby. She had three children and loved her life as a wife and homemaker. She loved finding new recipes to cook for her family, enjoyed painting and wallpapering, and even did an occasional plumbing job when the washing machine broke down. She liked buying clothes for her children and arranging parties for their birthdays and holi-days; she particularly enjoyed Christmas—baking cookies and arranging for Santa Claus. She found that organizing her chil-dren's lives, going to their school plays, taking them to their piano, dance, and art lessons was more than a full-time job. And it was! She enjoyed being her husband's wife, picking up his shirts at the laundry, and meeting his train at night. She felt her life had direction and purpose, and when her children were successful in school she felt she had achieved her goals. And then, in a flash, her children grew up. They wanted to stay at school for extracurricular activities and were not home as often for dinner. Elsie found the structure of her life changing. As she turned on the TV one morning shortly after her fortieth birth-day, she realized she felt bored, restless, and uneasy. Her hus-band was on a diet and had asked her not to bake as much, her oldest daughter had just started college and would not be home until Thanksgiving, her two younger children were busy with school activities and would be home only to have a quick sand-wich for dinner, and she'd already cleaned the house.

Elsie remembers that day very well. When she wondered what to do with her time she thought about calling several women with whom she had been friendly. It was then she realized they would not be at home, for they were now working. That evening she called one of her working friends to discover how she might get a job with the same insurance company. She thought they might travel to work together.

That day was over twenty years ago and Elsie has been working for the same company ever since. Her job duties have changed somewhat: She has learned to use a word processor instead of a typewriter and she is earning more than twice her original salary, but the routine is basically the same as it was when she started. She likes the schedule of her days and she enjoys the camaraderie of the office situation. She is friendly with many of the women in her office and she likes that their ages are varied. She is a competent and diligent worker and a valued employee. She would probably consider working until her sixty-fifth birthday except that most of her friends are leaving or have left, and her husband will be retiring next year. Not only did the young Elsie never think she would go to work outside of her home, but she certainly never dreamed that she would be considering retirement.

Until the 1970's, most women defined themselves by the work they did in the home. In 1980, however, 45 percent of the women in our society were employed outside the home, and that number rises every day. The fact that women are spending more time in the workplace has made tremendous changes in the way women identify themselves. When men are asked to tell something about themselves, they most frequently describe the kind of work they do. Men have always considered their work to be the most important part of their identity. Until recently, women, when asked, would state their marital status and tell how many children they had, if any. Married women who work outside the home now have new definitions of themselves, separate from "wife and mother." Even those who spent most of their lives at home and then went into the work force have added a new identity.

This change in women's lives, this entrance into the workplace, has changed the way women feel about themselves. A new dimension was added to the married woman with children. When she went beyond being wife and mother, she found a new sense of self, separate from her life at home. Single women as well have changed the way they feel and identify themselves.

Now when women retire from the work force, they too leave behind a significant part of their identity. Women need to know the impact of this new identity so they can assess their retirement needs. Whether she has worked in or out of her home, a woman will need to discover the essence of herself in her work life in order to go forward successfully into retirement. Preretirement is an important time for women to evaluate what their work means to them. Women have special emotional work to do in preretirement, for their emotional needs are different from men's and they need to be armed with specific information about the meaning of their work. Your retirement future is in your hands. The more information you have about yourself and what your work has meant to you, the more options and opportunities you will be able to use in negotiating your successful retirement.

Some women who have worked most of their lives look forward to a life of leisure during retirement. Many of these women are content to put off any detailed retirement plans. Whatever their work may have meant to them, it doesn't matter; they just want to be finished with it. If this is how you feel, you should know that most women with this feeling discover that they thoroughly enjoy the first years of their unstructured retirement, but that they begin to feel restless and unproductive after three or four years. So you may want to hold on to the information in this chapter for future use.

The questionnaire that follows is designed to help you determine the meaning of work in your life. It is divided into four categories: money, duties and routines, social aspects, and prestige and identity. Each questionnaire and discussion will be separate, to allow you to evaluate your responses more easily. All four categories apply to everyone to one degree or another. You will probably have several responses in each category. Each response is an important part of your evaluation. As you evaluate each response you have made, keep in mind that you may have gone to work for one reason but stayed at your job for quite another reason. Evaluate in terms of what is current. Your life has changed and so have your needs. Remember as you answer the questionnaire that there is no right answer, only *your* answer.

The Meaning of Money in Your Life: Questionnaire

It would be foolish to attempt to write anything about the meaning of work and not address the issue of money. Your financial resources are the most important part of your retirement future. Money is society's scorecard of success, but we want you to consider its meaning in your working life in a slightly different perspective. (If you need help in assessing your finances for retirement, or if you have other questions about investing, refer to our resource guide. There is a list of publications that will help you determine your financial situation.)

Consider the following statements and check the ones that apply to your situation.

a) I went to work because it was necessary for me to earn a living.
b) I went to work to supplement the family income.
c) I could never financially afford to be without a job.
d) When the income was no longer important, I continued to stay in the work force.
e) Money was not the reason for my working, although it was nice to have.
f) I am married and I have some money separate from my husband.
g) I consider myself financially independent.

The Meaning of Money: Assessment

If you found that any of the first three statements (*statements a, b, c*) apply to you, will this continue to be true until you retire? If work was and is a financial necessity, you may believe that you were interested in your work and stayed at it only because you needed a way to support yourself. You may be correct, and only you know this about yourself. For many women who grew up in the 1950's and early 1960's and went to work in the late 1960's and the 1970's, the most important consideration of going to work was economic. Many did not stop to consider if they had special interests or skills. Whether married or single, they often took jobs based on the proximity to their home or the availability of flexible hours. They usually obtained sales jobs, clerical jobs, or service jobs that did not pay well. Their work outside the home was often sedentary and monotonous. If you fit into this picture and feel that the meaning of your job never went beyond the paycheck, think back. Once you earned money, did you begin to experience yourself in a new way? Money brought to women in the work force a different sense of purpose in their lives and a feeling of success they had never before experienced. We do not mean to imply that food, shelter, and clothing are not important, and money obviously gave you access to those basics; but, in addition, money gave women access to other important intangibles. When women went back to work they felt, for the first time in their lives, a feeling of self-worth, a sense of achievement, self-reliance, and pride. Women who never experienced themselves as independent or self-directing began to have a new image of themselves, sometimes because of the job itself, but often because they were earning a salary. Evaluate this component of your work carefully before you dismiss the fact that your working life has been simply a matter of economics.

If you stayed in the labor market after your children finished college or you paid off the mortgage (*statement d*), your salary was not the necessity it once had been. (There will be opportunity to explore this question later in the chapter.) But did you remain despite the fact that your job offered you little satisfaction? Do you know why you stayed? Many women could not quite identify what had kept them on the job. When we talked, we found that money was the deciding factor, even though the dollars-and-cents need was no longer operating. But, more important, money means independence and is often a measure of self-worth. Many women do not realize this. At the time of retirement they are reluctant to give up their independence. It is important for you to know if money means any of these intangibles to you. If so, be very sure that you will have enough income to allow you to continue to feel good about yourself. The amount varies for all, and you need to know how much will suffice for you.

If money was not the reason you went to work (*statement e*), but you did enjoy having it, look carefully at what the money bought for you in the intangible areas we spoke of above. Also consider carefully the issues of financial independence. For some married women, having their own paycheck gave their relationship with their husband another perspective. Many married women began to rethink the way they wanted to manage not only the family finances but their lives as well. More women, however, had conflict when they considered *statement f* (I am married and I have some money separate from my husband). Some of them did . . . "but." Some considered their money separate but began to consider the way they would negotiate their separate money when they retired. Most retired couples we spoke with had a fixed income and usually considered their money to be held jointly. The way you will feel about money in your retirement if you have had some prior autonomy can be essential to a successful retirement.

Laura, whom we will meet in Chapter V, Family Attachments, came up with some interesting insights for herself when she evaluated this section of the questionnaire. She had gone back to work after her children had grown and until that time had always received an "allowance," which was usually well accounted for each week. When she began to bring in income, she and her husband Michael worked out an equitable arrangement so that a good portion of her salary was hers to spend as she wished. She enjoys the freedom to spend without any accountability. When she considered retirement she never thought about the possibility of returning to a situation of less autonomy regarding money. She does not feel that she and Michael have conflict over money, and he does not control the way she spends money, but she is concerned. Before she began working, he knew every penny she spent. She does not want to return to this scenario for many reasons. One reason concerns her grandchildren. It is important to her to be the benevolent grandmother. Part of her pleasure in her job is the pride she feels at having money with which to indulge her grandchildren. Although Michael is every bit as devoted to the grandchildren, he doesn't think he needs to spend much on them. Laura likes to be able to give them special treats, and she knows that in retirement she will want enough money to be able to continue such beneficence. She knows that should the money once again be jointly managed she may need to request and explain every expenditure. She knows Michael would be willing any time she really wanted to buy something, but she does not ever want to be in the "asking" position. She is thinking this through and planning how she will build this need into the financial part of the retirement plan she and Michael negotiate. Retirement will change some of the independence Laura has achieved, but retirement does not have to be the time to give up her autonomy completely.

Statement g (I consider myself financially independent) is an issue that is basic to successful retirement for many women. Only you know how important an issue this is for you. Some of the women we spoke with considered this question to be moot; they had never given it much thought and did not feel they needed to begin at this time. These were often the women in traditional marriages who had enjoyed a sense of security about the family income for most of their lives.

The concrete aspects of your financial situation can be easily planned, but do not ignore the emotional pieces of financial independence, which may be central to your well-being.

Duties, Purpose, and Routine: Questionnaire

In this section you will get a picture of the specific duties and activities involved in your work. Choose the statements that apply to your job and give some thought as to how important or how meaningful each aspect is to you.

a) My working day has a regular routine to it.

b) I perform the same tasks on a regular basis.

c) I work for someone who clearly defines my job duties on a consistent basis.

d) My job is not the same from day to day.

e) Most of the time I work independently.

f) Most of the time I am in charge of my own work.

g) My job often puts me in contact with people inside my company.

h) My job often puts me in contact with people outside my company.

i) My job often puts me in contact with the public.

j) My job involves work with projects or special research.

k) My job involves work with statistics.

Duties, Purpose, and Routine: Assessment

This section proved to be straightforward and easy to respond to for most of the women we interviewed, and yet many of them were surprised at how much information about themselves they obtained from this evaluation. The manner in which you have lived on a daily basis and the daily activities you have been involved in can tell you much about who you are and what you need to have in your life. Examine your responses carefully.

If *statement a* applies to your working situation and you rather enjoy the routine of your working day, you have an important factor to consider as you enter retirement. For most people the structure and continuity of a job give life a sense of purpose, and routine is often an important aspect of working life. If this is true for you in your job, when you retire you will probably want to plan activities that will give your days a similar structure and continuity. The kind of activities you do may actually be of less importance than the fact that you have places to go and things to do with a certain amount of regularity. You may decide to do volunteer work, join a special-interest committee or organization, or perhaps go to school. Think about this carefully as you continue your evaluation.

Elsie is quite aware that one of the reasons she went to work outside the home was to replace the routine that was no longer present in her life as a housewife. Elsie enjoys her working life outside the home, has many friends, and enjoys feeling that she is a productive worker, but what she likes most about her job is that she feels comfortable and purposeful performing her set responsibilities. She is determined not to find herself in retirement in the same place as she was twenty years ago when she went to work outside of the home. She is considering how she can plan her days with activities that interest her so that she will feel organized and productive. She is currently thinking about taking some courses with a friend at the local community college.

If you determined that you have plenty of routine on your job but you do not like it, you may be a woman who in your retirement is looking forward to oceans of unstructured time. You may view retirement as a time to make your own structure, to reflect, rest, and put your life in order. You may symbolically walk on the beach and revel in the fact that your working life is over. If you determine that this is your need, retirement can have an ebb and flow without an external structure. Be aware that your needs may change, and if they do, you have options and opportunities available. Many women enjoy this unstructured style in the early years of their retirement but feel the loss of a routine as time passes.

Rachel had worked as a bookkeeper for the twenty years she had been employed after her husband died. For the last twelve years she worked for a mail order company. She had kept the books, done the billing, and handled the payroll. She had enjoyed the routine of it and liked working with figures. For the last two years, however, she became impatient with the sameness of her daily life and actually accelerated her retirement date because she felt she didn't want to do bookkeeping any longer.

She retired, stayed at home, and moved at her own pace for three years. She saw friends, went to the theater, went to lunch, took a course at the university, and baby-sat with her grandchildren . . . and she was content. Gradually she began to feel uncomfortable about her aimlessness. To cope with this feeling of being disorganized she started to make a list of things to do each day. She found at first that she didn't necessarily need to follow everything on the list, but she needed the activity of making the list to reassure her that she had a direction. Now, to her surprise, she is beginning to feel ready again for some actual structure and direction in her life. She is in the process of searching for some options.

As Rachel evaluated her feelings about her retirement she realized that she missed not only the routine but the regularity of her work. The payroll (which did not change much from week to week), the monthly billing, and the yearly tax preparation all had a flow that gave Rachel a great deal of satisfaction and comfort.

If *statement b* applies to your job, and you perform the same tasks on a regular basis and enjoy this part of your job, you know an important part of yourself. You probably do not like surprises or too much change in your life. You are more comfortable with what is familiar. Retirement can thrust you into routines that are known and will be pleasant for you if your life outside of work is as well organized as your job situation. If this is not your situation and your personal life is more complex, be aware that you need some sameness and routine in your life in order to be emotionally comfortable. If you determined that you perform the same tasks on a regular basis but this is an area you disliked about your job, you may experience retirement as a welcome rite of passage and a time to leave a routine and perhaps frustrating job.

Wilma had started work in the post office when few women thought of being hired for that civil service position. As a single parent, she had worked long hours, putting in a good deal of overtime at a job she never enjoyed, but she had little chance to leave. She is looking forward to retirement with great expectations. She wants the freedom to explore new options, and she wants to have a new beginning. She never felt in full control of her working life, and she sees retirement as a time to develop herself, with hobbies, travel, time with her grandson, and a freedom she has always dreamed about. She sees her retirement as a time to begin the next phase of her life, a time to have life on her own terms. She feels energetic and knows she has the ability to enjoy the rest of her life to its fullest.

If *statement c* applies to your job—if your work has been clearly defined for you on a consistent basis—you too may experience a loss of external structure when you retire. Even if what is assigned to you is not the same each day, and even if the assignment alters your daily routine in fairly predictable ways, you do not have the opportunity to plan and make your own choices as to how you spend your time. There are many women who went from their parents' home to their marriage to a job in which they had supervision, and many of them never strove to be more autonomous. If you are one of these women and this is a pattern that has worked for you, be aware of it and carefully evaluate its importance to your sense of well-being. If this pattern has been successful for you, you have probably chosen your authority figures well and will probably continue to do so. You are likely to be more comfortable when you have someone to consult on a consistent basis. You may need to continue this pattern in order to have a successful retirement. If you are married and this is the style of your marriage, then you will not have a problem. If, when you retire, you will not have the authority in your life that your work provided, you will need to replace it in some way.

Lorraine graduated from college in 1952. She worked at a succession of jobs until she found one she liked as a secretary to an executive in a large hotel in her city. Dennis, her boss, was a married man with two children who was ten years her senior. The two of them got along beautifully from the beginning. He was an authoritarian person, much like her father, and he structured her work and her time. He helped her to understand the business and gave her more and more responsibility, but always under his supervision. He depended on her for many details of his job. Lorraine never married, and over the thirty-one years she worked for him she was promoted to executive secretary, to administrative secretary, and then to assistant to the vice-president when Dennis got his promotion. She enjoyed working in the hotel, loved her boss, and considered herself very lucky to have such a good life.

Very suddenly, a few months after Lorraine celebrated her thirty-first anniversary with the hotel, Dennis had a heart attack and was never able to return to work. The man who took over for him was considerably younger, and at first relied on Lorraine for information and advice. He was also extremely authoritarian and soon had his own systems and procedures. He structured Lorraine's day and her time just as Dennis had, but she no longer enjoyed going to work. Something about the way that her new young boss supervised made Lorraine uncomfortable. He was not respectful or interested in her feelings and did not share events with her. He just directed. He made her feel like an underling after all those years of feeling like a partner.

Lorraine has been working in this situation for three years. She is eligible for retirement, although her pension is not what it will be if she holds on for three more years. Through self-assessment and evaluation she has become aware of her job situation. A friend who is involved in women's issues suggested that she should have been promoted to Dennis's job when he had the heart attack and that her disappointment is the source of her trouble with this new supervisor. Lorraine is absolutely sure that her friend is wrong. She is certain that she does not want this job for herself—she never wanted the autonomy or the responsibility that goes with being an executive. But she also knows that she doesn't want to work for or be dependent on someone who treats her as this new man does. She is struggling with this problem and at this time is seriously thinking of retiring from her job. She is considering relocating to be near her older sister, with whom she has always been close. She is aware that her sister has been a good authority figure in her life, and living near her will be comfortable and reassuring. She has other areas of her life to consider before she takes this step, but at this moment she has an important piece of information about herself that will help her as she faces retirement.

You may be working for a company where the hierarchy is clearly defined, and like Lorraine you may be comfortable knowing your place in it. Many of the women we spoke with were in this situation but were not always happy with it. Some of them found they were undervaluing their importance or that others were undervaluing them. Many women we interviewed admitted having feelings about the fact that they never truly worked to their full capacity. You may feel you have hidden capabilities. If this is you, retirement may be the time to take some more determined steps, try new things you never thought you could do. This may be the first time in your life that you can take risks with lessened fear of the consequences of failure.

Rachel, too, felt that her capabilities had gone largely unused. She had always had her bookkeeping job clearly defined for her. But she often wished she could be more autonomous in some areas of her work. She liked it when she could work independently (*statement e*) and when she was in charge of her own work (*statement f*), and she had tried to set her own daily schedule for doing each task. She began to realize that she had been eager to leave her job because her boss was becoming more and more involved with her duties as his business began to grow. She realized that this interference with her autonomy was probably as much the reason for her wanting to be free of routine as was the routine itself.

Rachel is looking to put some structure back into her life, and she has been considering returning to the labor market on a part-time basis. As she evaluates the possibilities she now knows that she must consider her need for autonomy and independence in her work. She is realistic enough to know that this is difficult to find in part-time work. She has begun to think about starting her own mail order business on a small scale, selling one or two choice items. She feels that she has the expertise to do so after running the financial part of a similar business, and if she is able to bring this about she will have the structure, routine, and independence she needs in her life.

Issues of autonomy and independence often appear as women evaluate their lives. If you have strong needs in this area, your work situation probably fulfilled them, and your adjustment to retirement will be smooth only if you carefully consider the ways you can continue to be autonomous. If you are married and have these needs, retirement brings its own special issues. Your idea of freedom and autonomy may be different from your husband's. Many married women retire from jobs or careers that give them independence and autonomy only to discover during the first years of retirement that they have automatically reverted to being the kind of wife they were before they went to work.

Most of the women we spoke with did not realize that this was what they were going to do, and it just happened to them. Susan, who retired with her husband, Larry and moved to Arizona in Chapter I, found that in leaving her work as a successful executive, she left her independence as well. She had not realized just how basic this facet of her job was to her sense of well-being, and she did not realize how discontented she would be when she lost it. When she did become aware of her feelings, she took action on her own behalf and is finding that her volunteer job as a museum docent is fulfiling her needs.

For many married women, retirement is a time to exercise caution so their hard-won autonomy will not be lost. The roles women were taught as little girls are still inside them, and women in transitional situations may revert to what worked at an earlier time of their lives. It happens in marriage, in divorce, and in any times of change. Often during the transition to retirement this regression occurs. It can occur without your knowledge, until one day you wake up to discover that your life has taken a direction you did not desire.

Wendy, who was mentioned briefly in Chapter I, is wrestling with just this issue as she faces retirement. She went back to law school at the age of thirty-seven and has been working as a lawyer for twenty years. Unlike Lillian, she does not want to go out with her boots on; she would really like to pursue other interests and have less stress in her life. She knows how important her independence is to her, but she also is aware of her husband's attitudes. He accepts her career but feels that her duties as wife and homemaker come first. Wendy knows that she will have difficulties maintaining her independent state should she stay home full-time. She values her marriage and loves her husband. She will be spending time in the next few years making a plan for her retirement that will balance her individuation needs with her marital responsibilities.

If you feel that you will be coping with these issues as you move into retirement, you may want to review Chapter I on the women's movement and Chapter VI, which deals with couples.

If *statement d* (my job is not the same from day to day) applies to your job situation, it is likely that your job is a challenging one. This variety may be what has kept your job zestful and alive for you. Over a period of many years, however, a job of infinite variety takes on a certain sameness of its own and the challenge becomes less. The stress of these work situations becomes more intense when the challenge of the job wanes. These are the jobs that feature burnout as a possible component. You may be retiring from stress and winding down from the challenges of the past. Although you may be retiring from stress, remember that you may still need a variety of experiences in your life.

Stacy and Lorraine both knew that they would miss the variety in their jobs. Lorraine had always felt that working in a hotel had given her the opportunity to have a variety of experiences with a variety of people as well as the opportunity to handle a variety of situations; and she knows that she will miss this in her life. Although Stacy's work in the job placement firm had become routine, the situations she had to deal with were varied and often interesting, and she knew that she would miss this in her life. Planning a variety of activities to be involved in during her retirement was part of Stacy's plan to fill this void. Lorraine is still exploring her retirement options, but she knows that she will need to replace the variety she had at her job when she makes her retirement plans.

If you are in the same situation you will need to find out

what resources are available to you in your community. Finding activities will be an important objective. Before Stacy relocated she made a card file of the available resources in her area of Florida. She did this by looking in the yellow pages, reading the ads in the local PennySaver, and listening to friends and acquaintances as they spoke of the ways they spent their time.

If you determined that your job often puts you in contact with people inside or outside your company on a business basis (*statement g* and *h*), or if your job puts you in contact with the public (*statement i*), you are accustomed to having daily interactions with many people. Evaluate the way you feel about this aspect of your work. This kind of social interaction can be demanding and exhilarating at the same time. Women who work at this type of job and enjoy the casual interchanges and relationships obtain self-esteem and personal enhancement from these contacts. Many women we spoke with experienced a sense of loss upon retirement because this particular aspect of a job is difficult to replace. Decide if this sort of contact is a part of your job that you enjoy. If it is important you will need to find a way to replace your people contacts when you retire. In your retirement, you will need to have activities in which you can feel engaged and connected with people. For many women with this need, political activity provides a needed high level of people contact.

Beth, who worked as a probation officer, had many contacts at work with people outside her office. She frequently spoke with school principals, employment counselors, lawyers, and policemen. She enjoyed all of these contacts and throughout the years developed an extended social network. These contacts enhanced her and brought her feelings of satisfaction while she performed an important service to her clients. She knows she will need to replace that part of her life in her retirement. As she prepares for relocation and a new career as a paralegal, she is aware she must work with others, for she needs contacts to maintain her positive sense of being an accomplished woman.

June works in the complaint department of a large department store. She has dealt with the public for twenty-one years and knows she is finished with that part of her life. She believes that she has spoken to far too many people in that time and is looking forward to a life of complete solitude. She knows that this is completely unrealistic since she has many friends, a husband, and several grandchildren, but she fantasizes about it anyway. She is looking forward to less adversarial relationships and peace and quiet for several days at a time in her retirement. Often when she has a hard day, she thinks she has missed her vocation as a beachcomber; in retirement she wants to walk on the beach, hearing only the noise of the surf. She knows she will probably enjoy this for a while after she leaves her job, but she also knows her need for people contact is a big part of her.

If you responded that your job involves work with projects or special research (*statement j*), or that your work involves statistics (*statement k*), you probably have special skills that you can utilize in your retirement should you choose to do so. If you opt to cut down your working hours, you might arrange for part-time employment either with your present firm or with a firm with similar needs.

Social Aspects: Questionnaire

Some women find it difficult to evaluate just how meaningful the social aspect of their work life is until they no longer have it. For many, work provides a social structure unavailable in any other area of life. At the time of your retirement you will be leaving people who have been a part of your life, not necessarily because they are your friends but because they have been part of a built-in structure that makes up your working life. It is important for you to evaluate this aspect of your working life with care.

Choose the statements below that apply to your situation at work.
a) I like to have a place to go every day.
b) I enjoy dressing to go to work.

c) I look forward to seeing the people with whom I work.
d) I have at least one friend at work with whom I share events in my life.
e) I spend lunchtime more than once a week with a co-worker.
f) At least once a month after working hours I spend time together with co-workers.
g) When I entertain or plan special parties I often invite some of the people with whom I work.

Social Aspects: Assessment

Even if you do not socialize to any extent with people at work, the lives of your fellow employees intertwine with yours. You may not have any substantial contact with other employees, only chatting with them in the rest room or greeting them on the elevator. You will probably notice their new clothes a new hairdo, whether they have lost or gained weight, their general manner and demeanor . . . and they may notice the same things about you. These people make up your everyday world although they may be only a peripheral part of your life, and for most people this familiarity and sameness is comfortable.

If you responded that you do like to have a place to go everyday (*statement a*) and that you enjoy dressing to go to work (*statement b*), you like to be part of a larger social scene. Many women we spoke with who had already retired mentioned that although they enjoyed being able to dress casually most of the time, now that they were home they missed the involvement they had in shopping and dressing for work as well as for the people they saw every day. When we spoke with Lillian, Lorraine, Stacy, and Elsie about this aspect, they all, despite their varied occupations and backgrounds, agreed that dressing was something they enjoyed about going to work and something they would probably miss.

If you determined that these statements apply to you and your feelings about your job, do not minimize their importance. Just as the actual routine of your job may be meaningful to you, the fact of having a place to go each day and a reason to look good can make a difference in how you feel about yourself and your life. You need the feedback you get from the social inter-changes, the social routines, and the social relationships. You should research organizations or activities you can be involved in so you can replace some of the social structure you will lose when you retire from work.

Many working women interviewed mentioned the impor-tance of having a place to go each day. If you retire from a job, how will you feel about spending a good deal more of your time at home? You must decide if part of the reason you like to be away from home is that it limits the time you can spend as a caretaker for your parents, your grandchildren, or other family members. Working is an excellent reason, as well as an excuse, for limiting distressing contacts and their concomitant demands. When you retire, you may feel you will be more vulnerable to demands to be the family caretaker.

Laura and Judy, whom we meet in Chapter V—Family Attachments, determined that although they liked having a place to go each day because of its intrinsic value to their lives, they also liked that it curtailed their free time and therefore limited their family availability. Laura uses her job as an excuse to avoid excessive baby-sitting, and Judy knows that she would be inundated with family problems if she had the free time that retirement can give her. Knowing this, each is planning her time with this issue in mind. If this is part of your conflict, you need to separate out the issues with which you are involved. Perhaps you need to evaluate your circumstances more carefully in terms of your family life rather than in terms of your feelings about your job.

If you are married and know that you like to have a place to go each day, you must be thoughtful about the way you plan your time in your retirement. Many women we spoke with had been sure of the fact that they wanted to stop working but had not considered that they might not be content to stay at home. If you responded that having a place to go and to dress for on a daily basis is important, recognize this and plan to have some social structure in your daily life, aside from your marriage, so that you will continue to have a feeling of satisfaction about your life. Refer to Chapter VI, For Couples Only, to evaluate the way you and your husband have arranged your lives.

If you responded to this questionnaire with any, several, or all of *statements* c through g (looking forward to seeing people at work, one friend at work, lunch and evenings out with co-workers, or entertaining people from work in your home), you are probably aware of the importance of the social aspects of a work situation. Sociability is one of the areas in which there is a subtle difference between men and women when each evaluates the meaning of work for themselves. Men generally do not consider this an important issue, and the social aspects of work are viewed by them as less important—although they are probably more important than men believe them to be. When women speak of what they will miss about their work, one of the first things they say is that they will miss the people. Many stay too long at jobs because they are attached to the people. Most of the women interviewed, whether involved in a career or doing work they simply see as a job, expressed how important their colleagues were to the feelings they have about their work.

You may have responded to this questionnaire with *statement* c (that you look forward to seeing the people with whom you work). Do not underestimate the significance of this in your life even if your involvement does not go much beyond this. At the time of retirement, you will be leaving people who have been a part of your life because they have been part of a built-in structure. You have a camaraderie, a sharing, when you are working toward a common goal which brings you a sense of accomplishment. You have a shared identity with your co-workers that makes you feel wanted, needed, and valued. These people make up your everyday world although they may be only a peripheral part of your life. When you retire you will need to replace to some degree the built-in structure of people in your daily life.

Stacy understood how important these contacts were to her, and told us about a woman in another department whom she saw and greeted most mornings on the elevator. Her work seldom involved this woman although they had worked together on a special project many years before. Stacy liked her and looked forward to their greeting each morning. Their only other contact was an infrequent meeting in the rest room when they would chat. When she heard from one of her co-workers that this woman's husband was ill and that she was going to retire, Stacy felt an unexpected sense of loss. She couldn't understand her feeling, for she knew in reality that this woman had little meaning in her life. People who make up your everyday world, although they are only a peripheral part of your life, are a connection with your work. Saying good-bye to them can be experienced as a loss and is one of the subtle changes that are made as you enter retirement.

If you responded that you have at least one friend at work with whom you share events in your life or with whom you lunch once a week or more (*statements a* and *e*), you should refer to Chapter IV on friendships. You need to understand the meaning of this particular friendship in your life, as it has provided you with continuity and a certain amount of intimacy. You should determine the possibility of keeping a place for this friendship in your life when you retire. Sometimes you cannot hold on to it in the same way and you must prepare to let it go.

Mabel and Rosalind had been friends at work for eighteen years. They had been hired within weeks of each other and felt drawn to each other almost immediately. They were both married and involved in the lives of their extended families. At work they spent their coffee breaks and lunch hours together, but at five o'clock each returned to her husband and family. They lived at opposite ends of a large city, and despite their instant affinity for each other, they came from dissimilar backgrounds. They enjoyed each other's company during the day and knew intimate details about each other's life. Mabel had told Rosalind she had had an illegal abortion when she was eighteen, something she had never told anybody before. They knew when they had menstrual cramps, when one thought she might be pregnant, and ultimately when they entered menopause. They knew details about their marriages, knew the way they felt about their mothers, fathers, children, and in-laws. But they never saw each other away from work, and had only met each other's husband and children in passing. Mabel is now thinking about retirement and she knows that she is going to miss Rosalind more than she will miss her work; but she feels awkward about making efforts to take the friendship out of the workplace. She hates to think about meeting for lunch away from work and feeling strained. She has decided that she will keep telephone contact with Rosalind and see where the friendship goes from there.

When Mabel evaluated her friendship style and her friendship needs, using our questionnaire in Chapter III, she realized that she does not need a lot of intimacy in her life. Most of her social life is with her family. If friendships are available in a structured situation, she accepts them, but she does not reach out easily. She knows she will not be able to replace her friendship with Rosalind; the kind of intimacy they had for eighteen years can never be replaced. This will be one of the losses Mabel will have to cope with when she retires. There are some parts of your life and some people in your life that can never be replaced.

If you spend time outside of work with co-workers, whether you go out together or invite them to your home (statements f and g), be prepared for the fact that retirement may bring some change. If you do not have a social network outside of work and if you depend on your co-workers for much of your social life, you need to evaluate the relationships with care. You may need to make special efforts to maintain the contacts that are important to you.

Elsie is giving thought to this aspect of her job as it relates to her retirement. Over the past twenty years much of her social life has been with the people in her office, just as previously it had been with her neighbors and the mothers of her children's friends. She has enjoyed going to parties at the homes of friends from work and has often invited them to her home. They have attended each other's special events such as bar mitzvahs and weddings. Elsie is aware that some of this will cease when the daily contact is no longer there. She already knows which of her friendships will survive the working situation and which ones she will have to give up when she retires. From working with the friendship questionnaire that appears in Chapter IV Elsie discovered that she has always found relationships wherever she has been. She expects that she will find another social network if she goes through with her plan to go back to school.

Identity, Prestige, and Power: Questionnaire

This section will help you evaluate the less concrete aspects of your job. As you evaluate your responses you will recognize issues of intrinsic importance to your working life which will strongly influence your retirement years.

Choose the statements that apply to you and your job.
a) I feel that my work is one of the most important things about myself.
b) I work for a company or an organization of importance in the community.
c) My job title is one that is considered important or prestigious.
d) I feel the job I do is important to the company for which I work.
e) I feel I am important to the people with whom I work.
f) My job is considered important by the people with whom I work.
g) I am considered to be an integral and important part of the company for which I work.
h) People tell me I would be difficult to replace on my job.
i) I supervise several people.
j) I have received several promotions over the years.
k) I had the opportunity for promotion but preferred to stay where I was.
l) I feel that with my work I perform an important service to society.

Identify, Prestige, and Power: Assessment

Work provides people with one of the most important sources of identification. From the earliest days of tribal living, when each person in the group had a specific job to perform to keep the economic and social structure viable, humans defined themselves by the work they did. Women in most societies traditionally were wives, mothers, and homemakers. The women in modern society who were born before World War II, who grew up in the 1940's and 1950's, expected that this would be their primary identification as well. Unexpectedly for most of them, they became the first generation of women to define themselves by the work they do outside the home. They were the first generation of women to struggle with the meaning of paid employment and its impact on their identity as women. Was their life as homemaker, wife, and mother their real job? If they had a job outside the home, what did their work in the home mean to their lives. Was their paid work just another job, or was it a more intrinsic part of their lives? How did their work outside the home change the way they thought of themselves?

These were the concepts these women wrestled with during their working lives. Either consciously or unconsciously, either overtly or silently, each woman who entered the labor market considered these issues and thought about her options concerning them. Now, after twenty or twenty-five years of work outside the home, how will these general issues influence the way women view their future in retirement? Most of these women did not start their working careers with the idea of retirement. For many, their work outside the home was only a beginning. They did not realize its importance and did not consider what the end of their working lives would mean to them until retirement suddenly was upon them.

If you answered that a large part of your identity is in your job, profession, or career (statement a), your job defines who you are and gives your life much of its meaning. Your work is probably your most valued activity. For you, retirement means giving up a part of yourself as well as giving up the activity of work. One woman who felt her work provided her life with its frame of reference described feeling a sense of physical loss—as though she would be giving away a part of her body—when she thought about giving up her career. Many women, like the attorney Lillian, obtain a major part of their identification and satisfaction from their work and feel they can never retire in the traditional sense. For Lillian, retirement will mean reducing the time she spends at work. She is fortunate, for as a lawyer she can continue doing her legal work and can shape her law practice as her needs change. Professional women who want to retire and relocate may be able to transfer their skills to other states. If this isn't true for you, you may be able to transfer your skills to another business or industry. The most important factor for you to assess is whether your work is so much a part of your personal definition and provides you with so much satisfaction that you must continue to do it in order to feel good about yourself. If, like Lillian, you know you must practice your profession or stay at your job, your retirement plans must include a careful assessment of the employment opportunities available to you. You must make specific efforts to continue to do the work, even though it may require some compromises.

There are many ways to handle your transition into retirement once you have recognized your primary identification. Ethel willingly retired from her job as an elementary school teacher knowing she no longer received the same satisfaction from working with young children each day. She found that classroom life had changed for her over the thirty years she had been working. The students were more difficult and less involved with learning; they demanded more than she was willing to give. She felt she was experiencing burnout, but she also believed she was less satisfied because of the impact of social change on the schools. But she knew she still defined herself as a teacher. When she talked to friends and acquaintances she would find herself wanting to explain things to them, and she referred to that part of herself as "the teacher inside." When she retired she was drawn to a volunteer adult-education program teaching English as a second language. When she taught in this program she felt at home and at peace, forgetting all other distractions. She decided to apply for a job at a local community college helping adults obtain their high school equivalency diplomas. The job demanded more time than she wanted to give, but she felt she needed the fulfillment of teaching in order to feel complete. She decided, at least for the time being, that it was worth the trade-off, and she made the compromise of having one less day for herself.

If you are a professional person, it is not difficult to contemplate taking this identity into retirement with you. However, there are many women who have worked at jobs that are not as easily identifiable, as prestigious, or as transferable, but nevertheless are as satisfying and important. And these women often feel deprived of this identity when they retire. This used to be considered a trauma experienced only by men, but as women work toward equality in the workplace they become equal in the consequences as well as the benefits. A loss of identity in this sense can be devastating for either sex, and to minimize its effects you must prepare for it ahead of time.

Josephine (whom we met in Chapter I), who received her MBA over thirty years ago when women were not looking for a career in business, is preparing to cope with the possible loss of identity now that she is seriously considering retirement. As we discussed earlier, she was never promoted to vice-president of the company although she thoroughly deserved the promotion. As a result, she began to experience her job as a dead end, and more stressful than challenging. Because of these circumstances retirement is closer now than she thought it would be. Despite her disappointment, Josephine thinks of herself as an executive of the personnel firm and is beginning to realize that when she leaves her job she will lose this part of her identity.

One of the difficulties Josephine will face as she attempts to reconcile this situation involves the manner in which this problem is viewed by society. Josephine is married for the second time, has two grown children, one grown stepson, three grandchildren of her own and one who is her husband's grandchild. The whole extended family lives within visiting range and they see each other often. Most of the people in Josephine's life, both in and outside of work, believe that she will settle into the role of wife, mother, and grandmother in retirement and not look back at her working life. Josephine almost believed this herself until she began to evaluate herself and her life.

Josephine knows now that she will not be content to view herself in the traditional role, and she is considering how she might find a new means of identification away from her job, possibly through political activity or volunteer work. She recently heard of an organization of retired business people who volunteer their time to people who are starting their own small businesses. She will look into this as a possible avenue to pursue when she retires.

Carefully evaluate yourself if you responded that your identity is tied to your work. Determine to what extent you are willing to let this identification go, and explore how you can maintain this important piece of you.

Many women told us they did not feel that their work was important to their sense of identity. If this is you, retirement may be another kind of transition for you. If you do not view your work as a main part of your identity and you have been employed outside the home, you may have gone to work for economic necessity and stayed because of the economic benefits. This retirement issue of job identification will not be a major concern for you.

A few women disliked the work that they were doing and resisted identifying with it. If this is you, you may view retirement as a time to become the person you really are deep inside. You may see your retirement as a rite of passage, a time to reflect on your accomplishments, and a time to put things in order and prepare for an unknown future. You may want to refer to the questionnaire in Chapter I to give you a perspective on this new phase of your life.

Adrianne has worked in civil service most of her adult life. She dislikes her job and has done little to advance herself for twenty-five years, counting the days to her retirement almost from the time she started to work. She dislikes identifying herself as a civil servant and prefers to identify herself by her avocation. She is an artisan and an artist, a person who creates beautiful objects in crewelwork and crochet. Her home is decorated with many fine pieces of her work and this is the primary source of her identity and pleasure. Adrianne thinks of her job as unimportant, certainly not one of the first things to tell anybody about. She looks forward to pursuing her artwork in a more relaxed manner in her retirement, perhaps even selling some of her less treasured pieces at art festivals. She isn't sure about this, for she loves being surrounded by her life's work. Adrianne's retirement may be the easy transition she anticipates—and it certainly will be in terms of identity—but she is now evaluating the other job aspects to ascertain if she is leaving behind more than she realizes.

If you have never worked outside the home and have devoted yourself to the jobs of wife, mother, and homemaker, you will not be dealing with retirement in the terms we are discussing in this chapter. You have maintained the traditional identity of your earlier expectations and of society's expectations as well. Your assessment will be within the structure of our other chapters, particularly Chapter VI, For Couples Only. Do not forget Chapter I on the women's movement and Chapter II on transitions as well, for although you will not have to deal with losing a work identity, there can be as many changes in your life as there are in the lives of your friends who have been working full-time outside of the home.

If *statement b* applies to your job, as well as to the company you work for, evaluate whether this has importance for you. We discovered that many retirees who had worked for large, well-known companies defined themselves by noting that they had worked for corporations such as IBM, John Deere, or MGM. Not only the recognition factor mattered to them, but also the feeling of being enhanced by association with a company of note. It was difficult for retirees to hold on to this identification for many years into retirement, and a few of the women we interviewed were even able to verbalize some feeling of being diminished when they lost their former connection.

Stacy had always known she was proud of being associated with her personnel firm. Although it had been a small company when she started, it had grown and become successful, finally going public. It was considered the fastest-growing employment company in the Midwest, and Stacy used to say this with pride. It had never occurred to her that this connection was anything to be missed, but as we spoke she realized how important the affiliation had been to her. It made up for an important part of her that she had lost when her husband decided to divorce her. Her whole sense of who she was had undergone reorganization at that time. She had put her life together and rebuilt her damaged ego, largely because of her job and all it encompassed. The approval of the owners of the company, the friendship and admiration of her co-workers, and her natural ability to do the work made her feel whole again. She felt she reflected the success of the company, and in many ways her work life took the place of her marriage. Stacy's situation is not too different from Josephine's, except that Stacy's identification was more with her company and its reputation than with the job she performed. Thus she has something different to replace.

If you consider your job title important or prestigious (*statement c*), do not minimize the value this may have for you. Women who have become successful at their work and who have prestigious job titles and responsibilites have often had to overcome many obstacles. Yet many women told us it was difficult to admit that the title and the prestige are what they really enjoy about their jobs. Many women told us that over the years work had become less interesting, but the prestige of the job title and its ramifications still provided pleasure. For many women who have little status in other areas of their lives, job titles and their concomitant perquisites have carried an unfulfilling job a long way. Many women in middle-management positions who do not see further chance for advancement and whose jobs have lost their luster still thoroughly enjoy the prestige their job title brings them. If this is you, you must determine if these factors are important to you as you consider retirement. If prestige is important, when you retire you will be losing part of your inner world that must be actualized in some other way.

Try to separate your feelings about the job duties you perform from the feeling you get from having the title. Stacy recognized that although she had been rather bored with her job, she always enjoyed the feeling of being "Manager—Clerical Job Placement Division." Stacy's self-assessment was becoming more insightful. She also chose *statements d, e,* and *f* as pertinent to the job from which she had retired. She felt her job was important to the company and to the people with whom she worked, and she knows also that she herself was important to her co-workers. She admitted to us, though, that she could never completely rid herself of the feeling that she could easily be replaced and that almost anyone could do what she did.

Stacy had never given much thought to just how much these areas of her job had contributed to her feelings of self-worth. She had never determined how much emotional satisfaction her status with her company and her status with her co-workers had provided her. She was enhanced by her affiliation with the company. She identified with her prestigious job title, and her self-esteem rose, not only when she was appreciated by her supervisors but when she was sought after by her colleagues for advice and companionship. Stacy may have been ready to begin a new life career, but she had not clearly recognized all that she was leaving behind. She was beginning to understand much of her discontent with her retirement and was ready to find a remedy.

Stacy had seen a newspaper article concerning a little theater group that was being organized in one of the local communities. Theater had always been an interest of hers, but she had never felt comfortable about pursuing it. She always felt she was not talented enough to be involved in this sort of enterprise. The self-knowledge she had acquired doing these evaluations gave her more courage and she went to a meeting. The group was just forming so there were many jobs to be done, which gave Stacy an opportunity to find a niche where she might be comfortable. She established herself as a writing consultant, and as such she became head of the committee that chooses the plays to be performed. She enjoys the experience and feels extremely comfortable with the jobs she performs. She has met people of all ages who are interested in her as a mentor because of her writing abilities. She feels respected and needed. The theater group itself is becoming well known in the area. Stacy is actually thinking of trying her hand at directing one of the future productions. This sort of involvement is what she needed to add to her life in retirement.

Though it is difficult to evaluate, do not underestimate the self-esteem you receive from your job. Try to tell yourself carefully and truthfully what this part of your job means to you. If the people you work with enjoy you as a colleague, value the connection with you, admire you, and ask for your advice about many aspects of their lives, this enhances your self-image. If the company you work for considers the job you do to be important to its success, you have another facet of your working life that contributes to your sense of self-worth. Do not lose sight of the fact that the admiration you receive has great impact on the feelings you have about yourself. It is too easy to forget this aspect of your job, particularly if the duties are no longer satisfying.

If you feel the job you do is important to the company, this status has been gratifying to you over the years. Whether the job is prestigious or powerful is not the issue here. The issue is that you are playing a meaningful role in a larger picture. Stacy looked forward to the quarterly profit figures circulated by her company, and liked to think that she had been responsible for 18 to 20 percent of the profit picture. Ethel, who had been teaching for many years, always felt enhanced when the reading scores in her school improved; she felt she made a real contribution to this. Consider now what you can do in retirement that can give you a similar recognition and sense of satisfaction.

If you are an integral part of your company, are difficult to replace, and supervise several people (*statements g, h,* and *i*), you have probably felt important and powerful at your job for many years, and your status, perhaps without your acknowledging it, has gratified many of your needs for power and prestige. The meaning of power in women's lives has been an important topic of the 1970's and 1980's. Many young women of today are actively engaged in the pursuit of power; but for women who grew up in the 1940's and 1950's, power was a new and uncomfortable issue that many women struggled with throughout their working lives. Women are often loath to acknowledge the amount of pleasure they obtain from having power, and many women tend to minimize or deny its importance to them. Many women are afraid of power, and many more are uncomfortable with it. Women's need for and use of power in the workplace has been controversial and not clearly defined. Women state that they have difficulty when they are supervised by or have superiors on the job who are female. Men, too, have problems with women in power. Is it any wonder that a woman who achieves power in the workplace feels confused by her status?

Gladys got a civil service job in The Social Security Administration shortly after college. Over the years she took the necessary examinations and became one of the supervisors in her state office. Civil service was one of the early avenues women could take if they had ambition for positions of authority; and although Gladys was not conscious of it at the time, she knows now that she entered civil service partly to be able to gain authority. She had her difficulties over the years with many of the men and the women she supervised, but she enjoyed the challenge of winning their respect. She is bright and fair-minded and for the most part is well esteemed by her co-workers.

For many years she enjoyed the work, but after a time it became routine and, on some days, boring. What she enjoys most about her job at this time, although she is reluctant to admit it, is the deference she receives from other employees. She loves being the person in charge, and she enjoys having this power. Many women who grew up in the 1940's and 1950's are almost ashamed, as is Gladys, to admit that they both need and enjoy prestige and power. In anticipation of retirement she has recently been looking for an activity that would be of interest to her. As she now evaluates her retirement needs, Gladys is aware that she will have to find not only an involving activity but a way to replace the intangible piece of her job that involves her need for power and prestige.

She is considering signing on as a volunteer patient advocate in one of the nearby hospitals. She has spoken with the coordinator and has discovered that the program has considerable power and prestige in the medical community. She feels that she would enjoy speaking out for others from the position this job would give her.

For many women, the power they achieved in the workplace became burdensome, and they look forward to less pressure and stress in retirement. They cannot deny, however, that they enjoyed and valued their power. If their retirement is to be successful, they need to acknowledge that power is fun, useful, and at times exhilarating. Do you enjoy the sense of importance, the power you have at work? Nobody need know your secret if you wish to keep it to yourself. Women in retirement, who no longer have power and prestige built into their lives, experience a loss. This was traditionally one of the problems that men had to face when they retired. It is no less true for women, except that those who grew up before the days of the women's movement may have more difficulty admitting it. If you have spent your working life denying that you enjoyed your power and prestige, you may assign your feelings of loss to the loss of your work, rather than of your power, when you retire.

Madeleine had been an executive in an insurance company and had supervised a large department for fifteen years before she retired two years ago. She had known that her job was important to her company, and she had looked forward to going to supervisors' meetings where her opinion and her input were valued. She had known her job was important to the people she worked with and she had always enjoyed having employees waiting to see her when she came to work, needing her instruction before they could start. She had advanced through the ranks and her department was an integral part of the insurance company. She had loved her job, but had been wearied by the stress and strain of thirty years. She had begun to disengage several years before she retired, when her company offered a preretirement financial course. She was shocked to discover many of her colleagues attending, obviously planning to retire in the next few years. Could it be time for her to retire too? She planned her financial future well and began to look forward to a life of leisure-time activities. She loved bridge and played often, and she took up golf.

We met Madeleine when she had been retired for nine months. She had become restless and she was reflecting on her feelings. She knew that her job had been the most important part of her life, and now that she had rested from the stresses and strains of the everyday grind, she knew that she missed it. She had already looked into finding a part-time job, but she found she was overqualified for anything that was available to her. She could have returned to her former company on a part-time basis but not at any level near the job she had left. She could not envision going back to a routine job where she had once been "so important." This statement gave Madeleine a clue to what she was feeling. She realized not only that she had liked her work but also that her need for power was strong. She was really missing her position of importance and control.

This put a different light on the options that Madeleine was considering. She did not need to replace the routine and structure of the job; but she needed to replace her feelings of power and prestige. One of the things she discussed was her peripheral involvement with the board of directors of the cooperative apartment building where she lived. She had researched some insurance possibilities for them and had worked on the safety committee. She had heard that they were going to hold elections for the seats of two members whose terms were expiring. She began to think that this might be the place to answer her needs and use her talents. It was an active board, and the tenants and apartment owners took their problems, complaints, and ideas to the various board members. It sounded like a job she would enjoy. She called the president of the board who was pleased at her interest. She feels her retirement is going to work out after all.

Women who need power have a special void to fill in their retirement. Simply obtaining another position will not make up for the loss they experience. Often they recognize their need to be involved and busy, and so they join community organizations. If they find themselves dissatisfied with one organization, they join another. They eventually find that they don't want to be just a member of an organization—they need to direct and manage it in some way. When they cannot do that, they become dissatisfied and move on to another organization or another activity. If they can acknowledge their need for power they can more easily move toward and perhaps achieve their goal.

If *statements j* and *k* (regarding promotions) apply to your work, they will help you determine an important aspect of your working life. They have to do not only with self-image, but they also reflect the hopes and dreams you had for yourself. Have you received several promotions over the years? How did you feel about these promotions? Were you pleased? Did you go for further advancement? Did you move into a supervisory capacity? If you were successful at your job and took the promotions offered you, you are a goal-oriented, ambitious woman, and in some way you sought a place of importance. Examine carefully whether or not you still have a need for personal power and success. If you do, these needs will follow you into retirement. These are not needs a woman of the 1940's, '50's, or '60's easily incorporates into her self-image, but if you are personally ambitious, it is a part of you. You need to recognize your ambition, enjoy it, and look for opportunities to express it.

If you were offered chances for promotion, but chose not to take them, were you content to stay where you were, or were you fearful of the advancement? Women with children often were in conflict as to where their future would take them, and to whom they owed loyalty. The idea of being on a career track was antithetical to them. Advancement could take time away from the family. Sometimes women had to make choices for advancement, such as spending longer hours at work or going back to school. Many women who were single parents could not get the financial or emotional support to take advantage of various opportunities. Many women who came from traditional marriages did not want to fight the necessary fight to obtain another identity. Many women never conceived of themselves as being successful and powerful. Some women were frightened of advancement, unsure if they could carry emotional burdens of responsibility, even though they had successfully managed the running of a home.

Perhaps you refused promotions because you do not have much personal ambition. You may have seen work as a way to make a living, a way to have friends and a structured life, but primarily you found your satisfactions outside of your job. You may be entering retirement relieved that your working life is over. You are ready to start the next phase of your life without the encumbrances of work. You may have preferred not to take promotions because you were doing other things and you saw your job and its routines as easy. In your retirement, you may be content to continue your life without the added stress.

Many women we spoke with who had not been offered promotions felt they should have been. Some of them had enjoyed their job because their co-workers came to them for instruction and affirmation, despite the fact that the management did not show them similar recognition. This was a common statement. These women felt they were often taken for granted and not considered for advancement when men were. When women allowed their self-esteem to be eroded by managers and supervisors, they frequently were disappointed in themselves and tended to undervalue their importance at work. If you have felt yourself to be in this sort of position for most of your working life, retirement may be the time for you to make some changes in your style. Although one part of your life may be ending, retirement offers the opportunity to continue your ambitions in new and different contexts.

Retirement is usually conceptualized as a planned-for option, but this is not always the case. Women near retirement age are eased out of jobs because of corporate takeovers or business relocation. Some are suddenly offered appealing retirement packages, or there may be subtle maneuvers that make them feel unwelcome. Older women today—just as their older male counterparts—unexpectedly lose jobs they value. These women, experience a loss in their lives akin to a death. Women who have been personally ambitious, who have defined themselves by the work they do, suffer this loss most acutely. They find themselves in a retirement they have not chosen and which has little meaning for them. As with any unexpected job loss, they may need months and a great deal of personal evaluation to work through this loss (see Chapter II on transitions). It is a time to rethink values, expectations, and present and future needs.

Mary Jane had been working for sixteen years in a large real estate office. She had great personal ambition which she was uncertain about expressing; but she knew she had many talents and was a capable worker. She was always sorry she had not completed her college education and felt apologetic about it. She never actively sought a supervisory or special job title, despite the fact that she would have liked it. She satisfied herself with the fact that her employer invited her to do many special projects, and she knew she was valued. Mary Jane felt secure and happy with her work and in the work situation.

During her sixteenth year on the job the circumstances in the office changed. A young woman came to work for the company who had few conflicts about her abilities and her desire to move ahead. She seemed to be under Mary Jane's feet when a job had to be done and in her way no matter what the occasion. She often seemed to do Mary Jane's work before Mary Jane knew there was work to be done. Mary Jane continued to call subtle attention to her own excellence, but the other woman knew how to be much more visible. Suddenly Mary Jane found herself in competition with this woman. She felt that she was doing well despite this, since she had the advantage of more experience and felt she understood the politics in the office well. Unfortunately, the real estate business generally and the company in particular experienced a mild recession, and when a choice was made as to who would stay and who would go, Mary Jane was asked to leave.

Her world fell apart. Although she was sixty-three and had thought about cutting down on the time she spent at work, she had never thought of retiring, and she certainly had never thought she would be fired. Her job had defined her and had given her the opportunity to feel independent and effective. Her work had provided her the opportunity to excel and to realize her talents. She felt lost without this major component of her identity, and without all of the other things her work had provided for her. Mary Jane had to pull herself together by herself. Her husband figured it was about time for her to stop working, and most of her friends agreed, saying she would be just as happy staying home, having free time, and keeping house. Unfortunately this was not what Mary Jane knew about herself. She needed options and a world outside her home. She took time to mourn her loss, and as time passed she began to feel stronger. The natural healing process was working. She made a list of her abilities and interests in ascending order of importance and began to think about ways she could use them. She made phone calls to people she knew, and thus she learned the power of networking. Through a contact at her former job she discovered Marlo, a young woman just starting out in the real estate business in a neighboring town. Mary Jane offered to help her by acting as a consultant. As the relationship developed, Mary Jane realized she was using her skills and felt valued by her new association. It wasn't long before Marlo asked Mary Jane to handle some difficult clients. Mary Jane found this work to be a satisfying replacement for the job she had lost. She established a new routine, and although she has not yet rid herself of the sense of loss she experienced, she feels she has done the best she can with a difficult situation. She has begun to feel her forced retirement is turning out better than she imagined it could.

If you feel you perform an important service to society (*statement 1*), work for you may be a way of life, an extension of your values and priorities. There may be a feeling of service, perhaps involved with religion, instilled in you from your childhood, which has guided you into certain activities throughout your life. You may have a need to feel that your life transcends the ordinary. Within that feeling is often a strong need to feel important to others. In many ways your emotional well-being has come from being and feeling necessary and valued.

Stephanie is fifty-seven years old and has worked as a receptionist in a mental health clinic for sixteen years. She loves her job and feels the most important aspect of her work is performing an important service to society. Her husband is planning his retirement and wants Stephanie to think about doing the same. He has been talking about relocating to a warmer climate. When we met with her, she was very anxious about the prospect of retirement. She felt that she wanted to retire when her husband did, although she had no idea what she wanted to do with her retirement time.

Stephanie comes from a religious family and was educated in parochial schools. In junior high school she realized she did not want to enter the convent, but fantasized that she would pursue a life as a nurse or teacher. She had little outside guidance and less available money, so when she graduated from high school she followed her friends and went to secretarial school. She took a job as a secretary, married soon thereafter, and left her job when she became pregnant with her son. She was a devoted wife and mother but always had a strong need to serve. As soon as her son entered kindergarten she did volunteer work at his school, helping learning-disabled children to read. When the school wanted to start a physical education program, they asked for parent volunteers. Stephanie offered her services and soon found herself running the program. She felt fulfilled doing this, but she once again was most interested in the children who had special needs. With enthusiasm and passion she designed a special physical education program for them. As her family's economic needs changed, Stephanie went to work outside of the home and reluctantly gave up her volunteer job in the school. She found a job at a mental health clinic, where she felt her work would be of service to the public. Her job has been rewarding; indeed, it has been one of the most important parts of her life over the last sixteen years.

As Stephanie reflected on her life, she realized some of her most meaningful and fulfilling experiences were connected with her volunteer work. She had never thought about going back to that work; she had considered that part of her life over. She now sees how vital that work made her feel, however, and she understands what she can do for herself to have a meaningful retirement. Before she retires and relocates, she is going to investigate the opportunities for working with children who have special needs. She is sure she will find a school that can use her services wherever she goes, and she now realizes she can happily replace her job when she retires. She knows she has not finished her life of service.

Women of the 1950's and 1960's who went into the professions that were designated for them—nursing, social work, and teaching—responded that with their work they perform an important service to society. If this is you, carefully evaluate just how meaningful service is to you. Many women we spoke with had entered these professions because they were the only avenues for college-educated women. The service occupations were traditionally for women, who were expected to perform this function either in the home or for society. Did you follow this path because it was expected of you? Or were you truly dedicated like Stephanie? Is it a combination of both? Many women who enter helping professions have ambition and a need for power and prestige they may have overlooked and undervalued. We spoke to many supervisors of teachers, nurses, and social workers who downplayed the pleasure and identification they received from their positions of authority. These needs for power and control, if you have them, may exist side by side with the need to be of service, and each should play a part in the way you structure the next phase of your life. Do not hide from them or submerge them unnecessarily.

Julie has been a nurse for forty years. She went to nurses' training school right out of high school, graduated, and worked as an RN in a private hospital for many years for low wages. This did not concern her at first, since she loved her work and felt committed to her profession. Halfway through her career she began to get restless, to see the work as routine and the salary as insufficient. When an opportunity arose for her to become a supervisor of nurses at the hospital, she decided to take the position. She is an efficient worker and has an easy way with people and a natural talent for supervision. She enjoyed this role and her position of power and prestige, not to mention the money. After several years she had another opportunity to rise higher in the hospital hierarchy by going into hospital administration, and she decided to advance her career.

Julie never gave up on the image of herself as a person who worked in a helping profession, and when asked what she did, she often said she was a nurse. She did this, she explained, because, although she enjoyed her position of power and prestige, she was never comfortable about letting people know about her importance. When asked to say what she enjoyed about her job, she focused mainly on the service aspects.

Julie began to realize she was not clear about what her work meant to her. Her decision early in life to be of service had encompassed many needs beyond the one to serve society. The form of service she had chosen gave her some opportunity to fulfill her needs to have authority and power at work even before she went on to become an administrator. Her need for importance and power lessened, however, as the stress of the job increased. Now that she has recognized and understood her needs, she feels she should continue to serve society in retirement. She is considering private-duty nursing. Her need to feel she is helping people as well as her need to earn extra money will be fulfilled.

You may have determined after answering this questionnaire that your work is so satisfying and rewarding, you do not want to retire. If this is your assessment you may try to negotiate a shorter work week or longer vacations to adjust to your new needs. Retirement for you may take the form of slowing down or cutting back. Remember, there is no right way to retire; in fact, for some the definition of retirement is a shorter work week. If you do not have anyone else's needs to consider, then you can use your own definition and your own timetable. Lillian envisions her retirement as a cutting-back but is aware she may have to contend with the needs of her husband, who will want to spend more time traveling with her and who may even want to relocate.

Among couples retiring in the 1990's, often the man has been working for thirty-five to forty years, while his wife has been in the labor market for less than twenty years. When he is ready to slow down and begin a new life, his wife is reaching full stride. The women know they want to retire someday, but they want to do so on their own schedule. An important aspect of marriage needs to be negotiated here if both spouses are to be comfortable with the retirement decision.

Perhaps you and your husband are in this situation of being "out of sync" in your working lives. To begin with, do not assume your husband needs you to be with him at home. We have spoken to several women who continued working with few problems for as much as ten years beyond the date of their husband's retirement. Do not assume that your husband will not accept the situation until you have attempted to work it out.

Bernice had gone back to school and then to work as a social worker when her children started school. She had started on a part-time basis doing psychotherapy two days a week. As the needs of her family changed and became less demanding, she began working full time. After ten years at the same mental health facility she moved into administration, and after twenty years she had become the director of clinical services. She loved her work, enjoyed supervising the clinicians, and liked being involved in the community outreach effort. Her husband, Daniel, worked as a supervisor for the Internal Revenue Service and had been with this division of the Federal Government since leaving the army after World War II. He had been ready to leave for three years before he did. At first he said he was waiting until Bernice was ready, but it became obvious to both of them that he might have to wait forever in that case, so they decided that he should leave. Both assumed that Bernice would follow soon after.

In retirement, Daniel plays golf every day he can. He spends long afternoons and leisurely mornings reading biographies and doing crossword puzzles, two of his favorite pastimes. He does some of the food shopping and once in a while cooks their dinner. When Bernice wants them to do something together on a Saturday or Sunday, he is willing to accompany her, because he has already played golf on Friday and will do so again on Monday. When Bernice wants conversation in the evening or wants to be social more than once a week, Daniel is agreeable because he has had his quiet time today and will have it again tomorrow.

Neither Daniel nor Bernice imagined it would happen, but they both agree happily that she will work until she feels she has had enough. She no longer feels pressed to retire, and may even do so sooner than she had thought. Daniel feels that his life is comfortable with the schedule he has.

If the retired husband wants to relocate, and his wife wants to stay in her job, it may be possible to negotiate this. Florida is a quick airplane flight from any place on the East Coast, and several of the upper midwestern states are a quick airplane trip from California and Arizona. Some couples have worked out weekend commuting arrangements, along with several short winter vacations for the working spouse, so that the separation does not have to be prolonged. Many women who do this find the traveling stressful and feel lonely during the time away from their husbands.

Several women we spoke with said that the distance at this time of their lives has afforded them an independence they did not have earlier in their marriage. Many noted that their husbands did not like the separation, but the women held fast, knowing that to leave their jobs before they were ready to retire would be perilous to the next part of their lives. (One woman, who wasn't sure she liked the long-distance arrangement but felt it necessary, laughingly told us that one of the up sides of the separation was that while she and her husband were apart she could eat crackers in bed without being told she was making crumbs.)

If you decide you do not want to retire and want to continue in your job, profession, or career, you may have to make certain concessions at your place of work. You may need to make peace with being one of the oldest people at work. You may have to accept that changes will go on around you, many of them frustrating and even unnecessary from your point of view. You may find that these changes violate your values and your attitudes. If you can accept these changes, then, and only then, can you continue to enjoy your work. When people cannot accept the frustration and sadness they experience as their life on the job changes, retirement becomes a necessary option.

When we began our research with women in preretirement it became apparent that the change in the identity of "the working woman" has brought new and complex issues into retirement. Women know their jobs are important to them, and although many feel undervalued and underpaid, their jobs have been an integral part of their lives. For those who struggled for equal status and equal pay, their jobs and their lives took on added meaning. Many of these women felt regret that when they retire they will leave inequality in the workplace as unfinished business. Many of them express anger that this issue seemed to suffer a reversal as the 1980's waned. Some women worry about turning over their battle to younger women who lack their experience of what it was like before the women's movement, and who may not be vigilant about furthering equality in the workplace.

What every woman must remember is that she will be the same person in retirement as she was at work. You cannot escape yourself, and that is why it is so important for you to know well your attitudes and feelings. Remember how you believed marriage would make you a different person? Remember how that didn't happen? In the same way, the retirement transition will not change who you are. What you enjoyed and needed emotionally before retirement will in many ways carry over into retirement; thus the continued importance of self-knowledge as you make that transition.

SHOULD I VOLUNTEER?

We have saved a special place in this chapter for the world of volunteering, which is so often considered the solution for women who are concerned about how they will spend their time in retirement. Women, retired or not, have historically been society's volunteers. They are traditionally the guardians of other people's welfare. Women have been viewed as caretakers with flexible hours; volunteering time and effort has been considered almost their duty.

To the extent that these beliefs are still entrenched in society, retired women may drift into volunteer work without due consideration of changes that have occurred in the status of women generally, and in the self-image of each woman personally. This is not to say that women cannot or should not proudly enter the field of volunteer work, or that it cannot bring the fulfillment promised and expected; you just need to acknowledge that volunteerism is not and should not be viewed simply as a way to fill time. Volunteerism is important work with important meaning for the individual and for society, but it is not for all women. Is it for you? If you're looking for a worthwhile experience, you must think through the issues discussed below. If you are sure that you want to spend part of your retirement doing volunteer work, and if you already know what you will be doing, you have probably already done this. If you are considering volunteer work as a possibility for your retirement years and have not conceptualized its meaning in your life, the following may be helpful to you.

Use the information you have about yourself from the previous questionnaires in this chapter. The following questionnaire will start you thinking about your priorities and needs when you consider volunteering. Remember, when you volunteer in your retirement, you have options and alternatives that you can use to help fulfill your needs as well as those of society.

Volunteering: Questionnaire and Assessment

Question 1. Do you measure the importance or the meaning of work by the money earned for it?

Question 2. Would you be comfortable with the fact that people doing work similar to yours are being paid, while you are volunteering your time?

Question 3. Among the following statements, choose those that match your reasons for considering volunteer work.
   a) I feel that I would like to make a contribution of my time, efforts, and expertise.

b) I need to feel useful.

c) I want to spend time with other people.

d) I want to add some structure and routine to my daily life.

e) I want to have new experiences and possibly learn new skills.

If you responded yes to the first question—that is, you measure the value of work in part by the money earned for it—consider this attitude should you volunteer your time and efforts on a regular basis after you retire. We live in a world in which our worth is often measured by the amount of money we earn, and in terms of self-worth, volunteering may seem like a demotion to some women. If you feel this way to any degree and you do volunteer work, you may find after a short time that you begin to perceive your volunteer work as less important than other aspects of your life, despite your good intentions. Without realizing it (because it may be difficult to admit), you may start to minimize your volunteer responsibilities and may put them aside when other commitments, to which you give greater importance, come into your life. This attitude of minimizing the importance of unpaid labor may be the reason some women have difficulty transferring from paid employment to volunteer work, and this is a valid consideration.

Some women find they have a problem volunteering for work that they have trained for and formerly did for pay. They may not have the same difficulty if the unpaid work is unrelated. Ethel, the teacher we spoke of earlier in the chapter, was not happy about volunteering her time to teach English as a second language, although she enjoyed the experience. When she realized she felt unhappy, she obtained a paid position in another teaching program. She does not, however, have a problem about working a few hours a week for the American Cancer Society, answering phones and helping in the office. Other women feel differently and are glad to be able to volunteer their expertise and skill to people in need. Lillian expects to continue devoting some of her time, even in semiretirement, to the Legal Aid Society, a service she has been doing for many years.

Women in volunteer work sometimes discover that others in the organization are doing similar work and being paid for it (*question 2.*). This pointed up Ethel's predicament. She discovered she was working just as hard assisting the teacher, who was being paid for the program. It is important for you to consider and honor this feeling if you answered yes to this question. When you volunteer, you are more likely to find yourself side by side with paid employees if the work you are doing takes you into the administrative or office part of the organization. Most charitable organizations have a paid staff of administrative and clerical workers who are basic to their functioning. You will be more cognizant of your unpaid volunteer status if you choose to work in these areas. If this is your area of choice or expertise, be prepared for this scenario. You may want to make a careful choice of the department of the organization you become affiliated with. If the satisfactions of volunteering do not outweigh your frustrations, perhaps paid employment is the best place for your talents.

If you have no negative feelings about unpaid work, this is time to look at your motivations for volunteering. Many women who want to contribute their time and effort and feel useful, (*question 3, statement a* and *b*), have told us they had little difficulty transferring from paid work to volunteering in their retirement. The satisfaction they receive comes from the pleasure of the work itself, the acknowledgment of doing something useful and worthwhile and contributing to society in a meaningful way. The appreciation of the people whom you are helping is also enhancing. In retirement, women can contribute their time and effort to causes that are of particular significance to them. Many women do volunteer work for organizations such as Gray Panthers, Older Women's League, or the American Association of Retired Persons (AARP). Many work in hospitals or in schools, or do fund-raising for special organizations. Some women, such as Josephine, the MBA we mentioned earlier, will seek to use their business expertise and will volunteer appropriately. Many cultural and civic organizations attract volunteer workers who want to help these organizations continue to perform their valuable service. Many women volunteer at social service agencies that are poorly funded and in need of personnel. Historically, activities related to religion have been a focus of women's volunteer work, and in retirement this is where many women will find meaningful volunteer activities.

It is important to determine if you have other motivations for volunteering. Many women want to feel useful and want to contribute time and effort, but they also do volunteer work because they need contact with people or a structured life, or perhaps because they want to broaden their life's options (*question 3, statements c, d,* and *e*). Volunteering can serve any or all of these purposes. Choose your job to match your needs. Remember, you are volunteering to do the kind of work you like to do. You have the opportunity to decide if volunteering will provide you with contact with people, and/or with a routine and structure you need.

Remember, too, you do not have to make as many concessions in your volunteer position as you did in your paid employment. Many women who were self-effacing and who needed to be subservient in their work for pay told us that in their retirement they had little to lose by making their volunteer job work for them. This was not always easy, but armed with the feeling that they were their own boss in retirement, the women were able to go for what they wanted.

Mildred decided to volunteer at a local hospital. She thought it would be fun to help out for five hours once a week. She knew she wanted to get out of the house one day a week as part of her retirement routine, and she also knew that she wanted a fairly structured job, preferably in an office. When she went for her volunteer interview, she was told the hospital policy meant she would have to spend a full day, from 8:30 until 4:30. The woman in charge of the volunteer department gave her the job of wheeling patients from floor to floor for therapy or special services.

Mildred was eager to volunteer, so she accepted the assignment, although she knew she did not want to start work that early and really did not want patient contact. She went for one day, and knew after two hours that what she was doing was not right for her. She felt uneasy about asking the head of the volunteers for a change in her time and assignment. She decided she would not go back the following week. She talked it over with her husband and with a friend and she began to see the situation in perspective. Her job at the hospital was not regular employment; it was a place she had wanted to go to, not only to serve others but to meet some needs of her own. She had little to lose by asserting herself. She worked up the courage and the next week went in to ask for the office job she really wanted, with hours that were better for her. Much to her surprise, her assignment and her hours were changed immediately. The volunteer department was pleased to have her and was willing to bend its policy to keep her.

If you decide to do volunteer work after considering your needs and motivations, there are considerations that should be highlighted if you are moving from paid employment. Volunteers often are closely supervised, and your work may be checked, at least initially, more than you feel is appropriate. Be prepared for this. Remember, this is a new situation, and you have not yet proven yourself. On the other hand, this is *your* retirement and you do not have to allow yourself to be exploited.

When you first start volunteering you may have the feeling that your autonomy and independence are being challenged and you are being controlled. You will be told when you are expected to arrive at work and when to leave. There may appear to be little flexibility and too much structure, which may frustrate you. But the volunteer work you are doing has an element of choice that gives you options. If you are looking to enjoy yourself, to feel needed and productive, you can probably find a place for yourself despite the problems you may encounter.

Some of the women we spoke with who had taken volunteer jobs were surprised to discover they were once again involved in office politics. Even in volunteer organizations, people who have authority and those who don't vie for power at other people's expense. If these events occur on your volunteer job, you should evaluate the meaning of volunteer work in your retirement. This work will have a different place in your life, and office politics should not stop you from finding your place in the structure. Your status as a retired person allows you to laugh at pettiness in the workplace and then work around it. This is like life with grandchildren: You enjoy the experience but finish with it at the end of the day.

Perhaps you are thinking of something new for your retirement years. Many women in retirement have used volunteer work as preparation for a new career, or as a means of enriching their later years by an involvement with a completely new activity (*question 3, statement e*). You may be thinking of going back to school for a new career. If you volunteer for a job in the area you are contemplating, you can be in an excellent position to test the waters for your future, to learn new skills and retain yourself. Even if you've done only one kind of work up to now, that doesn't mean you can't do something else from now on.

Several homemakers who had wanted to be teachers when they were young found volunteering in the schools so satisfying that they went on to community colleges and trained to become teaching paraprofessionals. One woman volunteered in a hospital and discovered that becoming a laboratory assistant was a viable option for her for the next ten to fifteen years. Another woman, for a lark, volunteered and was accepted by a group that was going on an archeological dig in the Yucatán in Mexico. She enjoyed this so much that when she returned she went back to college to study archeology. She really had no plans for doing much more digging, but she loves studying and knows it has enriched her life.

Volunteerism in retirement serves many purposes, both for the individual as well as for society. Society benefits from taking advantage of energy and skills that would otherwise be untapped. For the individual, volunteering can fulfill the same needs as paid employment. Volunteering can be an extension of your working life, or it can provide a way to use previously unused or underutilized talents. As more women retire with the knowledge of their talents and ambitions, they bring to volunteerism many new aspects of themselves which they can share with the community at large. You will find volunteerism in retirement to be self-fulfilling and productive if you plan your volunteer work carefully.

IV

Styles of Friendship

True Happiness
Consists not in the multitude of friends
But in the worth and choice.

BEN JONSON (1573–1637)

Robyn is fifty-three and her husband Saul is sixty-one. They have been happily married for thirty years. Saul's company is in the process of being reorganized and he has been offered early retirement. He feels ready to retire and perhaps relocate. He has worked steadily since he was a young man and feels ready for rest and change.

Robyn, who went back to work after her children started school, has been working outside of the home for eighteen years. She feels unsettled about Saul's decision. Although she likes her job, she is not particularly committed to it. She is not quite sure what she wants to do with the rest of her life.

Robyn is an attractive, outgoing, enthusiastic, interesting, and interested woman who makes connections with people easily. She is the kind of woman who doesn't wait for friends to call her. When she needs to be in touch with people she picks up the phone and calls them. She is seldom without a friend when she wants to go shopping or out for lunch. She is the person in the marriage who makes the majority of the social contacts, and most of the couple's friends have been brought in by her efforts.

She has a large circle of friends from the various stages of her life—from her childhood years, from several jobs, from the days in the park when she was raising her children, from her church, and from the Republican Club. She has kept these people in her life with varying degrees of intimacy.

Although Robyn enjoys her work as an office manager, she knows that what she truly enjoys is being involved in the lives of the people in her office, visiting with them each day, going to their parties, christenings, bar mitzvahs, and now to their children's weddings. She is what younger people refer to as a "popular person."

When Robyn contemplates retirement and relocation, she feels concerned about leaving all her friends. She would miss her place in their lives as well as their place in her life. She knows that her friendships comprise a very important part of her life, and she cannot imagine life without the proximity of these relationships. Robyn needs to evaluate her needs and strengths in the area of her friendships before she makes a decision about her retirement.

Martha is fifty-eight and her husband Mark is sixty-two. Martha has worked as a probation officer most of her adult years and her work has been one of the most satisfying parts of her life. Although she has many acquaintances and some close friends, it is not of the utmost importance to her that she have many people in her life.

Martha has shared a deep friendship with a woman cousin with whom she grew up. She speaks to her cousin several times a week and they see each other at least twice a month. They have been close for most of their lives. Their friendship is supportive and sustaining for them both.

Martha is happily married for the second time and she and Mark enjoy each other's company, so that in addition to the love they have for each other, they are good friends. In addition,

Martha also has two grown children to whom she is quite close. These relationships with her husband, her cousin, and her children are often all Martha feels she needs, since her work as a probation officer drains much of her emotional energy.

Martha never had problems bringing people into her life and establishing close relationships when she felt she wanted or needed them. However, she has not felt the strong need to hold on to these friendships as her life's transitions occurred: her second marriage, the move to a new home, and a series of job transfers. Although she has had several other close relationships during specific periods in her life, her friendship with her cousin has been the most consistent and sustaining.

Martha acknowledges that there may come a time when her need for friendships will increase, and she takes comfort in knowing that friends can exist for her if she wants them.

Hope is a sixty-four-year-old widowed psychologist. She retired as a college professor three years ago and looked forward to a small private practice in psychotherapy and time with her husband Edgar. Indeed, they had a wonderful time for two years before Edgar became ill. Hope nursed him through a terminal illness. During the last year of his life she had little time to think about herself or about being retired. She had barely enough energy for her practice and for Edgar.

Hope has been widowed for one year. She sees patients three days a week as she had planned and feels content most of the time. Primarily she feels content to be at home. She always enjoyed her life as a homemaker and enjoyed being a mother to her two children. She loves to cook for herself and still enjoys the domestic life.

Hope never had many friends. Relationships always seemed complicated and she finds it difficult to stray from her routines to accommodate other people. She is lonely on occasion and this feeling concerns her, although she often had this feeling even when Edgar was alive. She can busy herself, however, and because she has many interests, the loneliness quickly passes.

She realizes she should not be alone as much as she is. When she starts to feel isolated, too insular, she contacts professional acquaintances and enjoys their company, as long as they do not make demands on her time.

These three women portray three distinctly different styles of relating, three distinctly different needs of women in relationships. There is no "way" to relate; there is only the way in which *you* relate. There is no "right" level of need, just what *your* need is for and from a friendship.

Friendships are essential to our emotional well-being. Women's friendships in many ways sustain their emotional lives. From the very first "best friend" of childhood to the proverbial peer group of the teen years and the college roommate, women use friendships to meet specific needs. Women have developed many ways of finding and forming friendships. They know how to maintain loving ties in their complicated relationships.

The women's movement of the 1950's and 1960's helped to conceptualize what most women intuitively know—that women need other women. Many women of the 1940's and 1950's grew up learning that women need men—for love, status, and financial security. But so often it was another woman—a mother, sister, or friend—who was sought out in a time of crisis. Women's friendships survive petty jealousies, envy, competition, mistrust, marriage, children, retirement, and even relocation. If the statistics are correct, most women will spend an appreciable amount of their retirement in the company of other women. It is important, therefore, for women to understand their feelings about the nature of their friendships and relationships with women.

The friendships a woman has reflect her personality and her basic personal needs. In addition, her friendships will reflect her emotional needs over a given period of time.

As we talked to women about their friendships, many similarities became apparent. We discovered that although women think about their friendships, and have many different kinds of friends, most of them had not examined their friendships. Their friends and friendships simply existed.

All valued their friends, and most felt they could not live without them. Everybody remembered at least one situation when a friend really "came through" for them. All of the women we interviewed loved talking about their friendships and the specific way in which friends had supplied support, comfort, warmth, and, perhaps most important, loyalty when their lives seemed to be faltering. One comforting moment from a friend could extract lifelong gratitude and a feeling that one had been made whole by having a friend.

In 1978, the magazine *Psychology Today* conducted one of the largest studies on friendships that has been done to date. The 40,000 respondents, most of them women, listed keeping confidence as one of the most important ingredients of a friendship. Loyalty, warmth, affection, supportiveness, and frankness followed closely behind. Friendships that are based on trust and affection enhance our self-image. Our friends are perceived as compensating for deficits we see in ourselves. The choosing of a friend involves much the same process as choosing a good mate, and we expect our friends to come through when the going gets rough.

THE DIFFERENT FACES OF FRIENDSHIP

In the following questionnaire we are not discussing husbands, significant others, or other relationships you may have with men. We want you to evaluate your female friendships. This questionnaire will help you to consider your unique thoughts, feelings, and needs concerning your friendships. Go with your feelings. That's what these questions are all about.

The questionnaire is in four parts; each one considers a separate aspect of friendship. One aspect of friendship may be more meaningful to you than another, but work with them all. Approach each question as a separate entity. Under each question choose the statement or statements that apply to you and your friendships. You may choose several answers to each question.

As you answer the questions, think about the way you feel today and the way you have experienced yourself this past year. Remember, there is no right or wrong answer, just your answers.

Friendships: Questionnaire

Question 1. Who are my friends?
Choose one or more responses.
a) I have one friend I spend time with or talk to at least once a week.
b) I have more than one friend I spend time with or talk to at least once a week.
c) I have several friends I am in touch with and visit with at least monthly. I enjoy keeping in touch with them.
d) I spend time with friends because we are involved in work, projects, clubs, and activities. I am not sure I would see them as often otherwise.
e) I keep in touch with several friends but do not see them more than a few times a year.
f) My friends are current neighbors or members of my family.

Question 2. How much intimacy do I need?
For this section think of a friend or friends whom you consider closest to you and then choose the appropriate response or responses. If you have more than one friend to whom this questionnaire applies, consider each relationship separately.
a) We enjoy talking about movies, books, television, shopping, and current events.
b) We share the things we are currently involved in, for example, jobs, vacations, children's current status, family events.
c) We share how we feel about events in our lives.
d) We talk about how we feel about relationships and we share details and feelings about our earlier lives.
e) We talk about the way we feel about each other.

Question 3. How do I find my friends?

Choose one or more of the following.

a) I have at least one friend from my childhood or my school days.

b) My friends are from clubs, organizations, classes, or committees to which I have belonged.

c) My friends are from my work situations.

d) My friends are women who have been or are my neighbors.

e) My friends are members of my family.

Question 4. How outgoing am I?

Use this scale to assess the way you felt this past year. You may find that you have made subtle changes in your friendship style over the years without being consciously aware of it. Choose one or more of the following.

a) I am the one who usually calls and keeps in touch with friends.

b) I will often call a friend to make arrangements to get together.

c) I will often invite my friends to my home.

d) I belong to and am involved with one or more organizations.

e) When I am invited or have an opportunity to go someplace I am pleased and will go.

f) I would rather wait until my friends call me.

Friendships: Assessment

1. *Who are my friends?* If you answer that you have a special friend whom you see or speak to a few times each week (*statement a*), you probably think of this person as your "best friend." This answer indicates that you need a particular kind of intimacy in your life. You probably have always needed one person you can go to for friendship, comfort, and solace, and you will continue to do so.

Have you had the same best friend for many years, or do you find a close friend as your situation changes—for example, with a new job or a geographical move? Many women have both. Robyn has a friend from childhood who has remained close for almost forty years. In addition, she has had close friends at various stages of her life.

If you have found close friends during various stages of your life value this aspect of yourself, nurture it, and remember it when you think about retirement. Close friends whom you can share with are important to you. You will need to have people you can relate to in this manner when your retire.

If your "best" friendship has been a long-standing relationship, reflect on the effort and energy that went into making and keeping that relationship. It will be difficult to find a replacement. You probably will not need to, nor will you want to, when you retire. The expectations from this relationship are far greater than from any other relationship, but so are the rewards.

When asked who her friends were, Martha gave two different answers. She considers her cousin to be her closest friend (*statement a*) and acknowledges that this friendship is of great value. She does not feel she can do anything to damage this friendship, but she is careful to nourish and protect it. There is no reason to expect that Martha or her cousin will ever need to replace this relationship. It has survived geographical moves as well as two husbands each and three children collectively. Martha occasionally wonders what it would be like if anything were to happen to her cousin.

She also responded with the statement that she has several friends she is in touch with on a monthly basis (*statement c*). She only needs a close relationship with one person but she does enjoy the relationships she has with the other women in her life.

At various stages of life friendships fulfill different needs. There are times when women are more available and more open to friendships because they have a particular need. Women take the opportunity to bond as they live through their life stages. Many lifelong best friendships began on a park bench as two women sat and watched their toddlers play in the sandbox.

Robyn remembered a close friendship that developed on her first job. She and another woman, also on her first job outside of the home, started on the same day. They gave each other support and friendship during the first difficult year and remained close for several years until the friend left to take another position. Many relationships like this end when the particular need is over, but this does not diminish the importance of the closeness at the time.

Martha had been more open to friends during her first marriage when she and her husband were not as companionable. Friendships filled her need to communicate and feel connected during that time of her life. She sought friends with similar needs. As Martha's job became more emotionally demanding she had much less emotional energy for friendships. She would come home from work with just enough energy to care for the needs of her children. She would then look for solitude to recoup for the next day.

As Martha began to discuss her friendships she thought of all the women she had known in her life. She realized that she did not have any difficulty finding friends at her various jobs and on the park bench when her children were younger. Martha had actually chosen not to follow up on these friendships, but she realized that when she wanted friends she could find them. In planning for her retirement Martha needs to know that she needs friends. Martha's past tells her she will be able to find them when she needs them.

If you answered that you have several friends you speak with frequently and enjoy keeping in touch with (*statement b*), you are the kind of person who enjoys social relationships and you need people in close proximity. You are likely to have a cross section of friends and acquaintances from various times of your life. Frequent contact with others helps you to feel caring and cared for. You are a "people person" and you need to plan a retirement that includes the opportunity for social contact. Do not go for the desert island or the cabin in the woods.

Robyn's assessment of this questionnaire was enlightening to her. Robyn knew that her friendships comprised a good part of her life. Retirement and perhaps relocation made her think about starting a new life. As we spoke with Robyn she expressed moments of worry. What if she needs to talk with several of her friends frequently? How can she keep in contact with them, particularly the friends at work? How will she keep these connections after she retires?

As she reflected she began to speak of how easy it was for her to find people with whom she was compatible. She hated to think of losing the friends she had, but she had never lost friendships she valued. People who need other people often feel anxious that they may not have enough people in their lives. What they forget is that they will always connect, because that is what they need to do.

Robyn began to recognize that she needs to continue to be where she will have groups and organizations available to her. She needs continuity with people. Once in those situations her natural ability to connect with people will continue to operate.

If you responded with the statement that you have several friends you are in contact with monthly (*statement c*), you may value your privacy and feel more comfortable with fewer relationships. Hope responded to this part of the questionnaire in this way.

Hope enjoys her own company. As she assesses her need for friends in retirement she does not feel particularly concerned. She is content that her inner resources will sustain her as they have in the past. Hope does not consider herself alone or lonely. She feels bonded to those friends with whom she has kept in contact.

Hope has had a successful career and a successful marriage despite the fact that she does not need people the way that Robyn and Martha do. Only you know how important friendship is to you. If your true need is for fewer people and more privacy, don't change this style to fit the expectations of others.

If you answered that your friends are from your involvement in work, projects, or other activities (*statement d*), your friendships have a basis in the other facets of your life: job, hobbies, or other activities. You choose your friends because of a commonality of interests.

Your first consideration as you move into retirement is to evaluate whether you will be able to continue with these interests. Sometimes it is difficult for people to continue with the same activities when they retire. If the main involvement is your job and if your social contact centers on the workplace, you will need to find an activity involving people to replace the friendships you will be leaving. If you are going to relocate, you may not be able to pursue the same interests. Are you satisfied to move on to other interests and find relationships there? If you have always found friends who were involved with similar interests, you may rightly expect to continue to do so. Remember that for you the common interest is what brings you together with others, so you will need to replace the activity. This is important information for you as you enter retirement.

If you responded that you keep in touch with friends but do not see them often (*statement e*), you need to feel connected with the world but find it easier to do so on a less personal basis than if you had selected any of the previous choices. In friendships of this sort, the telephone and the mail play an important role, allowing you to maintain strong ties despite distance. Perhaps your friendships are like this because you moved frequently, whether residentially or from workplace to workplace. If not, you may simply be more comfortable when you have this level of contact with others.

Eileen had a majority of her friendships with women whom she did not see more than once or twice a year. She felt that she had as many friends as she wanted, although she spent much of her time in her own company. She kept in contact with friends from various stages of her life primarily by telephone and mail. She would occasionally be surprised to discover via postcard that one of her friends was traveling in some far-off place. The last time this happened Eileen had been thinking of sending away for theater tickets and thought that this friend might want to go with her. She knew she would be in touch with her friend soon and that they would spend some time together in the near future. This is the way Eileen plans catch-up visits. If you negotiate friendships in this manner it should not be difficult to continue to do so when you retire.

Martha had many friends from various times of her life and she kept in touch with them primarily by phone. She did not see them more than a few times each year but she looked forward to their time together, catching up on children, husbands, and jobs. She considered these friendships important and cared deeply about each woman. One of the reasons these friendships were important for Martha was her expectation that these women would be there for her when she needed friends. She was aware of her need for friends although she is not the people person that Robyn is.

If you responded with the statement that your friends are from your family or neighbors (*statement f*), you have a much more traditional style of life. Family means not only the nuclear family but the extended family system. The family used to be the primary source of emotional sustenance for its members, and for many people it is still the most stable and gratifying source of friendship. Many women we interviewed spoke of their family members as easy to be with because they shared the same values, concerns, and memories. The women who did not have significant friendships outside of their family valued the familial experience as the most important element in their friendships. The family gives them feelings of intimacy, of belonging, and of being needed.

If you responded that most of your friends are your current neighbors (*statement d*), your style of friendship may involve many of the same aspects as those who have close family ties. In today's world of transient relationships and family dislocations, neighbors can provide a structure and support system that is often highly valued. Several women expressed the feeling that they considered their neighbors to be as close to them as family.

If you answered this question with a variety of statements, then you have several styles of friendships. Many women have a "best friend" and then different degrees of other friendships. Some women do not feel the need of a close relationship with a woman but have many other kinds of friendships. Many women have friends from various times of their lives whom they do not see more than a few times each year. They tune into the relationship at different junctures in their lives and value the contact each time they do so.

No matter how you answered this series of questions you will note that in one way or another you need people. Unless you are under the most adverse conditions, nobody is truly alone. Friendships, in whatever form they exist, are crucial to the well-being of the human condition.

2. *How much intimacy do I need?* When discussing intimacy in relationships, women revealed extremely varied ideas about the concept of closeness. For every woman this has a unique meaning in terms of her own personal needs. A solid, close friendship to one is a superficial relationship to another. An intimate friendship between two women seems ridiculously involved to a woman who has less need to connect and bond. What became very clear is that, again, there is no standard measure. In evaluating, the only method you can use is your comfort level and the needs that your friendships supply. When you know yourself you can begin this new phase of your life with a feeling of power.

If your response to this questionnaire was that you enjoy talking about things like movies, books, and television (*statement a*), and if this was your only choice, the sharing of intimate details is not important for you and you enjoy your privacy. You have a need for a certain kind of aloneness since you do find it easy or necessary to share your personal life. You enjoy the daily interaction with this friend or friends and you feel you have good solid friendships in your life, sharing what you wish. If you have several friendships, you may appear to be much more social than you feel, and people may think they know you a lot better than they really do.

When we spoke to Augusta she told us that she most enjoys talking with her friends about what she does with her day, the television shows she sees, and current events. She enjoys many activities and hobbies such as bridge and folk dancing and she always keeps herself busy. Her friends enjoy her company and she is always included when her friends make plans. Because of her easy style and the few emotional demands she makes on people her friends enjoy her company and she inspires their confidence. She keeps her own counsel, however, and does not have any need to share her feelings. She prides herself on her ability to make and keep friends.

If you answered that your closest friendships are those in which you share the things you are currently involved in (*statement b*), you, like Augusta, are a private person and prefer to keep friends at an emotional distance. You have a strong sense of what you want people to know about you and you are probably quite selective about what you reveal. You tend to feel intruded upon if you are asked to talk about yourself in a more intimate way. It is important for you to control the way you let people into your life.

Anita, whom we met in Chapter I, felt that her closest friendships are those that involve talking about movies, books, and the like (*statement a*), as well as sharing facts about jobs, vacations, and family events (*statement b*). She has several friends she feels close to and she enjoys spending time with them. She does not, however, enjoy sharing feelings about her personal life and feels intruded upon if a friendship takes this turn. Anita is quite comfortable with her style, and as we spoke she became aware that over the years she had developed ways that made it clear to her friends she is not interested in discussing personal matters. She realized that she has resisted the attempts of friends to be more intimate, but she knows what she needs. Anita will continue easily with her friendship style into retirement.

If you answered that your close friendships involve sharing events in your lives and your feelings about these (*statement c*), you are the kind of person who needs intimacy in your life although you are probably not comfortable talking about deeper feelings. You have very definite things that you will share with friends, but you probably have difficulty letting your friends know about any deep hurts and longings. You keep many of your feelings inside and you keep your public life and your private life separate. You want things to go well and you want people to think well of you.

Harriet said that she shared with her friends the things she was currently involved in and her feelings about current events in her life *(statements b* and *c)*. She felt that talking only about books and movies did not give her enough emotional closeness. She did not feel comfortable talking about her deeper feelings, and did not like to talk to her friends about the way she felt about other people. She considered these feelings personal and private. The most fulfilling relationships for Harriet were the ones she had at work where she could share the current details of her life. She told us that when her nephew was married the event was enhanced by talking to her friends at the office about her new niece, the rehearsal dinner, and the wedding itself. She did not share with anybody, certainly not with her friends at the office, the hurt she felt that her brother and sister-in-law did not seat her at a place of honor at the wedding reception. Harriet was used to keeping these hurts to herself.

This level of intimacy, which Harriet finds satisfying, is found most often in structured situations such as work, school, clubs, and organizations. These friendships can transcend the specific situation if the people have other common interests that make them compatible. Harriet has one good friend at work with whom she often spends weekends and vacations. This friendship will carry over when Harriet retires. What she needs to know as she enters retirement is that many of the other relationships will end when she leaves her job and that her adjustment to the new phase of her life will depend in part on her ability to replace them. The best place for her to begin will be to seek other structured situations.

If you answered as Harriet did, you know that you need people with whom you can share your life. You also know that you are most comfortable when the degree of closeness is limited. This is important for you to know about yourself as the structure of your life begins to change.

Robyn answered that *statements a, b,* and *c* best described her close friendships. She needed to feel bonded, and talking about the current status of her life and sharing the lives of her friends gave her a strong sense of the connection she needed without an intimacy level that might make her uncomfortable. She had many friends so that there were many available relationships to give her the bonding opportunities she needed.

If you stated that you like to share details and feelings about your life (*statement d*), you enjoy the involvement and intimacy that come from sharing feelings with your friend. You are probably interested in understanding the unconscious motivations of yourself and others. You enjoy analyzing your thought processes and your inner life, and you need to share this with a friend. You are not fearful of exposing some of your private self to another person. You are able to trust this friend.

This kind of sharing takes time and effort, and if you have friendships of this type you know they cannot easily be replaced. As you move into retirement you must consider ways to maintain the relationships you have; if this will be difficult, you must look for opportunities to form new friendships based on this kind of sharing.

Roz and her husband Tom moved from their home in western New York to Tucson, Arizona, because of his severe arthritis. They had put off the move as long as they could, but they were both able to take early retirement from their jobs and the move was a physical necessity. Roz had grown up, lived, and worked her whole life within a fifty-mile radius and she had many close friends and a "best friend" she had never expected to be separated from. Her friendships with many of these women involved sharing feelings about their lives, and her friendship with Ethel, her best friend, was particularly close. Roz found these friendships to be a particularly sustaining piece of her life. The separation from these friends was the only devastating part of the move, since Roz and Tom had known it was inevitable and had planned accordingly.

She cried often during her first year in the Southwest, although she spent much time on the weekends and many evenings on the telephone with her friends. Ethel came to visit for a month during the first winter, and Roz and Tom had several visits from other friends over the year. Despite these visits, Roz continued to miss her friends intensely. She and Tom played bridge, and joined the church, and she joined the women's group there, but she could not seem to find satisfying friends among the women she met.

As we talked with Roz she realized that she would never

replace the friendship she had with Ethel. Their weekly or twice weekly phone calls would have to suffice until perhaps Ethel too would retire and move to Tucson. Roz also realized, however, that she needed to find women friends with whom she was more compatible than those she had been meeting until now. Friendships had been an important part of her life and she needed them even more now that she was not going to work each day.

As Roz evaluated her style of friendship and the degree of intimacy she found satisfying in friendships, she realized that she would have to seek out women who were interested in sharing their feelings and analyzing relationships. Sharing bridge or church concerns was not enough; she needed relationships with more intimacy.

She has now joined a national organization of college women which has a subgroup of women who come together to discuss interpersonal problems. She has found several women in the group who share common feelings about being relocated, and she feels that here is where she will probably find the friendships she needs to make her life satisfying.

If you answered that you talk with your friend about the ways you are feeling toward each other (*statement e*), you feel reciprocity, commitment, and trust with this friend. Relationships that reach this level of intimacy are unique. You are not afraid of making yourself vulnerable and you know what it feels like to share your inner life. By risking intimacy of this kind you have gained an unusual kind of emotional closeness. In this friendship you feel accepted, loved, and valued just for being you. If you have this kind of emotional closeness with somebody, you must continue to have easy access to the person. You have a friendship that is of great importance in your life.

Martha knew that she likes to talk about her feelings and thought that *statements d* and *e* characterized her close friendships. She enjoyed talking about the details and feelings of her earlier life, and she enjoyed the feeling of intimacy when she shared this with her friends. Martha understood that her most meaningful friendships over the years had been those in which she shared her feelings and the intimate parts of her life. This was one of the reasons that Martha particularly enjoyed her relationship with her cousin. She also enjoyed sharing memories of her past and analyzing her present actions in relationship to her past. This was fun for Martha, and it gave her a sense of well-being. Martha did not particularly enjoy relationships in which she could not achieve that level of closeness. She would rather be alone than talk with friends for any length of time about what she considered trivia.

Whether you are like Martha or more like Anita or somewhere in between, you must remember that there is no one who can tell you how to be. It is important that you become aware of what you need to make you comfortable and fulfilled with the friendships in your life.

3. *Where do I find my friends?* In order to plan for a successful retirement, you should think not only about who your friends are and how close you are with them, but also about where you found your friends. Retirement and especially relocation will bring new issues about finding friends. Many retired women felt that the need for friendship during the early years of their retirement was more intense than at any time since adolescence. This had surprised women who had looked forward to having time alone or with their husbands and to being able to live at their own pace.

Margo told us this story about the first year of her retirement. She had been content with the friendships in her life when she was working, but she had never given thought to the importance of any of the relationships. There were many women in her office and they had lunch together and found time during the working day to gossip and visit. She also had a busy social life with her husband which involved friends and family. She rarely visited with her work friends outside of the office.

Shortly after Margo and her husband retired she began to yearn for some friendships that did not involve her husband. She had not realized that except for work she had no independent relationships. Although she felt close to her husband and they had many conversations, the conversations were usually about movies, television, the children, or other family members. She felt unsatisfied with this. Her husband had never been comfortable talking about feelings, either theirs, his, or hers. Margo had thoughts and feelings she wanted to share with other women. She was looking for a particular kind of intimacy that women provide for women. She had never realized how important it was to her. She is now looking for a group or an organization that will enable her to find compatible women friends.

Katherine, a recent retiree, told us what she had learned about her need for friends during her first year of retirement. Katherine never married and willingly retired from a job she found stressful and annoying. She felt her job had not been conducive to making friends, and she had minimized, if not devalued, the meaning of the friendships she had at work. When she retired she did all of the things she had planned but often with a certain kind of loneliness. Many of her friends had not yet retired and she found that she was more alone than she wanted to be. She had not thought of the daily contact with the people at her job as important, and she was surprised that she missed it. It was only when she was telling some friends about a movie she saw that Katherine realized how much she missed sharing the details of her life on a daily basis. She needed friends with whom to share her plans for the weekends, her thoughts on the television shows and movies she had seen, and her family stories and events.

Katherine needs to find a way she can replace the daily camaraderie she had at work. She needs to establish a new social network and has started to do so by becoming involved in community service.

In order to have a successful retirement, you should begin to evaluate the ways in which you found your friends, so that when your life changes—and it will—you will be in charge and able to shape it to your liking.

If you answered that you have at least one friend from your childhood or your school days (statement a), you have a strong sense of continuity in your life and a strong need for roots. The friend from your childhood is a very important person to you, although you do not necessarily see this friend very often. The childhood friend remembers your parents, your siblings, and—most important—*you* at a time you remember as being only yesterday. Your childhood friend binds you to your past, giving your life a continuity you find comforting and reassuring. If you have remained in touch with friends from your childhood you will take these friendships into your retirement, for connections are important for you. You will make every effort to remain in contact with the people you value.

Sarah had a friend from her childhood she was in touch with two or three times each year. They always remembered each other's birthday and kept each other informed of current events in their families. They enjoyed remembering their first encounter when they couldn't decide what game to play, and had memories of each other's family and friends that went back forever. Nobody else remembered teachers, friends, and neighbors as they did, and they often fell into reminiscences when they were together. They were not intimate, but they felt strongly connected, each one valuing the friendship as a strong tie to her past.

It is not by chance that Robyn has two friends from her childhood. She has kept in contact with these friends as part of the way she relates to people. Bonding to people is a part of her identity. She needs connections and prides herself on her ability to hold on to relationships. It had certainly taken some effort to keep in contact with both of these friends. Remember, keeping in touch included over thirty-five years of calling and writing. Robyn never thought of it as an effort and had always enjoyed knowing her friends were there.

If you answered that most of your friends are from clubs, organizations, classes, and committees (*statement b*), you are probably the kind of person who mingles easily with people. You enjoy the camaraderie of groups and you can pursue these sorts of relationships with comparative ease. To reach out in this manner is not easy for everyone, and many people consider the ability to do so a special talent. If most of your friends are from the clubs and organizations you have belonged to, you can expect that you will continue in retirement to find people through the same channels. Just keep in mind that you will need to be where you can join groups centered around your various interests. As you plan for your retirement you need to give yourself every opportunity to fulfill your needs.

Robyn correctly assessed that most of her friends are from the various activities in which she has been involved. She knows she will need to have access to clubs and organizations when she retires because this is how she has built the network of friends that makes her life so satisfying. As she knows she will be relocating, Robyn is exploring opportunities to join various organizations and committees in the retirement community.

Women upon retirement traditionally are counseled to keep active by joining clubs and organizations. This is not necessarily the way for all, and if you feel differently do not allow yourself to be intimidated.

Hope answered that she did not need to join organizations or clubs and, even if she did, it would be extremely difficult for her to make friends in that situation. Structured activities made her feel uncomfortable and she was not able to negotiate those situations without feeling self-conscious. When Edgar died she joined a widows' support group and found this experience extremely helpful. When she left the group—feeling that she had received all the support she needed—she did not keep contact with any of the women. Hope will continue with this style into her retirement. She may join a special-interest or needs group, stay with it until she is satisfied, and then leave with apparent ease.

If you answered that you found most of your friends through your work situations (statement c), you have utilized a built-in social structure to build relationships. Proximity and commonality of interest are important elements in your friendships. If you have carried any of the relationships beyond the workplace when you left the specific work situation, then you have successfully nurtured a friendship that obviously had value for you. You may need a structured situation in which to develop relationships, however, and you may need to find such activities to enable you to find new friends if you wish to do so when you retire.

If most of your friends are from your current work situation, the closeness probably stems from a common interest that keeps the relationships intact. Perhaps you have not thought of the relationships in your place of work as friendships, but they are most often a particular kind of relationship and their importance in your life should be assessed carefully. Think about the daily interactions with your friends from work. Perhaps you share your interest in a television show you each watched the night before, or perhaps you tell your co-workers that yesterday's mail brought a wedding invitation. You enjoy sharing a portion of your life with these friends and that sharing gives you the feeling of belonging. Think about how much fun you had when you shared your vacation with your friends from the office.

This is a good time to evaluate the importance of the particular friends you have at work. If you decide that you value any of these relationships and that you want to maintain any of them after you retire, you will want to discover if the relationship can transcend the workplace. Since relationships change after you leave work, you need to find out what you can while you are still working with the person. You might plan activities away from the office and have dinner together or spend some time visiting on a weekend. Perhaps you can join a club or take a course together. Find out if you feel comfortable in the new relationship. Learn if you have things in common besides work.

It may also be helpful to discuss your retirement plans, your concerns, and your feelings with your friends from work. Their attitudes and feelings toward your retirement can help you decide who is in tune with your needs. Some of your friends from work may be having the same questions about their own retirement.

Many retired women reported that for the first few months of retirement their friends from work were eager to see them. After a time, the office gossip and politics were not interesting enough to the retiree to last through more than a quick lunch. The women who were still working were involved with the tasks of the job on a daily basis and wanted to talk about it. There was not much else to share, for the common bond that had sustained the friendship had disappeared. The time spent together became strained and the meetings became less frequent.

Anna, an office supervisor, is considered by others as well as by herself to be somewhat of a loner. As we talked with her she became aware that most of her friends were from her current job. Relationships that she had not considered friendships have been fulfilling her need for friendship.

Anna realized that although she enjoyed the built-in convenience and the commonality of interest, she did not wish to pursue any of these friendships when she retired. She recognizes her need for social interaction and friendship, but she does not feel connected with any of the women at work. As she approaches retirement she recognizes that she will best fulfill her need for friendship if she seeks it within an existing social structure, and therefore she will have to replace her work situation with another organization. With this in mind, Anna, who is interested in politics, is now becoming involved in her local political club.

If you answered that most of your friends are either current or former neighbors (*statement d*), you count on proximity to enable you to find relationships. You also are likely to enjoy intimacy and continuity in your friendships, because neighbors who are friends often become like family. In this situation you have daily contact, and emergencies large and small often are shared due to your easy access to one another. Strong ties probably are meaningful to you. If you are not changing your residence when you retire, you will probably have little difficulty in maintaining your friendships, although you may find that you need more from them.

Several women who were neighbors described the closeness they felt for each other. They had lived in the same community for most of their lives and everything that mattered to them was in close proximity. They spoke of retiring to a drier and warmer climate but they expected to do it as a group. They have been researching areas during vacation time together. None of them wants to cope with feelings of loss and separation at this time of their lives.

If you grew up in a small town or a small suburb of a large city, you may be accustomed to finding your friends in your neighborhood. If you decide to relocate you will want to find a community with people who have backgrounds similar to yours.

If your friends are mostly family members (*statement e*), and if you do not relocate when you retire, you probably will not experience much change in your relationships. These friendships will probably continue for you throughout your life and you will not have to consider replacing them. If this is your friendship style you have a need for stability and continuity of which you should be aware.

As you evaluate the other aspects of friendship through the questionnaires in this chapter you will recognize the needs that you have from these family relationships. Keep in mind the possibility that others in the family may have their own plans. Depending on your needs, you may want to change your retirement plans to fit the needs of others. Remember this and evaluate it carefully as you plan for the future.

Several of the women we spoke with told of sisters or cousins who had relocated because of the needs of husbands or children. Many of these women felt that they had been deserted; some decided that they too should relocate.

4. *How outgoing am I?* There is no standard or appropriate way for women to reach out to each other. Each woman has individual needs for friends at different times of her life and she reaches out accordingly. The way women feel about a particular friendship or about friendships in general can be a barometer of their needs during a certain period of their lives. You will remember that there were times in your life when it was easier to call a friend, and certainly some friends are easier to call than others.

As women get older and their circumstances change they often find that their need for friendship changes. Some women who needed many friends when they were younger told us they did not need as many casual friends as the years passed, and thus they became more selective about their friendships. Some women who had jobs that drained much of their emotional energy found that when they retired they looked for more social involvement.

Are you as outgoing as you need to be in order to fulfill your needs for friendship? This is an important evaluation for you to make at this time. Do you have the intimacy level you want in your relationships? Do you have the friends that you want in your life? Do you feel comfortable about the idea that you may have to make some changes as you move into a new phase of life? If you can gain an understanding of the way you operate in terms of your outgoing behavior, you will have an easier time ahead.

If you answered either that you are usually the one to call and to keep in touch (*statement a*), or that you often call to make arrangements to get together (*statement b*), you have strong social needs and you are direct in the way that you fulfill them. If either or both were your choice, you probably enjoy many friendships and feel that your friends enhance your life's experience. You know how to go after what you want and you like to be in control of the way friends enter your life.

Robyn was usually the one who called and kept in touch with her friends. She did not think who had called whom last time. When she wanted to hear about a friend or follow through with a friendship, Robyn communicated with ease. Robyn will bring her gift for friendship and her outgoing nature into retirement and she will continue to seek relationships as she needs them.

Cynthia answered that she was the one who usually called her friends to make plans because she enjoyed herself a lot more when she went places with friends. She would not go to the movies or out to dinner alone and she looked for company when she shopped. People who need people in their lives usually are outgoing enough to find them.

Merle is a woman with a vast assortment of friends. She never married, she feels her friends to be family, and she keeps in touch with them consistently. She calls to make plans to see a show or go to a concert. Merle often calls friends just to say hello. She needs this contact in order to feel connected with the world. Even when she travels she keeps in touch. She has her friends' names copied on labels and when she goes on trips she pastes the labels on envelopes and mails notes to her friends. At Christmas she prints a newsletter about what she has done for the year and sends it to her friends all over the world. She is outgoing in a more impersonal way than Robyn or Cynthia, but Merle's style of friendship involves less need for intimacy. She is outgoing in just the right way to fulfill her needs.

If you answered that you often invite friends to your home (*statement c*), you too can reach out easily. When you invite people to your home you are showing a very special part of yourself to the world and this takes courage and confidence. You enjoy being in control of a social situation and you feel comfortable when you make the plans.

Joan said that she usually calls and keeps in touch with her friends and she enjoys having friends come to her home (*statements a* and *c*). Joan prides herself on having a lovely home and her home is an important part of her identity. She remembers that when she was a child, her mother kept plastic covers on the living room furniture; indeed, the living room was off limits to her brother and herself except on special occasions. Joan's mother did not enjoy having company because it disrupted her routine. Joan vowed that when she had her own home she would make it comfortable and without plastic. Joan frequently invites her friends to her home and experiences a feeling of accomplishment after her friends have spent enjoyable times with her in this intimate manner.

If you answered that you are involved in one or more organizations (*statement d*), you too have found a comfortable way to reach out and be involved socially. This is a way to seek friendships without necessarily risking a one-on-one encounter. You are outgoing in your own way and should have no trouble continuing this style into retirement.

Many women who said that they belong to one or more

organizations (statement d) also said that they call and keep in touch with their friends (statement a). If you answered in this way, you are comfortable socially and probably enjoy many friendships.

If you answered that when you are invited places you are pleased to go (statement e), you enjoy socializing and being involved with friends. You enjoy the idea that you are wanted and you enjoy being engaged in life. Eva loves to be invited places since she is on a busy work schedule and seldom finds the time or the energy to make plans in advance. She appreciates that invitations structure some of her free time. Eva is looking forward to retirement as a time to enjoy her friendships and do some of the things she has been unable to do while involved with her job.

Perhaps there are times when invitations feel like an imposition and an intrusion on the structure of your life. Many people feel safe in the world they have constructed for themselves and do not like having their routines interrupted. Hope feels comfortable about her life and likes her style; she said that often she was not pleased when she was invited places. She would have the feeling that the invitation was an imposition on her time and space. She finds that she refuses as many invitations as she accepts. What is important for her is that she feels okay about her style of friendship and expects to carry on in the same way. Remember, there is no way to be, just the way that helps you feel content.

Hope does not anticipate many changes in her life over the next years. This may not be so for you; retirement may bring a restructuring of your life and you may have fewer routines. You may then have more need for outside contact. If you think this may be so for you, and if you have an outlook similar to Hope's, you may want to think about modifying your style. It is important for you to assess how your life will be different and how your needs will change.

If you answered that you would rather wait until you are called (statement f), you tend to be more reticent with your friendships. It is possible that friendships are a serious commitment for you and take a good deal of your emotional energy. Perhaps you have some anxiety about reaching out to people and have some fears of being rejected. If you are satisfied with the friendships that you have and the level on which they are conducted, then your more passive style is working for you. You will need to evaluate what changes will occur and how your network of friends will be altered when you retire. If there will be any major changes you will need to give some thought to your ability to reach out to others.

Several women said that they are pleased to go when they are invited places and yet would rather wait until friends called (*statements e* and *f*). If this was your assessment, you are a person who needs to be sure of your welcome. Only then can you feel that your friendships are within your control and you can reach out and be comfortable. Many of these women wished that they were invited places more often because they felt hesitant about making plans. They were shy and somewhat fearful of rejection. Although they liked to go places, they needed an impetus from outside.

If you answered that you wait to be called but like to go places, this is a good time to evaluate your style in terms of needs. You may be more outgoing than you think if you enjoy yourself when you are out in social situations. You may want to try to get some understanding of your reticent behavior to enable you to modify it to some degree. Shyness cannot be eliminated but it can be controlled and modified.

Lenore said that she calls and keeps in touch with one friend but she usually waits until her other friends call her (*statements a and f*). Lenore said she had one close friend and many other friends whom she thought of as acquaintances. She said that she seldom called anyone except her close friend. Lenore remembered rejections in her childhood, and although she is a successful career woman, she cannot get past feeling cautious in her friendships. She is always responsive when people call her and her friends understand and accept her style. This has worked so far for Lenore, but it may cause some difficulty for her in retirement. Many of her social contacts are from her work, and

retirement brings many changes, particularly in these friendships. Lenore may find herself isolated if she waits for friends to
call.

If you evaluated yourself similarly you may want to be
aware of the possibility of modifying your style. If this is your
need and if retirement will make changes in the structure of your
social life, you need to plan in a practical way how you can keep
a circle of friends who will fulfill the needs you do have.

After using the assessment questionnaires you may have
discovered many things that you did not completely know about
yourself. Perhaps you have a different style of being with your
friends than you believed, or you may have discovered that what
you thought you wanted is not the same as what you do want.
Perhaps you just confirmed what you already knew about yourself in this regard. Perhaps you picked up one point that was of
interest to you as you reflected on your answers.

Martha felt that she had put her friendships into a different
perspective as she analyzed her ability to find women friends
when she sought them. Hope felt that she knew about her need
for privacy and found no surprises. Anita became more comfortable with the idea that she did not need the intimacy some of
her friends seemed to want. Robyn was able to be less worried
as she realized that her strong need to connect will enable her
to have new friendships even in another place.

A friendship is an important piece of a woman's emotional
life, and many women have found retirement to be a time in
which friendships are particularly important. Midlife women
have a lifetime of experiences to share with each other, and in
retirement they have a unique opportunity to offer each other a
personal kind of emotional support. Know what your needs are
and what you have to give as you begin this new chapter in your
life.

V

Family Attachments

All happy families resemble one another, but
each unhappy family is unhappy in its own
way.

LEO TOLSTOY (1828–1910)

Laura and Michael have always been a family-oriented couple. Michael was an only child who had been raised by his widowed mother from the time that he was five years old when his father died, and he had always looked forward to a large family of his own. Laura came from a close family of five children and expected that she would have a similar family life when she married. In the early days of their marriage and when their children were growing up, they were considered by their friends to be the traditionally happy couple and family. And they were! Michael had a good job that provided well, and Laura stayed home and took care of their children and the home. She did not work outside the home until all of her children were in high school, and even that job was on a part-time basis. She was an available and caring mother during the years before her children left home.

Now that her three daughters are all married with their own children, Laura has a full-time job as an administrative assistant which she truly enjoys. The children live within easy driving distance so that, in addition to speaking on the phone with each of them several times each week, she and Michael can visit often. They all look forward to the phone calls and the visits. Laura is beginning to be aware that she feels somewhat smothered by the family obligations, which give Michael great pleasure. In the past two years her children seem to be calling her more frequently requesting baby-sitting or other favors. Two of her daughters expect Laura to enjoy and appreciate all the opportunities to be with her grandchildren. They feel resentful when she hesitates or at times refuses to baby-sit. Laura enjoys her children and her grandchildren but feels that she would enjoy them more if she set the schedule. Michael will be retiring from his job within the next two years and Laura will probably do the same so that they can travel and do more things together. As Laura contemplates this she is concerned about her role as mother and grandmother. What is her commitment? What is her obligation? What does she want to do?

Judy, aged fifty-eight, who never married, is involved in a close relationship with her mother, who is seventy-nine. They do not live together, but they speak daily and visit weekly. They have always been close, for Judy's father died when she was fifteen and Judy then became her mother's companion for many social obligations, most of which revolved around the family.

Judy is also the family reference point for her extended family, which consists of her three aunts, their children (Judy's six cousins), and the grandchildren. Judy has always enjoyed this role, which evolved for her as part of the fact that she never married. She always seemed to be available to help emotionally as well as in practical ways. She has a job as an office supervisor for a large corporation and she will be able to collect a sizable pension in three years when she reaches the age of sixty-two. She will be retiring at that time and she sees the family burdens increasing as her aunts as well as her mother are growing older and their needs seem to require more of her time. She finds that she is being called upon to fill in for her cousins, who seem to have less time to care for their mothers than she does. She needs to evaluate the importance of these relationships. Does she wish to devote the next years of her life to maintaining and sustaining them? How will she get time for herself when she is no longer working? How much of the family obligation does she wish to carry into retirement?

Relationships, particularly family relationships, are always in transition. Although many women at the time of their retirement feel that their relationships with their family have stabilized, some relationships women hoped would go in a straight line start to curve in unexpected ways. Relationships with daughters- or sons-in-law complicate relationships with children. Children who were expected to live in close proximity relocate. Grandparenting brings unexpected demands. Grown children return home with or without grandchildren, parents or other relatives become ill or frail, and retired women unexpectedly become caretakers. When these situations occur, women—particularly those who grew up in the 1940's and 1950's—have difficulty finding for themselves the indistinct line between obligation and commitment. Are they sacrificing time and emotional energy for dependent family members because they feel obliged to or because they want to? The message from today's society and from the women's movement is that women are responsible first and foremost to themselves. The duties society traditionally has imposed upon women, and that women have traditionally imposed upon themselves, often conflict with this message. This conflict runs deep as voices from the past intrude on women's present needs and desires. Now is the time to explore and then exercise your options.

For the following questionnaire think about the people in your family with whom you have meaningful contact. Are they your children, siblings, parents, or other family members? With that person or persons in mind, choose the statement in Part A —Frequency that applies. If there is more than one person, respond separately for each. Then look at Part B—Feelings and choose the statement that best fits the feeling you have about your contact with this family member. Evaluate your response to Part A in relationship to your response to Part B. As you begin to assess your important family relationships, your responses to Part A will give you a true idea of the extent of your contacts with each person.

Your Part B responses will illuminate your feelings about the contact that you have. As you evaluate your responses to Part B you will begin to see the line between your commitment and your obligation to the people involved. As you define this for yourself you can begin to see if you want to make any changes when you move into retirement.

Remember, this questionnaire does not include your relationship with your husband. That relationship will be addressed in the next chapter.

Family Attachments: Questionnaire

PART A—FREQUENCY

a) I usually have some contact with this person on a daily basis.
b) I visit with this person, either by phone or in person, at least one time each week.
c) I have regular contact at least once a month.
d) Although I'm in contact, it is irregular.

PART B—FEELINGS

e) Most of the time I look forward to my contact with this family member.
f) I would look forward to my contact if it were less frequent.
g) I would look forward to my contact if it involved less of my time.
h) I would look forward to my contact if it took less of my energy.
i) I would like to have more choice as to when and how I have contact with this person.
j) I often wish I didn't have to have contact with this person.
k) I would like to have more frequent contact with this person.

Family Attachments: Assessment

If you answered that you have some contact with this person on a daily basis (Frequency—*statement a*), this relationship is extremely meaningful to you, whatever you feel about the contact. You have a strong commitment to this person and perhaps strong feelings of obligation. Retirement may not specifically change your emotional ties with this person. Even relocation, which may alter the frequency of and kinds of visits, will not change the relationship appreciably.

If you answered in addition that most of the time you look forward to the contact with this family member (Feelings—*statement e*), this is a strong relationship that has a great deal of emotional meaning for you. Stop and think for a moment the way you feel about this contact. Do you feel enhanced after the contact? If you have positive feelings, this relationship enhances you and you probably think of this relationship as a friendship. This may be the person you identified as a best friend when you evaluated your friendships. This person provides warmth, acceptance, trust, affection, and support for you, as in a close friendship. This is a relationship that defines you in the best possible way.

Norma has been in daily contact with her parents for most of her life. Her father is ninety-two and her mother is ninety. They are a close-knit family, and although they had their conflicts they enjoyed the comforts of an extended family. Norma, who was widowed two years ago, had made arrangements several years before for her parents to move into an apartment one block from where she lives. She wanted them to live close by, feeling she would be better able to care for them. The extended family still gathers frequently and is a source of great pleasure to Norma's sister and brothers and now their children. Although Norma anticipates retiring within the next two years she does not see any need to change her family relationships. They are interdependent and all of the family members are comfortable with this situation.

If you have contact on a daily basis your feelings may not

be as clear-cut as indicated by the statements in Part B—Feelings. You may find yourself vacillating between looking forward to the time (*statement e*) and wishing it were less frequent (*statement f*), or perhaps wishing that you had more choice about the contacts (*statement i*). If no one statement seems to fit, ask yourself these questions about your feelings: When you have contact with this person, do you enjoy thinking about the things you have talked about, or do you have faint—if not strong—feelings of disappointment? Even if you look forward to the encounter, do you feel that you do not get what you need? If you feel disappointed, frustrated, or even angry after a contact, you may need to reconsider what this relationship means to you. There may be ways to change the relationship if you can identify what is lacking. This may be the time of your life to make this change.

Marilyn, aged fifty-seven, has a close but conflicted relationship with her thirty-one-year-old daughter Kim. Marilyn, who is divorced, may need to retire and relocate because of physical problems. She has been divorced since she was thirty-two and Kim was six. She has lived as a single parent, dating on occasion, with one long-term affair with a married man whom she knew she would never marry. (She liked her independence and did not want to remarry.) Marilyn and Kim had a volatile relationship since Kim's adolescence, although they consider themselves close friends. Kim lives nearby in her own apartment. Marilyn continues to feel that the relationship is fraught with conflict. She feels Kim demands too much emotional energy from her and gives little back emotionally. Kim is engaged, and she and her fiancé enjoy visiting Marilyn frequently. Marilyn is flattered by their visits and feels a strong obligation to see them, but she feels drained emotionally when they leave. She worries about her strong feelings of obligation and wonders how much they may be connected with feelings from her past. She wonders if she can change the relationship.

Another factor is Marilyn's concern about her physical health. She has asthma and has been told she would feel better if she lived in a warmer, drier climate. Because she will be able to retire in two years when she is fifty-nine and her pension will be fully vested, she has considered retiring and relocating. Up until now she felt she could not consider relocating because she could not leave Kim. Marilyn is starting to accept that her relationship with Kim will never be much different from the way it is now. The idea that she might not need Kim's proximity for her emotional well-being is emerging. Although she loves Kim, she feels more and more that she has less need for the kind of relationship they have. Through understanding her feelings toward her daughter, Marilyn has begun to separate her feelings of obligation from her feelings of commitment. She feels committed to Kim, but her obligation, her sense of duty toward her, has lessened. Thus Marilyn can make choices she never thought possible. One choice Marilyn has made at this time of transition is to become a paralegal, thus starting a second career with exciting opportunities and possibilities.

If you have contact with a family member on a daily basis but would like it to be less frequent, less time- or energy-consuming, or just more your choice rather than someone else's, examine this carefully. You are probably discharging an obligation rather than honoring a commitment and you may be unnecessarily angry at this person or unnecessarily dissatisfied with the relationship. Retirement may give you more time and this may ease the burden you feel, but as your leisure time increases, you or the dependent relative may feel that you should devote more of it to him or her. The obligation that you feel is probably real, but perhaps it is possible to deal with it better. These next years should be for *you*.

If the person whom you visit daily is an elderly parent who lives alone, perhaps you can make two or three visits each week in the form of a lengthy phone call. Or do you have a sibling or other relative or a friend of your parent who can take one of the days each week to visit? Is the visit absolutely necessary, or are you motivated by a sense of guilt and obligation rather than by a real need?

Janet discovered that by hiring a woman for two days a week to clean and spend some time with her mother she had those two days to take care of errands and other needs of her own. She had never really thought of it because the feeling of obligation was so strong that she never questioned or looked for an option. When she opened her parameters, allowed herself to expand and look for choices, she felt a strong sense of relief and a stronger sense of enjoyment during the time that she did spend with her mother.

If the elderly person has other social contacts, and many do, your visit may be welcomed but not necessary. If you're simply providing social contact, perhaps the needs of the elderly person might be equally well met if he or she spent a day or two a week at a senior citizen center. If you feel that you need to spend a whole evening or the better part of an afternoon, you may find that a ten-minute visit will do as well. Often just the "checking in" is all that is really necessary.

Look at your daily contact with your children or grandchildren within the context of your responses to Part B—Feelings. It is often difficult to admit that you can have too much of any loving relationship, but we often heard from retired women that they would like to be able to say "no" more often when it came to grandchildren. The daily contact involved more time or more energy than they really wanted to give. We heard many stories of working mothers who relied on their mothers for child care. Peg delayed her retirement for two years because of this. She could not bring herself to the point of telling her son and daughter-in-law that she did not want to take care of her two-year-old grandson. The grandson is now four and starting nursery school, but Peg is not off the hook because a new granddaughter was just born. She realizes that she will not enjoy babysitting on a full-time basis despite the fact that she loves her son and her grandchildren very much. She wants more choice over her contact (statement i) so that she can look forward to it and not feel burdened. She is aware that she must deal with this if she is to continue a loving relationship with her children.

If you can arrange any of these options for yourself, you will discover that your feelings about this person and the time that you spend with him or her will be of a more positive nature than ever before.

If you answered that you visit with this person at least once a week (Frequency—*statement b*), this too implies a strong committed relationship. Particularly if the physical distance is great, it is possible that this frequency can be as strong a commitment or obligation as a daily visit. If the weekly contact is a quick phone call, it may be weaker but is nevertheless a meaningful relationship.

It is important to examine your contact in conjunction with your responses to Part B—Feelings. If you do not look forward to the contact (*statement j*), look for other options that will enable you to fulfill the obligation you feel. If you would look forward to seeing this person once a month rather than feeling resentful about the weekly visit (*statement f*), try to arrange for this, as both you and the other person will be much better off.

Ruth had weekly contact with her mother-in-law who lived in a senior citizens' residence about forty miles from Ruth, who had recently been widowed. She made a monthly visit to the residence and always made a weekly phone call. Ruth was thinking of retiring and wanted to relocate to be away from the Chicago winters. The commitment she felt (or was it simply an obligation?) to her mother-in-law was a stumbling block. When Ruth spoke with us and answered Part B—Feelings of this questionnaire, she stated that she often wished she did not have to keep up this contact with her mother-in-law. They had never been friendly, and at times over the years they were not even cordial to each other. The current visits were strained and short, since the mother-in-law's disposition had not improved with age. Ruth had never really examined this relationship because she had loved her husband very much and they had been very close. She took his mother as part of the marital agreement. As we talked she began to realize that there was no reason to allow the obligation she felt to her mother-in-law to stop her from planning a life change. The weekly phone calls could be continued as long as they both wished, but there was no need to continue the monthly visits. There was no reason that Ruth could not begin to make plans to move if this is what she wanted to do.

Your situation might not be as straightforward as this, and

you may have more trouble sorting out the obligation from the commitment; but if you can begin to do so and begin to see options for yourself, your retirement years can be lived on your terms.

If you answered that you have regular contact at least once a month, the commitments and obligations you have in these relationships are probably less important than those toward persons you might see on a daily or weekly basis. The latter are often stable relationships with family ties from the past helping to keep them nurtured.

Pauline described her relationship with her Aunt Bertha. Bertha, her father's sister, never married and had always lived alone. Pauline described many happy memories from her childhood: Aunt Bertha taking her to her first Broadway play and her first fine restaurant with linen tablecloths; buying her pretty underwear that her mother always thought much too frivolous. Out of strong loyalty to her father, who died eight years ago, and other strong familial feelings, Pauline calls Bertha at least once a month and looks forward to spending time with her. The feeling that Bertha is a connection with her father keeps Pauline in contact with Bertha. When Pauline thinks about retirement she knows that she will keep the connection. She thinks it will be possible to see Bertha more frequently when she has more time, although she feels that the relationship is as good as it is because it is not on a more frequent basis.

She has acknowledged that she will probably be the caretaker when Bertha is unable to care for herself. If Pauline is to relocate she is not sure what plans she may have to make for Bertha, but she knows she will care for her in some way. Pauline feels both commitment and obligation to Bertha and feels positive enough about their relationship to keep it willingly and with love.

Many women have contact with their grown children on a monthly basis, and therefore are not involved in the daily activities of each other's lives. They consider themselves friendly but not close. Frequently after grandchildren are born these relationships change. Parents and children will renegotiate their relationship in order that parents can enjoy their role as grandparents.

Sara's daughter Heidi moved from New York to Colorado after she finished college. Sara, who lives in New York, kept in contact via the phone and with summer visits. The daily nuances of their lives were lost to each other but the strong family ties prevailed and each time they spoke they picked up where they had left off. When Heidi was married the same relationship continued, but after Heidi had a child each felt a stronger need for more intimate contact. The phone calls and visits became more frequent, and Sara and her husband are now considering the possibility of relocating to Colorado. There they can have a good quality of life and also participate in the life of their grandchild.

If you answered that your contact with the family member is irregular (Frequency—*statement d*), you may want to reassess the meaning of this relationship and ways it may change when you retire. Because you kept in contact for many years, the relationship has some value for you; it might have been closer if you had had more time. This sort of relationship can take on new parameters when you get older or when you retire. This may be a good time to determine if this is a relationship that can enhance your retirement.

Naomi has had a cordial relationship with her sister-in-law for the past twenty-five years. They always looked forward to seeing each other during family visits and often spoke about getting together for lunch. The boundaries of the family relationships and unspoken family taboos, however, prevented this, but now that their children are grown and they are both entering a new phase of their lives, Naomi feels it could be the time to break the barrier and perhaps find a new friend.

If you answered that although you are in irregular contact (Frequency—*statement d*) you would like to make it more frequent (Feelings—*statement k*), this may be the right time to make some changes. One of the people with whom you kept in irregular contact may be a sibling. Preretirement is often a time when women reshape their relationship with a brother or a sister, and siblings who have not been close often find retirement to be a time of renewal. Sibling relationships are among the most powerful. If you enjoy a good relationship with your sibling(s), the dynamics of reconciliation from your childhood rivalry have already taken place. If the contact has been infrequent with little intimacy, you may find the need or the desire for a change as your parents age. Siblings often discover that they must put petty jealousies of the past aside in order to plan for the well-being of their parents as the parents grow older. During these times when they are forced to be together, brothers and sisters discover how comfortable it is to have a connection with their past. They become aware that there are few people in their present life who knew them as children and who have so many of the same memories. Many women feel as they get older that they want this connection with their past and that their siblings can provide it for them.

Augusta's reconciliation came only after the death of her parents. She and her two older sisters were the survivors of seven children. The rivalry of the past had left the sisters quarrelsome and competitive but they were also at times lonely for each other. Augusta retired and relocated to Florida with her husband and was widowed within the year. When this occurred her sisters immediately called to find out what they could do. To the surprise of them all, they felt a need to be together and made plans for a visit to Florida.

Right from the beginning, old patterns of behavior emerged. Beatrice, the oldest sister, began to criticize Augusta, telling her that she had hung her pictures too high, that her dress was unsuitable, and that the soup was too salty. With no parents or husbands around to mediate, Augusta simply said, "You know, you hurt my feelings when you criticize me so often." This was a new beginning for them; they began to talk about their feelings and the way they behaved with each other. This visit gave all of them the feeling that they would like to give their relationship with each other a second chance. Now, and albeit with caution, they have reached into their past for another try.

Judy had more work to do on this questionnaire than most other women interviewed. She has several family members with whom she has meaningful contact. As the family caretaker, she defines herself as a helper and enabler, and although she sometimes feels burdened, she needs these commitments. They define her and bring satisfaction to her life. Her responses to Part B—Feelings were nevertheless interesting to her, as her feelings varied greatly from person to person. She saw clearly that she is in weekly contact with one aunt with whom she would prefer to have no contact at all.

As Judy considers retirement, she is becoming aware that she needs more options and choices in her role as the family caretaker. She is emotionally acknowledging that her mother is growing older and will not be with her forever. This fact became startlingly clear for her when she and her mother took a trip together two years ago. Judy couldn't help but notice that her mother's pace and stamina lagged well behind her own. She realizes that she needs to plan for the ways she might feel when her mother or other family members for whom she cares become frail or ill. She knows that her retirement will include caring for her mother and she will do so out of choice, commitment, and love.

She is fairly certain that as the unmarried woman in the family she will become responsible for the other family members and recently she has found herself as the family caretaker in more concrete ways. It is not that Judy minds this role, but she sometimes feels angry that so many of her relatives expect it of her. She realizes that when she cares for some family members she does so more out of obligation than commitment. This explains some of her anger. She does not want all of her retirement time to be eroded by being a caretaker. Good for Judy! She anticipates the problem and can begin to make plans accordingly.

Several cousins have gladly turned the job of caretaker over to her, so Judy has decided to hold a family conference to enlist their help and set some limits. The amount of time she wishes to contribute will be an important agenda item in her meeting.

Judy, as a single woman in retirement in the 1990's, is entitled to fulfillment in a way that is different from ever before. She does not have to accept the role of family caretaker as if it were her duty. She too must separate commitment from obligation and she is starting to do that. Judy must keep her needs in sight as she experiences this new phase of her life.

As women move into retirement, the fact that they have become willing or unwilling caretakers of aging parents brings about a significant change in their lives. Even if women do not become caretakers, their relationship with a parent or parents will change. You cannot help but see facial changes, the slow-down in the gait of an older person, the difference in the energy levels and in alertness. In many ways these are not the parents you grew up with. This cannot help but change the structure and the dynamics of the relationship. Many women wondered aloud if they would be like their parents in their old age. The fact of their own aging begins to creep into their image of themselves. Thus, in many unforeseen ways, retirement is a time of transition.

Statistically, a woman is forty-seven when her last child is launched into the world. Thus, many of the traditional "empty nest" symptoms, if there are any, frequently are worked through by the time of retirement. When children first leave home they tend to be more dependent on their parents, but as children become more individuated, a more equal relationship forms between parents and children. Many women who grew up in the 1950's find the empty-nest syndrome to be an outmoded concept, perhaps even a myth. The empty nest today is not necessarily empty and meaningless. It simply means that parenting of a certain kind has stopped. For many women who grew up in the fifties the time after their children leave home has become their first chance to exercise a variety of options. They can now concentrate on their own needs, pursue new careers, and focus on their relationships with their husbands in a different manner. Without their children, many women greet their future with relief, as a time to find new freedoms.

Laura has a lot of thinking to do about her retirement future. Her family involvement, the most important part of her life, is changing. She must separate commitment from obligation as she moves into her retirement years. She knows that she wants more choice in the frequency of contact with her children and grandchildren (Feelings—*statement i*), and she knows that she would enjoy each contact more if it took less of her energy (Feelings—*statement h*). She is deeply committed to her family and their welfare, but she has begun to allow this to become an obligation that is increasingly difficult to discharge with pleasure. Understanding what she wants from her relationship with her children as she moves into her retirement has a different importance now.

Understanding a piece of her past will be helpful to Laura as she prepares for her retirement. She was brought up in a family where her mother and father put their relationship as a couple before the needs of their children. This had long been a topic of discussion among Laura and her siblings. Laura was determined that she would not do this to her children and, fortunately for her, her husband Michael felt as she did. Therefore there was little conflict about parenting in their marriage. She may now be paying a price for putting her children's needs first, however, for her children continue to have many expectations of her. They still want the same unconditional acceptance of their demands, and they are not used to hearing that their parents have different priorities and are putting their own needs first. Laura has been able to cope with this situation in the present structure of her life. When she feels that her children's demands are excessive, for example, she uses her job as an excuse to avoid baby-sitting and doing other things her children think she should do.

Laura is confused and conflicted about the way she wants to handle her new feelings of independence from her children. She needs to assess the reality of just how important she is to her children. Because she needed to be different from her parents, she may have overestimated her importance as a parent and this may be especially true in regard to her grown children. Do they really need her as much as she thinks they do? Laura needs to assess her children's needs in relation to her own needs, and she can do this effectively each time a request is made by one of her children. She has to begin to separate herself from her familiar role of a mother obliged to meet every need of her offspring. She needs to focus on a new role as a woman of the nineties who is ready to retire and begin a new life. She must separate commitment from obligation so she can continue to grow and develop.

The problem of grown children coming back home to live with or without their own young children when their parents are in their preretirement or retirement years is a complicated new phenomenon confronting many women. Many of these women told us that they had just launched a life with more independence than ever before, had just begun putting their own needs first, when a grown child had come home to intrude on preretirement or retirement time. Many of these women expressed the feeling that they did not want to reparent at this time of their lives. As a result there was often a clash between the two (sometimes three) generations and their differing developmental goals.

Patricia had been a housewife until her oldest son Ralph left for college. Although she had not considered a career until then, she felt her time had come and she went back to school to become a social worker. Her husband David, who was planning retirement, supported her plan to return to school, for they had agreed that when he retired and they relocated, Patricia would work. Patricia had obtained her degree and had been working for a year when Ralph returned home from college planning to stay until he could earn and then save enough money to afford his own apartment. Patricia had always had time to keep her home as she liked, and when Ralph was away at school she and David had worked out a comfortable schedule to accommodate their different hours. When Ralph returned home he expected Patricia to be the mother he remembered from his childhood and adolescence. He expected meals, cleanup, and laundry to be done for him, expectations that were easy enough for his mother to dispel. What was difficult for Patricia was that her house was always in disarray. Ralph treated it like a motel, and although Patricia and David made many house rules, Ralph was preoccupied with his own life in the fast lane. Patricia found she was doing a good deal more housework than she wanted. She discovered she was often annoyed for no discernible reason as she entered the driveway of her home. She realized, as this anger persisted, that something was wrong.

Patricia needs to sort out her commitment and obligation to Ralph and to herself at this time of her life. To whom does she owe what? She values being a good parent, and she has always felt obliged to meet her son's needs. But her life is different now. She is launching her career and establishing herself in a new profession. As she evaluated her feelings with us she began to realize that she saw Ralph's return home as a disruption and intrusion. She had not wanted to admit the fact to herself that she could view her child's presence as an intrusion. As she acknowledged that feeling, she began to understand that she no longer has an obligation to take care of Ralph as though he were a young child. Although she has a strong commitment to him, the most important person in her life now is herself. This realization has enabled Patricia to speak to Ralph and let him know some of her feelings. He is now contributing money for a cleaning person and as a result is more mindful of the physical condition of the house.

Women whose children moved back home often saw the homecoming as a mark of their failure as mothers. Their children, who were supposed to find success out in the world, had returned home to be cared for. The feeling of guilt engendered by grown children coming home can be stressful and explains why so many women revert, under these circumstances, to the old and familiar maternal role. They then find themselves doing things for their grown children that they really don't want to do. Parenting older children after they have left home and then returned is a situation that requires a woman to have a good understanding of her own feelings of commitment versus her feelings of obligation.

James returned home after he was divorced. He and his ex-

wife have joint custody of their child and James gave the apartment to his wife as part of the divorce settlement. He decided it
would be best for him to live with his mother, Helen, who had
been widowed three years before. Helen was just discovering
that life as a widow was manageable. With much trepidation,
she had enrolled at a local junior college for a course in art
history and had planned a trip to an Elderhostel the following
summer. She had not planned for, nor did she look forward to,
life as a mother and grandmother on a daily basis. She and James
had discussed his plan to move back home and both had agreed
that it was temporary, with time parameters of six months to a
year. It was a time that had to be lived through with as little
stress as possible. Plans had to be made not only for child care,
but for the interventions and negotiations necessary for a three-
year-old in the home two days during the week and every other
weekend.

Helen fortunately was able to visualize her position clearly
and to see that she could not be there completely for her son.
The first point at issue was to establish open and clear communication between James and herself. The second was for Helen
to make clear to James what time she had available to be a
mother and grandmother.

Helen needed to separate commitment from obligation, a
difficult task during this time of stress, but possible nonetheless.
She decided that she would try to be available for child care two
days of the week as long as it did not interfere with her school
schedule. She wanted to be able to plan her own weekends,
although she expected that she would spend some of this time
with her son and grandson. She wanted James to be responsible
for his son on these days, even though this meant getting up
earlier in the morning than he liked. All other baby-sitting time
was to be arranged on an as-needed basis. Helen's time was not
to be taken for granted. Although she felt guilty about not doing
more, she decided that she would rather feel guilty than angry.
The women's movement moved into Helen's life in a significant
manner, giving her permission to take on a different role as a
mother in her retirement years. She had never thought this
would be possible or that she would feel comfortable about it.

In order to prepare for a successful retirement, you need to understand the way you feel about your meaningful family relationships. As you begin to sort out obligation from commitment in this area of your life, you will learn the difference between the patterns that are no longer productive for you and the patterns that give meaning to your life. With this power you will be able to change those things it is possible to change.

VI

For Couples Only

*When men reach their
sixties and retire, they go
to pieces. Women go right
on cooking.*

GAIL SHEEHY (B. 1937)

Karen and Tom had been married for better or worse for thirty-eight years. They have been looking forward to retirement from their respective jobs as accountants and have spoken often about the problems that lie ahead. They are both practical people, used to dealing with practical situations. In particular, they both understand their financial situation and they feel prepared for their future. They have worked hard for most of their marriage and look forward to leisure time. They hope finally to get to Europe and perhaps the Far East, two trips they have spoken of often. Tom has a demanding job as a comptroller for a large private company. Karen currently is working as an accountant for special projects for a nonprofit organization. In addition to this and her household duties, she uses her Saturdays to work at her avocation, which is jewelry-making. Their busy schedules allow for little free time together and Karen is looking forward to the time when this will change—or is she? There are times when she feels uneasy. She hears Tom's description of retirement and the long, happy days they will be spending together and she finds herself becoming anxious. Tom speaks glowingly of all the fun they will have golfing, traveling, taking courses together. She does not always share his enthusiasm. She needs time to figure this one out. Why is she suddenly feeling the need to stay at her job forever? She has been waiting to retire for the past three years!

In the early years of her marriage, when her children were preschoolers, Karen opted to return to school. She earned her CPA and began her career as soon as she could with part-time help both for child care and for housecleaning. Tom never had a problem with Karen's busy schedule, although he never became involved in the arrangements she made to keep it going. She is a natural organizer and an extremely capable woman. She ran her household and the rest of her life with efficiency. When her children were grown and had left home for college and marriage she continued to manage her life with dispatch. She has recently been looking forward to winding down, leaving her job, and concentrating her time on jewelry-making and Tom. What is wrong? She loves Tom and they have had long and faithful years together.

Sadie and Dave were married when he came home at the end of World War II. They were engaged before he left to join the army in the spring of 1942, but he was twenty-seven and she was just turning nineteen and her family persuaded her to postpone the marriage. They were a devoted couple from the time they began the courtship and they remained so. They had one son, Simon, to whom, Sadie, particularly, was devoted, and she felt she had a pleasant life taking care of her house, Simon, and Dave. She had several friends, nice neighbors, and two sisters whom she visited frequently. Dave owned a small photography shop in a shopping area several miles away and he enjoyed going to work.

On their thirty-fifth anniversary, which was the year Dave was to be sixty-five, and the year their first grandchild was born,

Dave told Sadie he was closing the shop and retiring. He had been putting his money in a pension plan, he was eligible for Social Security, and he had the veteran's disability pension he had always collected. He felt they were financially secure and he wanted more time for himself. Sadie was surprised but not at all displeased and she looked forward to happy years.

Dave had always been helpful with the housework. He was amiable and loving and for years they had done the dishes together after the evening meal together, using it as time to share the day's events. He also agreeably helped with the heavy household chores. When he retired and was home most of the time he did more and more of this. He also began attending a gourmet cooking class in the local high school and began to shop and cook a few nights a week. Sadie was not angry with this gradual change in their life, since she had never loved these chores and was happy to be relieved of them. She began, however, to be somewhat bored. She was used to a structured day, chores to do, and dinner to prepare. She felt aimless too much of the time. As Thanksgiving approached that first year of Dave's retirement, Sadie began to notice help-wanted advertisements in the local newspapers. Many department stores were hiring extra help for the Christmas rush. She had worked in retailing while waiting for Dave to return from the war, but she had not been in the labor market for thirty-five years. She applied for a job! She began working in a large department store on the Monday before Thanksgiving. This was seven years ago and she is working today. She enjoys her job, likes her co-workers, and loves the contact with people.

It took Dave several months to recover from the shock, but he enjoys being home and at leisure. He is particularly devoted to his granddaughter and he baby-sits regularly. Sadie enjoys getting dressed and going out to work three days a week. She does not miss the housework. She loves having her dinner ready when she gets home. Life is not the same but Sadie believes it is even better now.

Retirement may alter the structure of a marriage. It will not change the relationship, but it will emphasize different aspects.

Problems may emerge that were not at issue previously, primarily because the external routine has changed significantly. Personality factors that the couple "lived around" or adjusted to over the years suddenly loom as obstacles to a life together. They are no longer spending time separately on a regular basis. The importance of this varies from one couple to another, but it is significant and cannot be ignored. Other factors that influence or cause problems for couples at retirement often refer back to this change in structure. The basic issues of autonomy and control are being dealt with, within a totally different framework. The familiar and comfortable routine of over thirty years is gone. The solitary extra cup of coffee and the newspaper in the morning have now become breakfast for two. The morning exchange with other women at work or in the neighborhood has now become a discussion of the previous or current day's plans with your husband. In retirement you and your husband want or need to know what you expect to do with your time on a much more specific and constant basis.

It is important as you move into retirement that you be aware and plan for this change. We have organized the questionnaire for this chapter into three sections which will be discussed separately. The first section deals with the allocation of time you now spend in the company of your husband; the second section deals with the independent activities and people that now figure in your life; and the third section helps you to assess your need for privacy and intimacy within your marriage.

These three dimensions will give you a better understanding of what retirement will mean for you in the context of your marriage. You may be looking forward to the extra intimacy and time you will finally get to spend together, just the two of you. You may feel that it will work out for you, and so it might. But look closely at the time allocation as you work on the following questionnaire. We found that most of the women we interviewed were unaware of the large amount of time they had to themselves before retirement. A realistic look at this, and an exploration of your feelings in relation to it, can help enhance your retirement living.

PATTERNS OF COMPANIONSHIP

Time Together: Questionnaire

PART A—WEEKLY TIME

The following statements will give you a picture of the time you are currently spending with your husband. Choose the statement or statements that apply.

a) We spend most weekday evenings in each other's company.

b) We rarely send an evening together during the week because each of us is involved in his or her own activities.

c) We spend most weekends in each other's company.

d) We have separate activities or obligations on weekends and our time together is limited.

e) Although we spend most of our weekends together, we are usually with other people

f) Although we are on different schedules we manage to spend a large portion of our time together.

PART B—FEELINGS

Consider how you feel when you spend time together with your husband. Choose the statement or statements that apply.

g) Most of the time I look forward to being with him.

h) We are very companionable and I like to do most things together with him.

i) We both look at life in the same way.

j) We have different outlooks on life.

k) I enjoy our time together although we often do not agree.

l) The pace at which I live my life is different from his.

Time Together: Assessment

As you reflect on the significance of your answers to this and to the other two sections of the questionnaire, do not focus on any problems your husband may have in adjusting to retirement. We do not mean to dismiss his issues, because you may be able to help him. We would like you here to focus on yourself and your feelings. This may be more difficult for you than you think, particularly if you were a child of the 1940's, '50's, or '60's, when you were taught to believe that the man came first. It is, however, of great importance to the next years of your life, particularly now that you are entering retirement, that you concentrate first on your needs. Remember, if you are tuned into your needs and feelings, you will not need to deal with your anger and frustrations at the same time that you are listening to your husband's problems.

Many of the women we spoke with answered with *statement a* (they spent most weekday evenings together with their husbands) and *statement c* (most weekend time spent together). If you answered in this way, look closely at your responses to Part B— Feelings, which pertain to the way you feel when you consider time together with with your husband. Your answers to these questions will give you a good understanding of what your time together after retirement will be like. If you look forward to the time you spend together *(statement g)* and you feel that your time together is fulfilling and rewarding *(statement h)*, you and your husband are companionable. The problems you may have in retirement will probably not stem from your time together. To affirm this conclusion, examine your answers in conjunction with the following two sections of this questionnaire. You will see that you are truly heading to the best years of your life.

Give your feelings careful scrutiny as you respond to the way you consider your time with your husband. Consider what occurs when you plan your time together. Do you look for the company of others more often than not? Are there topics of conversation that seem to come up constantly between you which create either anxiety or boredom? Do you approach life in the same fashion *(statement i)* or do you have different outlooks on life *(statement j)?* Is your husband more pessimistic than you are? Or does it go the opposite way? Does your husband depend on you to make plans for your time together? Are you prepared to do this on a full-time basis? Or does your husband handle that part of life, and are you prepared to let him do this on a full-time basis?

Are you both people who move quickly to get things done? Are you the procrastinator or is he? Do you both like a lot of relaxation time or is one of you always on the go? (These last three statements pertain to *statement 1*, that is, the pace at which you live your life is different from his.) Are you both people who tend to accept what comes in life? The fact of retirement is that whatever your life together is now it will be more so when you are retired and at home together. An understanding of what you can expect will enable you to modify and make changes to ensure a comfortable retirement.

We spoke with Maryanne, who has been retired and relocated with her husband Jim for over a year. Before they retired and moved they had a traditional marriage in which they were together weeknights and weekends, even after their children married and left home. They got along well together and enjoyed each other's company. Jim had always been a rather passive person with a pessimistic outlook who did not have a high energy level, but Maryanne had a cheerful outlook on life, energy for two, and a job she enjoyed so that Jim's moods did not affect her too much. She coaxed him along and made her plans. They did not go out as much as she would have liked, but they compromised and she kept busy with activities that gave her pleasure. Then they retired and relocated to a retirement community.

Maryanne made new friends, joined the church, went to art class, played golf, and made herself at home in their retirement community. Jim did not move out as easily and spent a lot of time at home reading and watching sports events on television. He made a workshop out of a portion of the garage and continued with his carpentry hobby. He did not seem as willing to participate socially, and Maryanne couldn't coax him along the way she had when he was working.

Maryanne found herself angry with him much of the time. He would be locked in the workshop or sitting in his favorite chair with the newspaper when she came in from a meeting or

golf. They were still companionable and spent good times together, but she wanted him to join her more in the couple-
oriented social life of the community. She felt he shouldn't keep
to himself so much. She was increasingly frustrated in her attempts to get him to move out socially.

As we talked with Maryanne she began to see what was
happening. Jim had not changed. He was the same person she
loved and married. He is caring, intelligent, and sensitive and
these are the qualities that had drawn her to him. He is, however, a passive person who looks at the world through gray
rather than rosy glasses. He is never going to have a lot of
energy. He worries about his health, their children, the stock
market, and the world situation. He is never going to be the life
of the party in company, and, if truth be told, Maryanne would
not like that very much. These personality traits, of which
Maryanne was well aware, became magnified the more the two
were together. She had not carefully considered what retirement would be like for them in this regard. Although she had
done thorough research on relocation and ways to occupy her
time, she had disregarded an important factor—the way she
might respond to Jim when she did not have her daily routine.

Once she became aware of her expectations of Jim she was
ready to solve her problem. Her anger had limited her attempts
at compromise, a technique that had served her well in the past.
In her anger she had not been able to sort out what activities she
could continue to participate in happily by herself. In her anger
and disappointment with Jim she had started to present each
invitation or social situation as a demand rather than as a special
request. This insight into the situation made it possible for her
to evaluate her needs in relation to Jim's so she could fulfill her
needs as a woman in retirement to the best of her ability.

Betty anticipates a different problem when her retirement
becomes a reality. She and Arthur also spend most of their
nonworking time together. As she evaluated her feelings, she
became aware of how differently the two approached life. She
was far more accepting of the people in their lives and of the
events that occurred. Arthur was often critical of her, their chil-

dren, their friends, and the world in general. Not that this was a surprise to her, as he had been this way for all the years of their marriage. Furthermore, she rather enjoyed and agreed with his sarcastic comments about other people, although she looked at life and relationships differently. He had a sardonic wit which gave her great pleasure. She saw, however, how it could affect her directly if he were around enough to become involved in her daily activities. It already affected her to some extent, and she resented the criticalness when it was directed at her. She does not have Arthur's ability to use language to advantage, at least not until the opportunity for a response has long passed. She just simmers or hurts silently.

She will be considering this problem from two aspects. She feels that she will have to structure their lives in retirement so that she has ample opportunity for independent activity that will give her the positive feedback she now gets from her job. She will also have to work on communicating her feelings to Arthur when she feels criticized. She is thinking about taking a course in assertive communication at the local community college to help her express her feelings. Her awareness of the situation and her preparedness will pave the way for a more comfortable retirement.

If you responded that you rarely spend an evening together during the week (Weekly Time—*statement b*), and that you often spend limited time together on weekends (*statement d*), you are in a minority group of women who grew up in the 1950's and 1960's. This marriage structure is more common in the marriages of the 1980's and 1990's. If this is you, whatever your wedding date, it is important for you to explore carefully what you believe will be the structure of your life together in retirement. You have little frame of reference for the way couples experience togetherness during retirement. Life will be easier after you retire if you do not allow yourself to just drift into retirement. If this is you, look closely at your responses to Part B—Feelings. Many women who have little time with their spouses are nevertheless extremely sensitive to what life together is about. If you are companionable (Feelings—*statement b*), and if you believe that you look at life in the same way (*statement i*), and if you and your husband live life at the same pace (*statement l*), you may know more than the questionnaire might indicate. Perhaps these retirement years together have been your goal and the reason you both worked so hard. We are not here to raise unrealistic doubts. You know yourself and your marriage better than anyone else. If you are sure of how it will be, then read on just for the insights you may gain.

To help you evaluate further, you may want to think about vacations when you spent two or three weeks almost exclusively with each other. This is not necessarily a true picture, since it is an artificial living situation which often has more stresses than most people realize; but this can give you clues as to what you can expect. You also may want to assess the reasons behind the separate time you now have. Is it because you live at a different pace or because you have different outlooks on life (Feelings 5 —*statements i, j, l*)? Will you need to resolve this as you move into retirement? Is the separate time purposeful, or just part of what happened because of the necessities of life? If you prefer and need the separateness, then just make sure that you plan for it in your retirement . . . and you will have to plan for it, because it does not just happen.

Joan and Lester had married, each for the second time, about fifteen years ago. He owned a home in a suburb about thirty miles from the city where Joan lived. They each had jobs near their respective residences and Joan had children who were still in school at the time of the marriage. They worked out a living arrangement that was agreeable to them both: They spent Monday to Thursday in their own homes separately, and Thursday to Sunday together in either place depending on the weather and social commitments. When they retired, they sold Lester's house and kept Joan's apartment, and they now spend the winter months in a warmer climate. This means that they are spending more time together than ever before in their marriage. It has been over a year now and the year has been full of adjustments and readjustments. They had known this might be the case and had been prepared to talk about and work out the difficulties together. They are companionable, look at life the same way, and live at the same pace (Feelings—*statements h, i, l*), yet they were surprised to find that each needed the separateness more than they had realized. As a result they are working on arrangements in terms of time, space, and activities so that they do not have to live apart to have the autonomy they each need.

It is likely that the time you spend with your husband is a combination of many of the alternatives on the togetherness scale. If you said that you rarely spend an evening together during the week (Weekly Time—*statement b*) and spend most weekends in each other's company (*statement c*), you should further evaluate your answer by examining your response to Part B —Feelings. Examine your feelings in relation to the time you spend with your husband. Do the same if you answered that you spend your weekday evenings together and your weekend apart (Time Together—*statements a* and *d*). If you added that despite different schedules you manage to spend a large portion of time together (*statement f*), you have another dimension to your responses which transcends the issue of physical time and gives you additional information about what life will be like for you in retirement. Reflect on your feelings about the time that you share.

If you spend most of your time together in the company of others (*statement e*), examine your relationship carefully. You may have less experience being together in an intimate way than you realize. Rose became aware of this shortly after Ken retired. She originally stated that they spent most of their free time together, both weeknights and weekends. What she did not take into account was that she and Ken spent most of their time together with Ken's large family. When she married Ken she became a member of his family of three sisters, four brothers, and two loving parents. Rose's parents died when she was in college. Her one brother lived in a different state and they were not close. Rose welcomed the opportunity to be a member of a large, caring family. As the years went on the family grew to include daughters- and sons-in-law, the numerous children, and finally grandchildren. Four of the siblings lived within a ten-mile radius of Ken and Rose so that even after his parents died, on weekends and on weekday evenings they spent time with one or another of Ken's sisters and brothers.

Shortly after Ken retired their only son was transferred to a job in Silicon Valley in California. He moved with his wife and their two children to a nearby suburb of San Francisco. Ken and Rose had often spoken of moving from the severe winter climate but did not want to leave the family. Suddenly there was reason to relocate and they were both surprised at how quickly they made the move. They are now living in a suburb of San Francisco, although not the same one as their son. They visit often, but the young family is busy building its own roots in a new area, which Ken and Rose realize they also must do. They have become aware that their life together has a new structure, without the family togetherness on which they had come to depend.

As Rose spoke about her life she realized that in actuality both she and Ken had over the years felt a little restricted by the close family ties, although the pleasure of them did outweigh the pressure. They had never been aware of how much they had shared with others and not with each other. They had never realized how diverse some of their interests were. Ken's involvement with sports had never given Rose a problem before because she had always had someone to spend time with while he watched a sports event. When she wanted to see a touring ballet company or a concert, she always had someone to go with. Compromises and sharing about these activities, which are quite common and worked out early in most marriages, had never been addressed by the two of them because there was no need to do so.

Ken and Rose are having a good time, although it is not always easy for them. They are learning to know each other better and to live together without the energy and activity engendered by a large family group. They are enjoying the quiet and leisurely pace. They have met some friends with whom they spend some of their free time. Retirement and relocation have given them a new beginning.

Independent Activities: Questionnaire

The purpose of this section of the questionnaire is to help you become aware of the level of independence you now have within the structure of your marriage. Many women interviewed, particularly women who did not work outside the home, did not realize the amount of independence they experienced as part of their daily lives. There was often more autonomy than they consciously realized despite a busy daily routine at home or on a job outside the home.

If you have no activities in your life that don't include your husband, then you probably won't have much difficulty feeling comfortable in retirement . . . unless of course you are thinking about changing your style of coping. You may want to concentrate more on the next section, Privacy and Intimacy. If you have even one interest that involves you in time alone and will probably continue into retirement, you should carefully examine your responses to *questions 3* through *6* of the questionnaire. If you are engaged in these activities during the time when your husband or you are at work (*question 3*), and if he encourages your involvement (*question 4*), consider how he will feel if you continue with this interest each morning at 9:00 A.M. when he would like your company over coffee (*question 5*). If you feel this may be a problem for him (*question 6*), decide beforehand how you will handle this.

In responding to this part of our questionnaire, try to evaluate each of your activities, both as to (1) time spent and (2) the feelings involved (yours *and* your husband's). You may know you have many interests and your husband has many also, and there will not be a problem. You may know you have many interests and that your husband doesn't like this at all, but you do not worry about this. If you can make either of these statements with assurance, then you should not have unexpected difficulties in this area.

Question 1. List the activities you are involved in that do not include your husband. Then:

  a) Estimate the number of hours you spend with each activity on a weekly basis.

b) Decide which activities you will continue to be involved in and list these separately.

Question 2. List any people you see independently of your husband. Then:

a) Estimate the amount of time you spend with each on a weekly basis.

b) List each person you will continue to be involved with.

Question 3. Which of the above activities are you engaged in while your husband is at work or during your working hours?

Question 4. Which of the above people do you see while your husband is at work or during your working hours?

Question 5. How does your husband feel now about your involvement in these activities?

Question 6. How does your husband feel now about your involvement with these people?

Question 7. How do you think he will feel when it takes from your time together or causes you to restructure your time together?

Question 8. If he does have a problem with any of your independent time, how do you feel about that and how will you deal with it?

Independent Activities: Assessment

Most of the women we spoke with had not given much thought to this issue and found it most enlightening when they did. Betty realized that although Arthur would not have a problem with her independent activities, she would be receiving plenty of critical feedback from him because of her specific interest in astrology. Arthur believed astrology to be nonsense and was uncomfortable with her curiosity. Before retirement, Betty had planned her astrology courses and seminars around Arthur's schedule, so that except for the occasional snide remark when she spoke about it, Betty's interest had never been a problem. She looked forward to spending more time in retirement with the study of astrology, but she was not sure that the interest would survive Arthur's sarcasm if astrology interfered at any time with his needs.

Betty is not quite sure how she will deal with this, although she is aware that the easy way would be to give up her interest, and this is always a consideration. She also knows that the easy way does not always satisfy, and she is pondering what to do. This is a typical problem for women: Pleasing and deferring to the wishes and ideas of others too often takes precedence over their own wishes and needs. Sometimes, as with Betty, the issue is the interest itself. Your husband may encourage and be willing to adapt to your daily aerobics class but be annoyed by your interest in bridge. He may like to see you utilizing your creative abilities in an art class but be inflexible toward your interest in returning to school.

It is not necessary now to go into your husband's underlying problems that come to bear here unless it will help you to cope with the situation. You need to evaluate the importance of the activities to you and your life in retirement. If any or all of your interests enhance your life, you will want to make plans to keep them as part of your routine. You may need to compromise, make schedule changes, or communicate your feelings with more forcefulness. Betty may find that explaining her interest in astrology and then telling Arthur how he makes her feel when he is so critical may make all the difference in her situation.

The other problem in this area is a more basic one and more commonly considered by the women we interviewed. Many women who had outside interests were concerned that these interests would interfere with their husbands' schedules. For the already retired women, lunch was a big issue. The comment, "I married him for better or worse but not for lunch," was not all that amusing to the many women who found themselves hurrying home from a morning meeting or golf game in order to prepare lunch.

Once you evaluate your responses to this questionnaire, you will know where you fit in this situation. Awareness is the first step to a solution. If you have many activities that interest you and do not involve your husband, don't consider giving up on them when you enter retirement. If you think there will be difficulties, you may need to decide which activities hold the most meaning and interest and begin to plan on how to continue them. If your interests are not wide but are intense, consider these interests carefully and do not casually put them aside.

It is important as well that you make every effort to anticipate what the situation will be between you and your husband in regard to your independence (*question 7*—How do you think your husband will feel when your interests take you from your time together? and *question 8*—Does your husband have a problem with any of your independent time?) These questions brought up another dimension to the problem Maryanne was having with Jim. She had not been aware of this problem, and only now is she beginning to comprehend its meaning. Part of Jim's reclusiveness in retirement is his response to Maryanne's energy, enthusiasm, and independence. Although these qualities are ones he greatly admires in her, he has not previously been living with them in such constant proximity. His response, because he feels so overwhelmed by her vitality and ability to function so independently, was to retreat into himself. Maryanne's understanding of this dynamic gives her another piece of information that will help her negotiate a more fulfilling retirement.

Try to respond to *question 2*, which involves the people you see independently of your husband, in the same framework as *question 1* regarding activities. If you do have friends you see without your husband and you expect to continue seeing them after retirement, look at your responses to *questions 3* through *6* very carefully. If you see your friends while you or your husband are at work or otherwise involved (*question 3*), evaluate your own and your husband's awareness of your involvement with these friends. Is he aware of your involvement? Does he expect that in retirement you will continue to see the friend or family member alone? Does he prefer not to be involved with them? What will his response be if you continue the relationship? If he will not have any problem with your daily or weekly contacts or your occasional afternoon or evening with your friends, then the way is clear. If he will have a problem but you do not have conflict, then you can more easily handle his feelings and you will have less of a problem in this area of your retirement.

As with independent activities, most of the women we spoke with had not seriously considered the area of independent friendships as an important factor in their retirement. Even when they gave this aspect of their lives thought, many of them did not see it as a problem area. There were many preretirees who did, however, see a potential problem, and many already retired women told us that they had more difficulty in this area than they would have anticipated.

Elvira had played Mah-Jong and visited weekly with a group of women who first met when their children were at the local nursery school. They had become good friends but they had never done much socially as couples and the friendships had remained separate from the marriages. Elvira and one of the other women had worked for a while on a part-time basis, but all in the group managed to be available most Wednesday afternoons at two. John, Elvira's husband, knew all about the weekly arrangement. It was never a problem since she prepared dinner in advance and was home before he returned home from work, which was usually between 6:30 and 7:00 P.M. When he retired two years ago he preferred an early schedule and expected dinner to be ready between 5:00 and 5:30. Elvira found that she was breaking up the game and leaving the fun at 4:30 each Wednesday afternoon. She was upset about her friends' resentment and the disdain she believed they felt toward her because of the situation. She found that she was very angry with John because she had to leave the fun. She felt trapped and unable to figure out what to do. This is a difficult situation for her since she is used to being the dutiful and nurturing wife, and she feels uncomfortable making any change in the structure of the marriage. As of this writing, Elvira is still leaving the game each Wednesday at 4:30 because she has been unable to discuss her situation with John. She has discovered, however, that talking it out with her friends has resulted in support and empathic reactions. She again feels comfortable and is able to enjoy the time that she does spend with them.

Connie works as an administrative assistant for a small firm that designs an exclusive line of women's clothing. She has been there for ten years and is thinking about retiring in two years. She has become very friendly with Bob, one of the designers. They go out to lunch several times a week and have shared confidences. He is a homosexual who is involved in a long-term relationship, and Connie was surprised at first at just how much they found to talk about. They have both come to value the relationship, but Connie has been unable to discuss Bob with her husband Don, except in passing casual references. Don grew up in the time and in a place where homosexuality was jeered at and condemned. Connie knows that her friendship with Bob would at best be misunderstood. She has time to wrestle with this situation and she plans on doing just that. She very much wants to continue the relationship and she will attempt to raise Don's consciousness and try to change his old-fashioned views. She may want to include Don in the relationship to some degree. She knows that somehow she will find a way so that upon her retirement she can continue to keep this important friendship in her life.

Activities and relationships that are of importance to you before retirement will not necessarily diminish in importance when you retire with your husband. You may need less involvement in some of your more casual relationships or interests. You need to determine which ones are dispensable and which ones enrich and enhance your life. If you give up any meaningful aspects of your life to please or adjust to your husband's needs, you may find problems where you did not expect to find them. The anger Elvira feels toward John for what she experiences as a deprivation is one of those many moments in a marriage in which the conflict has little to do with the event itself. Until retirement Elvira was unaware of how strongly she felt about an autonomous piece of her life, and she is now engaged in an internal struggle for more independence.

Married women who came of age in the early part of the twentieth century had no sociological context in which to pursue their need for autonomy and independence, so they had little conflict about the way to behave in their marriage. Because of the timing of the advent of the women's movement in their lives, women who came of age and married between 1940 and 1970 cross two generations. These women often have a deep internal conflict involving their drive for autonomy and independence. Married women who came of age in the 1970's and 1980's frequently are forced to address the conflict earlier in their lives and therefore come to terms with their needs concerning this. They usually will incorporate it into the structure of their relationships. Even women who came of age between the 1940's and 1970's and who do not have conflict about their independence in their marriage, may find it called to their attention as they watch their young friends and daughters handle their lives so differently. The drive for independence and the need for autonomy are valid and viable parts of a women's life today, whenever she came of age. If you are starting to feel they may be important in your life, you may have to struggle for them but you can gain ground.

Sometimes the need for independence is a moot issue within the structure of a marriage. The pattern of life together in terms of making a living and bringing up children may have fulfilled or bypassed this need. This is what happened with Sadie and Dave, whose marriage gave Sadie the needed autonomy in her life until its structure changed after Dave's retirement. As Dave took over more of her household tasks, she felt bored because her space was being intruded upon. She recognized as we spoke that she had lost a sense of the freedom she had when she was on her own for the day. She sees that her job gave this feeling back to her. Although Sadie did not consciously evaluate her situation and sees herself as acting on impulse, she did successfully fulfill her basic need for independence within her marriage in a society that was ready and willing to accept her need as valid.

Privacy and Intimacy: Questionnaire

Several women to whom we spoke could not relate to section two of this questionnaire, on independent activities. They had few meaningful activities or interactions with people (except at work) that were separate from their husbands. They did not anticipate problems in this area. Some retired women also stated that this aspect of life was not an issue. Many of these same women found that their assessment of section three provided them with much to reflect on. Evaluating privacy and intimacy will give you an objective picture of your need for private time and private space.

PART A—HOURS SHARED
For *questions 1* through *6*, estimate your waking hours only:

Question 1. How much time do you spend with your husband on an average working day?

Question 2. How much time do you spend with your husband on an average weekday?

Question 3. If you work outside your home, how much time daily is involved with your work (including travel time)?

Question 4. If you are not working outside the home, for how many hours is your husband away from the house?

Question 5. When you are together with your husband in the evenings, how much time do you spend actively engaged with each other or doing the same activity?

Question 6. When you are together with your husband on weekends, how much time do you spend actively engaged with each other or doing the same activity?

PART B—FEELINGS
Question 7. Within the context of your marriage, choose which of the following three statements apply:

    a) I often feel that I would like more private time and private space.

    b) I often feel that I would like less private time and private space.

c) I am reasonably satisfied with the balance I now have between privacy and companionship.

Privacy and Intimacy: Assessment

All of the women who had never given this much thought were surprised at how little time they spent interacting as part of a couple during working weekdays (*question 1*). When they considered this time in comparison to time spent in the same activity as their husband on a daily basis (*question 5*), it was even more revealing. Many women reported that by the time the evening chores were done, the amount of time they spent actually engaged with their spouse was between two and three hours on a daily basis. In addition, the time together was often spent with television, a book, or a newspaper, which is parallel rather than interactive time.

Margaret and Mark left for work at different times in the morning. She left earlier than he did, since her teaching job meant an early start to her day. His job required a long commute to Manhattan from the suburb where they lived. Although Margaret was home by 4:00 P.M., Mark did not come home until three hours later. She would do her work for school and prepare dinner before Mark's arrival. He would come in tired from the day and spend some time unwinding with his newspaper. Most nights they would have dinner, watch television, and then to go sleep. They found that after each had shared their day over dinner, they were both content to do no more than trade an occasional comment about the program they were watching. Margaret figured they had about two hours a day of any real togetherness.

Jackie, whose life was entirely different, totaled about the same two hours with her husband. She had never worked outside her home and continued her same routines when her children were grown. She sewed her own clothes, refinished her furniture, and did all of her own cooking and baking from scratch. She enjoyed this part of her life, which included lunch once or twice a week with a friend and an occasional afternoon of shopping or a movie. Jerry had a demanding position as executive manager of an electronic equipment company. He left home early and came home late. Jackie always waited for him so that they could share their dinner. Aside from dinner, Jackie arranged her weekdays as she wanted.

For many, the time together on an average weekend day (*question 2*) was proportionally far greater, often as much as sixteen hours (almost every waking minute). This was not an uncommon response, since when both partners work outside the home they usually do chores together, rather than separately, on weekends. Women who were principally housewives seemed to plan time to be with their husbands on weekends. This total time diminished considerably when each woman evaluated the time she spent actively engaged with her husband. On weekends, the fundamental tasks of living took them to different parts of their house and different parts of stores.

Margaret and Mark spend their weekends in each other's company except for an occasional ball game for Mark and his friends and some shopping and luncheons for Margaret and her friends. They usually plan to be with other people for one of the weekend evenings, and they try to spend the other evening alone together. They like to catch up on the things they do not have time to share on a daily basis.

Jackie and Jerry also spent their weekends with each other, but that time was primarily with one or the other of their children and grandchildren. They both enjoyed this family time and looked forward to more of it when Jerry retired.

The big surprise to almost all the women was the amount of time each spent involved with her own concerns (*questions 3 and 4*). One or both of the members of the couple worked outside the home between nine and twelve hours each day. Thus, for at least three-fourths of a working day these women were autonomous in relation to their husbands. It does not follow that a woman is therefore independent during this time, since there are obvious constraints with any job outside or inside the home. But, as each person considered this question, and as you consider it, you will see how much private time and private space you have as a result of your routine.

Margaret had never given much thought to the fact that

from the time she left school at 3 P.M. until Mark walked in the door some four hours later, she was on her own. There was certainly structure to this part of her day by virtue of the tasks she had to perform both for house and school, but she could do it at her speed and in her own way. She had over twenty hours of private space and private time in an ordinary week.

Jackie had over fifty hours a week of time for herself to structure as she wished. She was a private person with a private life and she loved it. It was not a surprise to her to discover this, but the fact of it was something that she had never given much thought to. She had certainly never thought about it in relation to retirement.

Question 7 is crucial for you to assess as you plan ahead. Most of the women we spoke with felt that they were satisfied with the balance between private time and time spent with their husbands (*statement c*), and most began to realize how the balance would change upon retirement. Margaret began to wonder how she could continue to have some of the privacy she was now enjoying. She knew that Mark was emotionally demanding of her time when they were together on weekends. She acknowledged that she often looked forward to an ordinary workday after a long weekend so she could have some private time. It will take some planning on Margaret's part, but now that she is aware that privacy could become a problem in her retirement, she will have control over the structure.

Jerry has been retired for almost two years and Jackie is just beginning to adjust. His retirement was mandatory and he had a difficult time at first. Jackie never realized the extent to which she had been the organizer and motivator of their lives together until she found that in retirement Jerry expected her to be in charge of their daily life. He was home all the time. She never seemed to be able to finish a thought, let alone a project. He wanted to know where she was and what she was doing constantly . . . and then there was lunch, every day. When their daughter decided to take a part-time job and called upon them for help with baby-sitting, Jerry was delighted. Jackie was aware that she was not.

She is good-humored and she and Jerry love each other

very much. She has therefore been able to keep her anger and disappointment in perspective. This is giving her time to figure out what is wrong and what she can do to change it. The realization that it is the loss of privacy that is the basis of her angry thoughts has relieved her. She had worried about the way she was feeling about Jerry and "his being constantly underfoot." She is now planning how she can engage Jerry in a dialogue about this problem so that she can have some emotional time and space to herself. In the meantime, he has been making plans of his own and will be doing some consulting work, so her goal may be easier to achieve than she thought. She plans to speak with him anyway, since she feels she has discovered something important about herself that she needs to share with her husband.

If you are satisfied with the balance of time in your life now and you are contemplating retirement, look carefully at what you believe retirement will be. You may feel sure that you will be able to continue this balance because of the way you planned the other parts of your life. You may be willing to curtail your privacy for the pleasure of more companionship. You may feel that the privacy you now have is not all that important to you. You know what is best for yourself and this is only for you to determine. The more you know about yourself, the more power you have over your life.

You may feel that you have more private time and space within your marriage than you want (*statement b*). You may feel deprived of your husband's company because of his working schedule or yours. Some women whose husbands worked long hours or traveled on a regular basis looked forward to retirement and an emotionally closer life together. Some women felt that, the time factor aside, their husbands would be more emotionally available when they were not so involved with their work. These women were looking forward to less privacy and more intimacy. Some women whose jobs were very demanding felt that they needed to keep emotionally distant from their spouse in order to conserve their energy level for their job. They looked forward to the time of retirement when they would be able to move closer and pick up the loving ties that were ready and waiting.

If your response to *question 7* was that you feel you would like more private time and space within your marriage (*statement a*), you probably have a time structure that allows for more togetherness than in the average marriage. If you do not work outside the home and your husband does his work from the house or has a business nearby, you may feel you do not have your own time and space. If you have a demanding job and you come home to what seems like stringent household demands, you may feel the need to get away on your own. No matter what the reason, you should review your responses to this whole questionnaire. The figures give you an objective framework within which to determine the following: Are you taking time for yourself that is truly available? When you are in each other's company (see section one, Time Together), is it possible for you to go to another part of your home and be involved in an independent activity? If you want, can you plan time for yourself to do something of interest to you, alone, on a regular basis?

This is a good time of your life to give some thought to this and to make some changes if you wish to do so. Often entrapment is an illusion that is self-devised and not the doing of the other person. Sondra felt that she had to be home each day to make lunch for her husband Daniel, who owned an insurance company in the small town where they lived. That demand on her time would often prevent her from making plans since it cut the day in half. As we talked, she began to see that she had never tried to negotiate or discuss this with Daniel. She had just done what she believed was expected of her. He had no problem when Sondra said that she would like one day each week for herself and that she would make him lunch or he could eat at a restaurant. He actually was pleased as he had been reluctant over the years to make appointments for lunch because he knew Sondra expected him at home. This structure of one day a week for private time will be carried over easily when Daniel retires in two years. Sondra feels she has made a good start as she begins the rest of her life.

If you feel you have little private time within your marriage and you wish to have more, carefully examine how you are now spending your shared time. There may be many more options for you than you believe. Sometimes it is as easy as recognizing that there are options and that they are there for you to utilize. If you identify these needs you can plan for fulfillment. Retirement will mean a change in the structure of your marriage but it does not follow that your individual needs will change.

Karen is wrestling with her problem in this area of togetherness now that she and Tom are planning to retire. They have spent less actual time together than most couples although they have been married for many years. In answering section one of this questionnaire, Time Together, Karen stated that she and Tom rarely spend a weekday evening together *(statement b)* and only spend Saturday nights and Sundays together on the weekend *(statement d)*. She feels they communicate well and are sensitive to each other despite this, and she feels that they try to spend as much time together as possible *(statement f)*. In response to Part B—Feelings, she said that she looks forward to being with Tom *(statement g)* and she feels that they both look at life the same way *(statement i)*. Karen was unsure whether they like to do most things together *(statement h)*, or if they live at the same pace *(statement l)*. They both like traveling and have enjoyed vacations together, but she always wants to see and do everything and Tom prefers to limit the sightseeing. She often feels she is much quicker to move and get things done than Tom. What will this mean in retirement? This is a part of her uneasy response to Tom's view of their life together.

Section two of the questionnaire, Independent Activities, made Karen aware that she had not been consciously thinking about Tom's response to her interest in jewelry-making. She had mentioned that she was thinking about marketing some of her pieces to local boutiques after retirement, but Tom had not seriously considered it with her. He never had a problem with her Saturday involvement, but he always worked at least half of the day *(question 4)*. She realized that when he spoke of their retirement it was in terms of what the two of them would do together. She was imagining her retirement within a far more independent framework. She began to wonder how he would feel about her scenario and how she would handle any negative feelings he might have *(questions 5 and 6)*.

As she responded to section three, Privacy and Intimacy,

Karen also became aware how little time she and Tom spent together. Although she said that she felt she would like to spend more time with him, she was reasonably satisfied with the private time and space she has now (*question 7, statement c*). No wonder she feels more and more anxious as retirement approaches! She and Tom are both private people who have led autonomous and independent lives within a loving marriage. The structure of the marriage has given each the opportunity to respect the other's routines, interests, and privacy and has enabled them to be independent people. This was not consciously done or discussed, so they have both been unaware of why life has worked so well. The understanding of this dynamic has never been important in their lives, but their approaching retirement has made it a crucial factor that must be clearly understood and handled.

Karen knows that early in her life she struggled for a sense of autonomy and independence. She grew up in a time and in a family where women were not expected to have these needs. She was the youngest child in her family and the first to graduate from high school. She fought to go to college. Her parents expected her to go to work and to contribute to the family income until she married. She compromised, working part-time and attending the local junior college where she got an associate degree. Unlike most young women of that time, she did not concentrate her energies on finding a husband. She took a lot of criticism for this from her family and friends but tried not to let it influence her. She felt she wanted to begin a career in business.

She met Tom on a blind date and they liked each other immediately. They found they had a great deal in common and they seemed to have the same goals in life. They both came from families that did not have much money and they both had a strong need to achieve and be financially successful. They married before the year was over. As we said, she returned to school when her children were small and began her career as a CPA.

Karen has been content within this marriage since it gives her love and independence. Now, however, she is hearing a threat to her autonomy and independence as Tom speaks of needing more of her time. When Tom describes how it will be, she becomes a little frightened and angry at the impending loss of autonomy. Karen had begun to think about putting off retirement, but now that she recognizes the basis of her feelings of discomfort she is evaluating just how she can retire, spend time with Tom, and still maintain the freedom she is used to. She is deciding how she wants life to be.

She realizes that when Tom speaks of their retirement she has to speak of the way she visualizes their lives. When she talked with him about her plans for her jewelry, his concern was that it not interfere with their traveling plans. She is planning in a practical way for the time that will be involved. If they both compromise, they do not have to think about changing anything; they just have to recognize and share their feelings. They are on their way to a comfortable retirement.

In many ways marriage is like a friendship, since it reflects the personality styles of two people. This will not change because of retirement, but preretirement is the time to reexamine and reevaluate the parameters and the dynamics of your relationship. Opportunities are available to continue on or to change, but a woman must know her needs in order to assess and determine her options.

VII

*. . . please yourself and at least someone is
pleased.*

KATHARINE HEPBURN (1909–   )

Sophie is fifty-eight years old. She is a senior financial analyst
for a large brokerage firm in New York City. She is single and
lives alone in a large one-bedroom apartment in a nice section
of Manhattan. She had never considered her life without her
work until three years ago, when as the result of a corporate
takeover, all employees over the age of fifty were offered a very
attractive early retirement plan. Two of her friends grabbed the
opportunity. One of them was a married woman of sixty-one,
whose husband was ready to retire, and the other was a single
woman of fifty-two who had always wanted to start a business of
her own. Several of Sophie's male associates were pleased with
the offer and readily accepted it. She passed it by easily without
any serious soul-searching, but the offer itself forced her to take
a look at her status as an older worker in the company. She had
not thought of herself this way until then, and it was somewhat
disturbing. Over the past three years, she has increasingly found
herself concerned with many issues involving retirement as well
as aging, and she considers herself now to be in a time of transition.

At work she is aware that her job feels more routine than it once did. She experiences a sense of challenge less often, and she does not have the same physical energy which at one time would keep her going from early morning to late at night. She is actually beginning to think of cutting down on some of her workload.

It is, however, the more personal issues which are the major concern for Sophie, who has never married. She is not uncomfortable with her private space, and she has always been content with her life, particularly because she has always enjoyed her career. She has several friends and one very good friend, Ceila, with whom she spends holidays and an occasional weekend. She and Ceila had become friends on their first job, and they continued their friendship when they both moved on. Ceila has also remained single and had a middle-management job with the telephone company for many years. Ceila is charming and vivacious, and has many friends. Sophie has always been part of Ceila's group of friends and has enjoyed being included.

When Sophie re-examined her life in the context of the retirement offer, she noted many issues which she had not considered before. She realized she had less need to plan an activity after work on the evenings she did not work late, and was pleased with the opportunity to have a restful evening once or twice a week. Her weekends too, when she thought about it, were taking on a new dimension, and she was experiencing more time alone, which she recognized often led to feelings of loneliness. When she and Ceila were younger they would spend many a Saturday together. They would leave early in the morning, shop, have lunch, shop some more and then take in a movie and perhaps have dinner. Now they both had less energy, and the days they spent together started later and ended earlier. They both tired more easily and didn't mind coming home much of the time, but Sophie was now alone more and it was taking some getting used to. She had never minded watching television or spending an evening reading by herself, but neither had she ever before done it so often. She began to envy her married friends for their built-in companions. She saw why, despite the subtle changes at work and in her attitude toward her work, she could not seriously contemplate total retirement.

An abrupt change in Sophie's life came two years ago, when she discovered that Ceila had been diagnosed with ovarian cancer and needed surgery. Ceila was very sick for over a year. She needed chemotherapy and radiation treatments. After treatments, she finally began to recover. She has never been the same physically and has taken early retirement. Sophie was supportive and available throughout the ordeal, despite her own fears. She still spends a lot of her free time with Ceila and talks with her daily, but the relationship has changed in many ways, even though the closeness and warm feelings remain intact.

Ceila's illness shocked Sophie almost as much as it did Ceila. She identified with Ceila and wondered what she would do if she became ill. She had always considered herself strong and in many ways invincible, but she started to feel vulnerable. The early retirement offer caused Sophie to begin to re-evaluate her life, and Ceila's illness accelerated the process. She looked around and saw the many differences in her life and in herself from twenty years before. She knew she needed to take a realistic look at her concerns and options for the years ahead.

Sophie's retirement issues are not as easily definable as those of many of the women to whom we spoke. Hers are overshadowed by the issues of aging and the changes which occur as life moves along. For the first time, she is looking at the fact that she will probably not die at her desk. She is beginning to accept this, but does not, at this time, feel she needs to make plans to change careers or make alternative life plans in a vocational sense. Like Lillian, the lawyer in Chapter III—The Many Meanings of Work, Sophie will be able to use her financial expertise for as long as she may wish to do so. She has, however, other work to do, both emotional and practical.

Sophie always felt she coped well with the sometimes disquieting knowledge that she was the only one in charge of her life. At times she needed to work hard to be optimistic, and she had had her share of painful experiences; but she felt she had survived and grown from each of them. This crisis period was the trigger for Sophie, but she sees now that this time of transition was waiting to happen. She had arrived at an age where she could no longer deny that life had moved on for her, as well as the others around her.

During the year that Ceila was so severely ill, Sophie was constantly forced to consider what would happen to her if she became sick. She had always thought that health insurance was all she needed to take care of her medical needs, but she soon realized there was more involved in an illness than insurance. She saw the way in which Ceila, as a single woman, was dependent upon and used her support system of friends. There was not only the maintaining of contact and the visiting, but Sophie had taken Ceila for some of her chemotherapy treatments, and another friend had a contact with a nursing service and had made arrangements for Ceila to get home nursing care. When you are ill or incapacitated, it is difficult to make ordinary arrangements for yourself. Sophie knew from her years of singleness that maintaining her relationships was essential and bolstered her against loneliness, but she had never before clearly seen how important these relationships could be.

When she first thought about her future in this new way she was overwhelmed with fears that bordered on terror. As a single woman with no husband, children, or family, she had only her friends on whom to rely—and what would she do as her friends left her? Ceila is still with her, but her weakened physical condition, and her limitations on how much she is able to do, had already caused Sophie to make changes in how she spent her leisure time. It also made her consider enlarging her own support system.

Ceila's illness accentuated to Sophie the extent to which she had always been on her own. She realized she needs friends on whom she can call in time of emergency, as she knows now that as one gets older the word emergency takes on a whole new meaning. She needs a plan to be followed in case she too becomes ill. She needs to think about who will care for her and what resources she has.

Sophie had given some thought to a living will before this

time, and because of her experiences with Ceila this became a priority for her. There had been a point at which everyone thought that Ceila would lapse into a coma and need to be kept alive with artificial supports. Sophie knew she did not want this for herself. She consulted with her lawyer and he drew up a living will for her which enabled her to give directions for any terminal illness, including the withholding or withdrawal of life support systems. Now was the time for her to put her wishes concerning this in writing and to leave the document with her lawyer and her doctor. She feels comfortable about this now that she has done so.

The lawyer also asked to whom Sophie could give the power of attorney. So much to consider! He thought it desirable for Sophie to designate someone to act on her behalf if she were incapacitated in some way. This representative would be responsible for paying rent, gas and electric bills, phone bills, and taking care of other necessary transactions if she were unable. Sophie was not sure if she should burden Ceila with this, or if indeed her friend would be able to handle it if something happened to Sophie, so she is considering several other options, including a younger woman who works for her.

One day, she left hurriedly for work and accidentally locked herself out of her apartment. Her neighbor has a key, and as Sophie rang the bell she thought for the first time that she did have neighbors on whom she could call if she became ill and needed some emergency food shopping. She hoped she would never have to ask, but she was comforted to know she could use this relationship if necessary. Her neighbor is a married woman with grown children who has recently re-entered the work force. She and Sophie have never been more than friendly neighbors, but Sophie is considering inviting her and her husband for a drink one evening to extend the relationship.

Looking around, Sophie became aware of other single women. There is a single woman at work whose sister has recently died. Sophie has known her for many years and likes her, but knew that she and her sister had spent most of their time together. She is now thinking about the possibility that this woman too is looking for more companionship in her life.

She recently received a flyer about an organization for single women over age forty-five called "Women Of Worth." Before, Sophie might have thrown it out, but now she thinks it might be a good time to investigate. Part of the answer to her fears of being alone is to recognize that she can make plans and that there are some answers. She needs to look at the world as a place filled with potential resources for her future. This is the pathway to feeling both physically and emotionally safe.

Sophie reflected on the way she had felt when her mother died and realized that this time feels much like that other transitional time of her life. Her mother's death had been a major loss, and there were times after she died that Sophie felt she would never be able to go on. After she had lived through the despair and disorganization associated with the mourning process (see Chapter X—Suddenly Single) Sophie reorganized her life. She purposefully set out to spend more time with her friends, particularly with Ceila, and had taken on more of a work load so she would be out of the house two nights a week. This time, however, she is not willing to increase her work load, and as for other activities, she doesn't feel as safe as she used to when out at night. Sophie feels that her major task at this time is to enlarge her people-support system.

Sophie spoke with Ceila about some of her concerns before visiting her lawyer, and learned that Ceila had left her small estate to her nieces and nephew. Sophie realized she needed to think about her other will as well as the living will. The last time she had seen her will was when her mother was alive. They had left their estates to each other. There will be money in her estate after her death, and unlike Ceila she does not have any relatives to inherit it. She has decided instead to make a simple will in which she will leave her money to her favorite charities. Her lawyer told her of a "Will of Friendship" in which she could leave certain possessions to her friends. This has given Sophie something to think about, and she will go through her cherished possessions to arrange for their future.

Her lawyer also discussed her current finances, including her insurance policies, and after listening to alternatives, Sophie decided to cancel her life insurance policy, which had made her mother first beneficiary and then Ceila. She feels she might as well use the extra dollars a year that this policy costs to spend on herself.

Sophie was always aware of her ability to take early Social Security at the age of sixty-two. Although she is determined to work as long as she can and does not plan on taking early Social Security, she finds comfort as she never thought she would by knowing Social Security would be a good supplement to her retirement income if she becomes unable to work before she is sixty-five.

Sophie also became concerned for the first time about where she could live if she was unable to maintain herself in her own apartment. She found that planning for the various contingencies reduced her anxiety about the future, so she began to research some alternatives.

She learned the truth of the adage that as soon as you learn something new you keep hearing it over and over again. Suddenly, Sophie began to find articles about alternative housing for retired women. She seemed to be besieged with ads for senior citizen housing. She heard of apartment sharing for older adults and found that this housing alternative was quickly catching on as the population aged. There was even a National Directory on Housing for Older People put out by the National Council on the Aging. She wouldn't have to be alone, if she chose not to be.

She met someone at a meeting who told her of the growth of continuing care communities, which are housing units built for seniors, both married and single, with provisions for nursing care and facilities built into the cost of housing, if the resident needs them. (see the Resource Guide, and also Chapter IX—Caretaking). This is of real interest to Sophie, if she can locate a community near enough to New York City.

She tuned in quite accidentally to a seventy-nine-year-old woman being interviewed on television who had just written a book on the intergenerational commune in which she had been living for the past 25 years. This woman described the friends she had made and the fun it was to live with men and women of all ages. Particularly inspiring had been the young people who had passed through her life.

Although Sophie feels she can never give up her own apartment, and it is too small to take in a boarder, she began to imagine what it might be like to house–share with another woman. She isn't sure she could ever do it, but if her support system falters she thinks this might be an option.

Sophie believes that getting older is different than she had expected, and different for her than for the friends who had been married. She feels more bereft when her support system flounders and feels she has more to be concerned about, particularly if she finds herself in poor health. She does, however, know that her successful life as a single woman, in which she has developed and maintained a strong sense of identity, will help her make sound future decisions. She knows now that in order to have a successful retirement she needs, aside from adequate income and good health, a continued good support system. If and when her support system falters she needs fall-back plans. She feels relieved to be in the process of making them.

Gladys has much conflict concerning her retirement. She has been working in civil service for thirty-seven years and has held a high–level position in the Social Security Administration for twenty-five of those years. She has a job with considerable responsibility and visibility, and she enjoys her prestige and power. (We met Gladys in Chapter III, The Many Meanings of Work.) She has, however, been starting to experience boredom and ennui with the predictable routine of her days. The problem situations which once posed a challenge have a sameness, and even the contact with various people has become ordinary to her. Many of the colleagues with whom she has been friendly have retired, and she is not completely comfortable with many of the younger people in positions on her level. In addition, she finds the newer and younger group of workers she supervises less able and involved with their jobs, so that supervising has lost some of its pleasure.

She has a decent pension available to her after working for the federal government for so many years, and a small inheritance from her parents which augments her income. She jokes with some of her friends that she would have more money available to her if she were retired, and that going to work each day is actually costing her money. She comes home after a difficult day at work and makes plans with herself to put in for retirement the following day, week or month . . . and then she changes her mind.

Gladys's marriage was early and brief. She had married Joe, her high school sweetheart, when they both graduated college in June of 1950. This was at the beginning of the conflict in Korea, and they had been "going steady" from the time she was sixteen. They married hoping he would be able to avoid the draft. Unfortunately, this was not enough to get him a permanent exemption and he was ultimately sent to Korea. Gladys had become pregnant during the early months of their marriage and gave birth to her son Anthony while Joe was overseas. When he came home at the end of the war early in 1954, everything had changed. Gladys was involved with her job and had made an interesting life for herself. Joe could not adjust to married life with Gladys. He was restless, anxious and angry, and didn't know what he wanted to do with his life. After much discussion he decided to go to Chicago to look for work. They called each other and wrote and he kept promising to send for her as soon as he found a permanent job. After more than a year and several trips back and forth, Gladys realized their marriage was over. She did not have too much difficulty getting a divorce because Joe had deserted her and he did not contest it. She was twenty-five with a three-year-old child, but she was not without resources. She had her job with the government, family to help with child care, and a large support network of friends.

As she looks back, Gladys is surprised at the ease with which she moved into her new life. She did not continue to live with her parents. She knew she no longer wanted to be their "other child," which was the way she had been treated as long as she had lived in her parents' home. She found an apartment for herself and her son although housing was at a premium. She had planned to continue working for the first few years after Joe came home anyway because she knew he did not have a job or career to return to. Therefore working was not a problem for her. Her mother was available and willing to care for her grandson even though Gladys no longer lived at home.

Life became even easier for Gladys when Anthony was old enough to go to school, because she did not have to be so dependent on her parents. She had appreciated her mother's help and was close with both of her parents, but she had always felt her mother to be too intrusive and too protective of Anthony, an agreeable child. He did well in school and had many friends. Gladys and he got along well together and enjoyed each other's company. As he grew into adolescence he became more and more self-sufficient, and by the time he left for college in another state Gladys felt assured that she had done a successful job of raising a child as a single parent.

She feels she has had a good life and is quite comfortable with who she is. She was hardly too old to marry again at twenty-five, even with a young child, and she did date. She never made a conscious decision to remain single, but by the time Gladys was thirty she knew she was a single woman with a child and lived life as such. She enjoyed being a mother and loved her son very much, but she never really felt that she wanted any more children. She often was quite pleased that she was on her own as much as she was. She received a great deal of satisfaction from her job and was proud of the various promotions she had received over the years. She knew she was needed both at work and at home and enjoyed this.

She and Anthony were close to her sisters, their families and her parents, and they visited frequently. There were strong family connections to other relatives as well, and they all helped to celebrate family occasions. She heard from Joe periodically and he sent child support when he was able, but he never made very much money, had married again and had a new family. He saw his son a few times a year, but Gladys was the main financial support and the main parental figure.

Her work is obviously essential to her life now. With Anthony married and on his own, despite her close family ties and several very meaningful friendships, it is Gladys's job which gives her life continuity and structure. The problem she now confronts is that although her work once gave her life a great deal of meaning . . . it no longer serves that purpose. Unlike Sophie, Gladys's job is no longer satisfying, and she does not enjoy her days at work. It is nevertheless unbelievably difficult to give up.

Gladys's main work issue is the power and prestige she receives from her job. She came to this realization with difficulty because, as with most women of the pre-Women's Movement generation, she had thought it unladylike or inappropriate to have these drives. It is fortunate that she is able to accept and understand this vital part of herself. It can be easy to assume that one must simply keep busy after retirement and that substituting another activity to replace work will be enough. The structure, routine, and social aspects of work have their importance for Gladys, but they are not basic to her self-fulfillment. She needs to find a place for herself within the community which will allow her to feel important as well as productive. Understanding and acknowledging her needs for power and prestige enabled Gladys to begin to make her retirement plan. .

She knew her work with the Social Security Administration had made her familiar with many of the available social service facilities in the community. She knew she wanted to use this expertise but she wasn't sure how. A close friend who had recently become ill had spent a month or two in and out of one of the large hospitals in the area, and Gladys had visited often. There had been some difficulty with the nursing care and with some of the consulting doctors, and Gladys had searched out the patient advocate. She had been impressed with the scope of the work that was done on her friend's behalf, and with the impact and importance the advocate had in the total hospital picture. Gladys began to think about this as something she would enjoy doing. The work itself would allow her to be involved with people and their problems, something she had always liked about her civil service job, and she believed it would fulfill her need to have power and control as part of her daily life. She would also be able to use her expertise about community resources for patients' aftercare.

Patient advocacy is a part–time volunteer program with a short training period, and Gladys is now enrolled as a trainee in anticipation of naming a retirement date in the near future. She is becoming more certain every day that she is ready to leave the daily routine of a full–time job. If the patient advocate position works out, she will have time to travel, visit with Anthony and just have some leisure to read and continue her regular bridge games.

When we talked with unmarried women it became evident that being single is a state of mind. Many of the women we spoke to who were widowed or divorced came to identify themselves as single at different periods of their "single" lives. Some felt "single" immediately, while it took others several years to move into that identity. Some women who were widowed or divorced, no matter for how many years, never did comfortably move into the identity of being single. They remained widowed or divorced in both their feelings and attitudes. If the women had children, the transition to the identification of being single was more complex. Gladys moved into a single life more comfortably than many of the women of her generation. This was because she accepted herself and her lifestyle early, although it was unusual for the time. Today, the single parent identity is more prevalent and socially acceptable. Women alone, with children and no husband, are more readily able to accept their singleness.

One of the discoveries we made about single women of today facing retirement is that their retirement issues are not intrinsically different from the retirement issues of any other woman. There are different emphases for some, but having a husband does not change a woman's basic needs, her retirement needs, or her future goals. In order for you to plan for your retirement you need to do the same self–assessment as any other woman. In this way you too can make a successful plan for your retirement.

As she discussed her retirement options, Gladys mentioned

an insight she had had about her decision-making as a single person. One of her closest friends is a teacher who is still working, although she is well past retirement age. Her friend can financially retire comfortably and has a husband who is retired waiting for her to do the same. But her friend knows that she does not want to leave her work. She knows her work maintains her identity and gives structure to her life, purpose to her routine. Gladys has thought that if she had a husband or somebody in her life who was retired and wanted her to be free of her work she would have her retirement decision made for her. But when she looks at her married friends she realizes decisions are not any easier if you are married. Not all of her married friends' husbands helped them to decide what to do, and even when they did the negotiations involved had not appealed to Gladys. At one time she had considered a career change and she wished for someone to be there to give her advice, but now she knows it would not have really have made the kind of difference she thought it would. Gladys did admit to having sometimes taken the path of least resistance because she was tired of deciding everything alone. Many of the other single women we spoke to, however, had one or several people they consulted so that they did not feel they did their decision-making quite as independently as Gladys had.

Gladys and Sophie both learned early on, as did many other single women, that in order to be successful they needed to take charge of the important facets of their lives. They must negotiate the tasks of personal independence and autonomy alone, and at the time of retirement they are taking charge once again. Gladys is wrestling with her retirement decisions primarily in terms of the meaning her work has for her. She does not have children or grandchildren to consider at this time, and there are no elderly relatives who command time or attention. Sophie is dealing more with retirement in terms of her relationships with the friends in her life. Many single women we spoke with found themselves having to consider obligations or commitments involving family members, and if this is your situation we refer you to Chapter V—Family Attachments or Chapter IX —The Caretaker.

Gladys had briefly considered the possibility of relocation, because the midwest winters can be formidable; but like many other single women we spoke with it never became a serious consideration. She has her friends and family and her life where she grew up; although one of her good friends had moved with her husband to the warmth of Arizona, Gladys could not see herself leaving her network and support system. She had visited their retirement community and was aware of its orientation toward couple living, which on further investigation she discovered is true of most retirement communities. The single women we spoke with who did relocate or at least seriously considered it moved to be near their family or a close friend. (See Chapter VIII—Relocation.)

Neither Sophie nor Gladys found the social aspects of work to be of great importance to their retirement considerations. Gladys evaluated the social aspects of her job and found that her main social connections are with her family and close friends from her childhood. Sophie was on an extremely competitive career track that kept her from forming close relationships at work. This is unlike a majority of the single women to whom we spoke. For many of them, the workplace had become an extended family, and for many others it was an important part of their social network. This was particularly true if they had lived through a divorce or had become widowed while working on the job from which they were retiring. If you are in this situation you should refer to Chapter III—The Many Meanings of Work, with special attention to the section on the social aspects of work.

When we spoke with groups of women concerning their retirement issues, one of the comments we heard from many single women, like Sophie, was that it is easier for a married woman to retire because she has someone to be with and does not have to be alone. It is true that having leisure time does make you more aware of aloneness. As Sophie told us, the time she spent with herself in her apartment increased as her physical energy diminished, and this made her more conscious of what her retirement years could be like. However, the more we researched, the clearer it became that for modern women retirement, just as work, has a special meaning and brings up issues which transcend the other factors of their lives—with no correlation to their marital status. The problems encountered by women facing retirement were the result of who each woman had become and the way in which she lived her life. Thus the best way for single women as well as for married women to resolve the problems of retirement is through increased self-knowledge.

Even the issue of aloneness does not truly distinguish single women from married women. No one we spoke with was more encumbered by family and less alone in her retirement than Judy, who never married (Chapter IV—Family Attachments), and she had much in common with Laura's (Chapter IV) obligations to her children and grandchildren in the way in which each needed to deal with their retirement. One particular and important variable in this discussion is the length of time the woman has been single. If you have recently been widowed or divorced and are dealing with retirement, you will probably be more interested in Chapter X—Suddenly Single. It is painful to deal with more than one separation in a short period of time, and if it can be avoided it is well to do so. Several women we spoke with who were considering retirement before their husbands' death held off on taking the step. Sometimes they waited several years before considering retirement again. Although it is not usually recognized as such, retirement involves loss and therefore often requires a mourning period.

Sophie's fears of loneliness and the absence of a caretaker should she become ill were shared by many single women. (Most married women we spoke with, too, were cognizant of the odds of the possibility of widowhood.) These are valid fears, but you can face them constructively—by shoring up your social networks, taking good care of your physical health, and investigating all the options that might become available to you. In any case, when you are dealing with the issues of retirement, it is most important to know yourself and then make compromises and decisions in the context of your knowledge.

VIII

Relocation?

*Fifty percent of the people in the world are
homesick all the time . . . You don't really long
for another country. You long for something in
yourself that you don't have, or haven't been
able to find.*

JOHN CHEEVER (1912–1982)

Phyllis is fifty-eight years old. She grew up and lived all her
adult years in a suburb of New York City. She has worked for
most of her adult life as a teacher and psychologist. She has a
son, Allen, from her first marriage. She has been married to her
second husband, Stan for more than twenty-two years. They
have a good marriage and Stan has been very supportive of her
career and ambitions. During the early years of their marriage,
and with his full cooperation, she worked full-time while she
returned to school and completed a master's degree. She felt she
had a busy and fulfilling life.

Over the years Stan became a successful executive in a large
personnel firm. Allen graduated from college, moved into his
own apartment, and then married. Stan's two daughters from his
first marriage, who had lived with their mother, were also living
independently.

In 1979, Stan and Phyllis went to a company convention in

Arizona. They both fell in love with the southwestern desert. They loved the stark, calm beauty. Stan, in particular, believed he had found Utopia. After several trips west, they bought a small house in a community south of Tucson called Green Valley, which they rented out for six months of the year. During the next few years Stan began to talk of "when we retire and move to Green Valley," It was not until he began to speak about being able to afford to retire and leave his job that Phyllis began to worry . . . a lot. She began to realize she had to face the issue of retirement and relocation.

You probably know by this point that Phyllis did move and relocate and that this piece of this chapter is autobiographical; names have not even been changed. I (Phyllis) probed, and evaluated constantly for two years before I made and began to accept my decision to move from my hometown of fifty-six years.

I have been living in Arizona for two years and I would like to be able to tell you that I made the right decision, that I am completely happy, and that you should join me. I cannot do that. I can tell you that during these two years I have made a good and comfortable life. I can tell you that there are many things about southwestern living that are better for me than living in a northeastern metropolis. I can tell you that moving to a place as different from New York City as is Green Valley, Arizona, has broadened my understanding of what life and people are about. I can also tell you that on a recent visit to New York City I was aware that I am at home there—dirty streets, cold weather, subway travel, and all. New York City is somehow still my home. Perhaps that will never change. Relocation is an involved issue, at least for me. It was not an easy step, and much of the internal adjustment was emotionally quite painful. In doing the research and the interviews for this book I have discovered that my experiences and feelings are not unique and in many ways are representative. Many of the problems I faced and came to terms with are the same as those of other women interviewed.

When I began my self-assessment prior to making my decision on relocation, I was fortunate that I could concern myself with relocation separately from retirement. Many of the women we interviewed had to deal with both transitions at the same time. I had already made my decision to retire from my full-time job as a school psychologist with the New York City Board of Education. I had done my evaluation of this decision and was aware I no longer had the interest or the fortitude to work under the conditions of this large bureaucracy. I also knew I had finished spending my days teaching children. I had been looking forward to leaving the Board of Education for about five years. I knew I was not finished with my working life, however. At the age of fifty-five I had plenty of energy, both physical and psychic, and I planned on using it. I had determined that I really liked to teach, and was planning to explore opportunities for teaching at a community college or in adult education.

The fact that I had retired psychologically from my work as a teacher and school psychologist was important in making the relocation to Arizona a reality for me. If my job had remained the most important part of my life, as it had been ten years before, I would have made a strong case and fought hard to stay in New York. I knew I did not want to leave my home, my family, and my friends. I was aware I would have had a problem putting my needs before my husband's, as I am a true child of the 1950's; but I had internalized enough of the ideals of the women's movement to know I had some entitlements. I would have assuaged my guilt about denying my husband his wishes with the feeling that I was entitled to have my work remain an important part of my life. As it turned out, I did not have a job or important work to keep me in New York, and could therefore more easily relocate to Arizona.

Another important consideration that brought me closer to Arizona was the high cost of living in New York City. Without the expenses of life in the Big Apple, Stan and I would have more money to travel and do all the things we enjoyed.

There was a third reality, another factor in my life that tipped the scales on the side of relocation. In the twenty-two years we had been together I had never seen Stan as committed to anything as he was to a life in Arizona. He is a fairly easygoing, flexible person and usually willing to go along with what I want, but this was different. There was an intensity and strength in his interest to relocate to the Southwest that was unfamiliar to me. I knew I could have refused to move and we would have stayed in the New York City area, but I decided I owed him the attempt to make our retirement in Arizona work. The decision to relocate seemed to flow naturally from these three facts of my life and I proceeded to work from there.

The work of self-assessment truly began. How would I fare when I found myself far from everything familiar? What internal strengths and experiences did I have that would help me get through a difficult time? Although I did not realize it at the time and I had not conceptualized it ever before, I had utilized the principles of the women's movement almost from the moment they were given public expression. I never marched or burned my bra and I never even joined a consciousness-raising group, but the way I handled my life from the early 1960's was right in step with the times. The women's movement helped me to look back and evaluate the earlier transitions I had coped with successfully.

Over the objections of my first husband I had returned to school to get teaching credentials as soon as my son was able to go to nursery school. This was in 1963 when my education professor was sneering at the small group of women in their thirties who were taking his education course to obtain teaching licenses. We were only doing this, he knew, so that we could carpet our homes and buy new refrigerators. He and some others in academia believed that women who were preparing to go to work were dilettantes. He gave us a hard time. My friend, who had been widowed and left with two young sons to support, and I, who was seeking a way to come to terms with a bad marriage, were furious but impotent. We took the only revenge possible: We got the credits we needed and began our careers.

The early murmurings of the women's movement supported me again when, over the objections of almost everyone I knew, I decided to divorce my husband. My mother and father told as few people as possible about this, and when I married Stan four years later many people they knew were surprised to learn that I had been divorced. In the context of the 1970's and 1980's, this divorce does not sound either courageous or unusual; but those of you who remember the early 1960's know how difficult and frightening a time it was. I had made an unpopular decision but I knew it was right for me.

As I looked back on my life I began to see that I was the first person on the block to do many things. It was a real surprise to learn this, as I had usually thought of myself as being conservative and passive in a social sense. I certainly had never thought of myself as innovative or different. I had returned to school before it was popular, had divorced before it was accepted, and Stan and I had lived together for about two years before we married. This was not what everyone was doing between 1962 and 1965. This look back and this self-evaluation gave me a different perspective of myself. Perhaps I would be the first person on my block to move to the Southwest and perhaps I could handle this decision. I had displayed courage before.

I started planning my future when I made the decision to retire. No matter where I might live, I knew I would not be content with only leisure activities. I am not interested in any athletic activities—I have to force myself to walk for exercise on a daily basis. I am not a game player in any sense, so neither bridge nor any other card games appeal to me. I do like to cook and bake for a while I toyed with the idea of being a full-time homemaker, something I had done only briefly when Allen was a baby. I thought I might learn to bake bread and maybe sew again, which I had enjoyed doing when I was young. I have always been a reader and have been in the middle of one book or another since age five when I began on *The Bobbsey Twins* and *Honeybuch: Her First Little Garden,* and I rather enjoy watching popular television; so the thought of staying home had a pleasant feel. What was interesting to me was that, for the first time ever, I was able to see that I had options. I have never seen my past life as a series of choices, because in a sense much of it was not. The early transitions of my life were not handled with independence. College was expected of me after high school. I was supposed to find a job after that, until I married, and I did all of these with little thought as to what I really wanted. I married my first husband because everyone I knew was getting married and I could not bear to be thought of as a failure, which was the way my world looked upon the unmarried woman. It is true that the events after this—the teaching, my divorce, my remarriage, and my return to school—had been autonomous choices, but, as I said, I had never seen them as such. This time I was able to see clearly that the rest of my life was mine. I began to plan.

One of the things that had attracted Stan and me to the community of Green Valley was its proximity to the city of Tucson and the University of Arizona. We knew we wanted to be near movies, theaters, and shopping, and I knew that if all else failed in my retirement and relocation I could always go back to school. Over the thirty-five years since my graduation from college I had returned to school every ten years or so to get another degree or just to learn. I had not yet gone to law school, and I figured I could follow that path with a university only thirty miles away. It is a possibility that I have not yet completely discarded.

In the meantime I was aware that here, in this part of the Southwest, I could pursue my extended teaching career either in a college or university or in adult education. This is a far less competitive field to enter in Arizona than in New York, so I knew I would have an easier time. I inquired and discovered that the county community college sponsored adult education courses in my local community, so I would not have to travel far from my home. I discovered also that there were no courses offered in my specialty, assertiveness training. I made the necessary contacts and arranged for my classes to begin shortly after we moved.

My biggest concern about the move had to do with the relationships in my life. I could not imagine being so far away geographically from either my sister or my son. I knew all about the telephone (and still do), so I was confident about not losing touch. But this was not particularly comforting. Generally speaking, we would not be spending holidays, birthdays, or special celebrations together anymore. Diana and I could not shop or have dinner together at least once a week and it would be difficult to pick up the phone each time something occurred that we needed to share. I could not come to terms with this at all. I still see it as the biggest loss of my relocation, and I look forward to the day when she too will relocate and be closer.

It was a little easier to reconcile the separation from Allen, who had married and begun his own business in the two years previous to our move. Although we have always been in contact with each other, he was raised to be independent and self-sufficient and had lived on his own since college. We were always emotionally close and we have remained so despite the move. We stay in contact with each other via weekly phone calls, and probably see each other almost as much as we would were we both in New York City.

I am a person who is involved with many people with varying degrees of intimacy, but with great concern and interest in them all. Robyn, whom we discussed in Chapter IV, Styles of Friendship, was someone I could easily identify with. I keep in touch with two friends from my elementary school days, and I have made friends and kept many of them each time my life situation changed. Stan and I have couple-friends we have become extremely close to over the years, and I could not imagine a life without this social network. My trepidations and my objections to the move to Arizona centered on this area of life. If I had evaluated myself with more insight, I might have had less anxiety, and I might never have given away half of my dinner service for twelve before we moved. All I could foresee was that my days of being social were over. I was sure I would never again know enough people to set a dinner table for twelve.

I had not given much thought to this part of my life before we moved, and it is only in hindsight that I see the true picture. I believed I would have to depend on contact with my friends from back home for any meaningful relationships. I was not planning on being reclusive and I expected to join an organization or two, but I had resigned myself to a social life of more casual contacts. I had not evaluated my friendship pattern to any extent; if I had, I would have seen that I have a need for friends. When this is a need, one sees that it is met. I have proven throughout my life that I have found friends wherever I am. This is, of course, exactly what happened this time as well. I have found women friends whom I enjoy, and Stan and I have found couple-friends we enjoy spending time with. As part of my usual pattern, these new friends are additions to the circle, not replacements for old friends. I did have to replace my dinner service for twelve.

Another relocation issue, which I again examined only in retrospect, involves the concept of conformity as opposed to a spirit of adventure. As I evaluated my life's transitions and my response to the women's movement, I saw that I had been more of a risk-taker than I had believed. There was a part of me that experienced a sense of exhilaration and freedom at the thought of beginning a new life in what was almost a new country. There were times when the possibilities seemed grand. This is a part of me I had never acknowledged or appreciated until retirement and relocation. I became sharply aware of it when Stan and I bought a motor home for vacations and traveling. With it we have had some of our best times ever, though the pleasures are incomprehensible to most of our old friends and totally foreign to the sophisticated New Yorkers we had been.

These past few years I have lived through some of the most difficult times of my life. The adjustments have been myriad and formidable. I still get depressed when Passover, Thanksgiving, and New Year's Eve come. When my son is ill, or my sister has a problem, or someone from home is in the hospital, I feel isolated and alone. Two of my aunts died in the past two years and I did not attend the funerals. Very close friends had an anniversary party we could not attend. When I walk in the midst of the beautiful desert scenery I miss walking down Fifth Avenue, passing Lord & Taylor, and the way I used to play the traffic lights in New York City so I would not have to stop at every corner. I see now that life is made of options and I have made a choice, not without regret, but it is realistic and viable for me.

More often than not, I now feel I am on the other side of the mountain.

The contemplation of retirement is quite often accompanied by the contemplation of relocation. Warmer climate, easier living, and new beginnings have a strong attraction at any time of life, and in considering retirement we are naturally tempted by these possibilities. An opportunity for a better life is one of our birthrights, and it is never too late and one is never too old to seek it. As the average life span increases and as the mobility of our society increases, relocation will more and more be a part of retirement. With life in the large urban areas becoming more expensive, crime-ridden, and dirtier, older people with no ties to their families, a job, or a career will be seeking safer, cleaner, less expensive places to live. Every preretiree has a friend who has found happiness in another area of the country and who strongly recommends it for everyone she knows.

Are you truly a candidate for relocation? If you have worked through the self-assessment chapters, you have a sense that there is no easy answer. You know that it must be an individual decision and that it may not be at all clear-cut.

Most of the retired and relocated women we spoke with had done the necessary financial planning, and most were fairly sure that the geographical location was appropriate for their financial needs. Geography and finances are, of course, the basic considerations. We have included several reference sources in both of these subject areas and you can find more material in libraries and the bookstores. This is the easy part for you to explore, and you can arrive at concrete conclusions as to the viability of relocation financially and geographically.

Many of the women we interviewed had friends or relatives in the area they moved to, so that they had some network of support in a social sense. Some moved specifically to be near family or close friends. Some moved to the Southeast or the Southwest to be warm in the winter. Some moved just to change their way of life. Some married women moved because their husbands thought it best that they do so. Their decision-making process involved no more than this.

What almost all of these women indicated to us was that they were sorry they had not done some self-evaluation and emotional planning before they moved. Although they did achieve their concrete objective—to be near a relative, to be warm, to have a different life-style—each discussed areas of her emotional life that became problem areas because of the relocation situation. Each believed she would have been better able to cope with her new situation had she recognized the possible problems beforehand. Most did not see the move as a mistake, and most were not unhappy with their lives, but they felt they could have been more comfortable with their relocation earlier had they been more emotionally aware.

Myra moved from her home in western New York State to West Palm Beach, Florida, because Harry, her husband, had retired and wanted to be able to play golf all year. Myra left her job as a bookkeeper with some reluctance, but her real problem with relocating was her feeling about leaving her mother, who was not well. Her father was taking care of her mother and she had two sisters who lived near their parents so her presence was not necessary for caretaking, but Myra felt a need to be close to her family at this time. Harry insisted, however, that they were only a few hours away and that she could fly back any time she wanted. They had owned their home in West Palm Beach for several years and had spent vacation time there, so the area was familiar to them and no one anticipated problems with this aspect of relocation.

Myra and Harry married in 1948 and had a marriage that was traditional for their time. Myra worked until she became pregnant with their first child, and she stayed home until the third and last child entered college. She enjoyed her life as a housewife and mother until the later years, when only the youngest son was home. She began to feel less needed as her son went through his last two years of high school. It was then she began to think of returning to work. She took courses to update her bookkeeping skills and learned the new computerized systems. As a result of this preparation she had little difficulty finding a job when she was ready. She had been at the same job for fifteen years when Harry decided to retire and relocate. She was disappointed to have to leave her job, but neither she nor Harry questioned that she had to go along with his decision. Her need to be with her mother was never an issue between them because only Myra considered it a necessity.

She saw no alternatives at the time, but neither could she control her feelings of resentment. As things happened, she spent a lot of time that first year in transit between Florida and New York, largely because her mother became critically ill a few months after their move. She was too concerned about her mother's condition to think about her resentment toward Harry, so it was not until after her mother's death a year later that problems surfaced. She hated the Florida climate and the life in Florida. She did not like the people she had met and she had nothing she wanted to do. She spent most of her time home reading and watching television. Harry played golf and Myra spent alot of time feeling miserable. At first she believed she was mourning her mother, and of course she was, but after a few months she began to realize that she needed to do something about the way she was feeling.

As we talked with Myra she began to gain some perspective on her situation. She had always been a resourceful person. She had raised three successful children, she had led some community organizations including the PTA when her children were young, and she had planned for and located a job when she felt it was time. In addition, she had been successful in her career as a bookkeeper. Yet when it came to her marriage and her relationship with her husband, it was as though this resourceful, successful woman did not exist. She felt her role as a wife was to subjugate her needs to her husband's and to follow his wishes. She had never assessed how some of her values from the early days of her marriage had changed, as some of the values of society had changed; and she had never taken credit for her personal achievements. As she talked, she began to see her strengths, and she also began to see her marriage in a different way. Harry was hardly a bully. He accepted certain hypotheses just as she did, so there was little question about Myra's needs when retirement and relocation were decided. There was a tacit assumption that Myra would resume her role as housewife, that she needed Harry, and that Harry needed her full-time in Florida. The possibility that she might spend a month or so at a time near her mother if she wished was never discussed. The possibility that they postpone the move for a year or so was never discussed because it never occurred to Myra to make this an issue. If Myra had been more in touch with her emotional self, she might have had an easier two years.

Recriminations and regrets are not productive, but they were helpful to Myra as she planned for what was ahead. Because she doesn't like the leisure life, she has opted to go back to work on a part-time basis. She is fortunate to be in an economy where this is possible and fortunate to have a marketable profession. At this writing she has had several job offers. She recognizes her role in the relocation scenario and therefore she has come to terms with her anger at Harry. He is eager for her to be contented again, and after they discussed her difficulties, he supported her decision to go to work. Her only regret at this point is that she did not have the opportunity to explore some of these feelings before, instead of after, the fact.

If relocation is in your mind, or in your future, it is important to remember that it is a time of transition. It is a time when you need to have as much information about yourself as possible so that you can make successful choices.

Abby moved from Charleston, South Carolina, to Denver, Colorado, as soon as she retired from her teaching job. She had been waiting to relocate to Denver for three years, since her son and daughter-in-law had moved there with Abby's three grandchildren. Abby had been divorced when her son was eight years old and had never remarried. She had devoted herself to raising her son and to her job as a fourth-grade teacher. She adored her son and she loved her work as a teacher. She had had several opportunities to leave the classroom and become a supervisor or a specialty teacher, but she knew that following her students throughout the year and watching them grow and develop gave her a pleasure she did not want to give up, even for extra money. Her son had married his childhood sweetheart and they had lived in Charleston for the first fifteen years of their marriage, so Abby had been able to maintain a close relationship with them.

She had a close relationship with her grandchildren, especially with the youngest, the only boy, who was five years old when the family moved to Denver. He had been ill as an infant and Abby had often baby-sat with him to give her daughter-in-law some rest. She looked forward to her retirement and relocation with great anticipation, because she missed the daily contact with her family.

She bought a condominium apartment in Denver within easy driving distance of her son's home. She assumed she would have almost daily contact, particularly with her three grandchildren. She expected to be serving milk and cookies after school a few times a week and hosting weekend sleepovers; she had even bought a two-bedroom apartment for this purpose. The reality was short of the fantasy, and ultimately too short for Abby to ignore. The children were now three years older than when they lived in Charleston—the girls were now sixteen and thirteen and her grandson was eight. The sixteen-year-old had a boyfriend who took most of her time and energy, and the thirteen-year-old was involved with her group of friends and moody most of the time. Her grandson had developed an interest in athletics, played Little League baseball, and was learning soccer. They were delighted to have Grandma nearby and they dropped in on occasion, but they were not willing to commit any large bloc of time to her.

Her son and daughter-in-law had developed a group of friends and had many social engagements. Her son was very busy with his corporate life. Abby's daughter-in-law now had a full-time job. Both she and her husband were delighted to have Abby around and available to fill in for them when they wanted to stay out on a weeknight or weekend. Abby had not counted on this. While she was working and while her grandchildren were small she was happy to be available when her schedule allowed, but she had not anticipated what it would be like when her life changed and she had nothing but free time. She had not seen herself as a housekeeper when she moved, but she had expected to be the welcome guest she had always been.

The other problematic aspect of her relocation was the loss she experienced being separated from her job. She had not evaluated the meaning of her work sufficiently. Teaching had been one of the most meaningful parts of her life. In addition, it had given her a social network she enjoyed. The sense of loss might not have been as acutely felt if things had worked out with her family, but her disappointment with the family scene, coupled with the loss of her work was overwhelming. She lived in this situation for over a year and tried very hard to come to terms with it. After all, she was seeing her grandchildren and her son, even if there was hardly any time for a real visit with them. They seemed to care for her as much as ever, and she got to see them more than if she had remained in Charleston. She was still unhappy, however.

An accidental meeting with a neighbor changed things for Abby. The neighbor was a widow who mentioned she was doing volunteer work in the pediatric division of the local hospital. She had begun a program for children with chronic illnesses that involved creative writing and creative dramatics. She was looking for someone to work with her. Abby began to say she was too busy with her family obligations when, as she told us, "a light bulb, just like in the comic strips, went off in my head." She began to talk with the woman about the program and realized she could bring her knowledge and expertise about children to it. Shortly after this meeting she began working in and implementing the new program.

Even before we spoke with Abby she had begun to see how her decision to relocate had not been as well thought out as it should have been. She had begun to realize she had not realistically evaluated her relationship with her family, her work needs, and her friendship needs. After her son and his family moved, she missed them so much she did not think about how she might miss her work when she retired and relocated. She underestimated her need for a social network. Her main social life was with her family, but she had friendships with many of the teachers. She had walked away from these friendships when she relocated, never realizing she would need and want to replace them.

Here, is an interesting aspect of Abby's story, one many women will relate to. Abby told us that her relationship with her daughter-in-law had always been cordial but never close. She had always wanted a better relationship, but had always encountered a barrier. When she looked more objectively at her feelings, she realized that a hidden agenda in her retirement and relocation had been the wish to grow closer to her daughter-in-law. Had she been more honest with herself she would have realized that this was not likely to happen. She also knew that her son was happiest in their relationship when she was involved with her work, social contacts, or other independent activities. He was least approving of her when she was intruding on his life. She now realizes that she can only be happy when she feels autonomous and independent.

Life is becoming much better for Abby. She is happy with the volunteer work in the hospital, and the program has expanded to other hospitals in the area. She was instrumental in helping this to come about. She has been socially active because of it. She actually has a schedule for seeing her son and his family similar to what they had when they lived in Charleston; she helps out when she can and visits with them on occasional weekends. She is now much more aware of her strengths and her needs and is therefore more comfortable with herself and her retirement.

Look back on your responses to the questionnaires in the previous chapters. Examine the information you now have about yourself in the framework of relocation. If you are contemplating relocation with any misgivings about your decision, look back on the impact of the women's movement in your life and evaluate the ways in which you handled transitions over the years. You may become aware of strengths which you have not always realized you possessed.

As we spoke with Roz (see Chapter IV, Styles of Friendships), she told us she had done just this evaluation, without realizing it, before she relocated. She and Tom had moved to Tucson because of his arthritis, although she did not want to relocate. Remembering how she had coped when Tom was in the army during the Korean war had given her courage to move into her retirement. She was pregnant when he went overseas, and she went through childbirth as well as the first year of child-rearing without him. He was away for two years, and for many months she did not know his whereabouts, since he was believed to have been captured by the North Koreans. She remembers this as the most difficult period of her life, but she persevered and survived. She tells herself, "If I survived those months, I can do anything" . . . and so she can.

Not everyone has as dramatic an example of courage in their lives, but most women have unrecognized and unsung capabilities to tap if the circumstances necessitate.

Were you taught, and do you still believe, that the man in your life comes first? Many women said they were just beginning to feel the pleasures of work outside of their home when their husband's retirement and relocation loomed. Many were not sorry to leave their jobs but did not want to leave their homes. Some felt helpless to fight the wishes of their husbands. Some told us that it never occurred to them to protest.

Shirley was surprised to discover that she was one of these women. She had never seen herself in this way until she began to talk with us. Her husband Jake is determined that when they both retire from their jobs they will move from their home in Cleveland to a warmer climate. He also wants an easier lifestyle, which he is sure he can find in a less urban area. He has settled on either Arizona or California.

Shirley has a job in the Ohio Department of Labor. She is a civil service employee and will be entitled to a pension when she retires in three years. Jake works for a large accounting firm and will be eligible for his share of a generous profit-sharing plan within the same three-year period. They have spent the last two years' vacation time visiting possible places to relocate when they retire. They have explored Prescott, Sedona, and Flagstaff in Arizona. They have explored Taos and Santa Fe in New Mexico. This year they'll travel to parts of California. Throughout all of their travels, Shirley has come to realize she likes Cleveland best. She has lived there since she and Jake were married and she likes life in a big city. She grew up in a small town in New York State and feels she did not belong anyplace until she moved to Cleveland. Her life is there. She has friends and is a member of several organizations there. She sees the benefits of a warmer climate for most of the year, but she doesn't really want to move west. Nevertheless she is traveling and seriously searching along with Jake. The more she sees the less she wants to go, but she says she cannot see a choice, since she cannot deny her husband an easier life and better weather.

As we talked, Shirley began to question these ideas. She began to see that her needs were as valid as Jake's. They had to be considered acknowledged and shared with Jake. Until this time she had been talking about all she would miss, but she never clearly stated to Jake that she didn't want to move. She had slipped into the position of feeling trapped and helpless and so she became resentful and angry.

Self-assessing in this way clarified many things for Shirley. She is able to see the myth she has been living with that a man's needs take precedence over a woman's. She understands that she has been viewing retirement and relocation as a threat to her independence, although she was not aware that this was an issue for her. Accepting the fact that she is entitled to consideration has eased some of her resentment, and as this happened, alternatives appeared to her. It has not been easy to discuss some of this with Jake, since he truly believes that what he wants to do is right for them. Shirley has difficulty with this, because she occasionally still feels that he is right. They have, however, come to a form of a compromise. They will continue to search for a retirement location, but instead of selling their home in Cleveland and moving once their retirement is a fact, they will

rent and try out a location for a year before making any permanent decision. Shirley believes that Jake will attempt to circum-
vent this compromise, but she knows that once he sees she is
firm in her intention, he will comply with the agreement.

Shirley is beginning to deal with her issues of independence
and autonomy. She feels that these issues, rather than Cleveland, may be the real problem she is having with relocation. She
is hoping that once she is in the situation on a trial basis she will
come to terms with the move. She will participate more actively
in the search and look for a retirement home near a cosmopoli-
tan area. She has more work to do before she will be comfortable
with her next transition, but she feels more in control of her life
now that she has conceptualized the problems she has with the
issue of relocations.

Is independence an issue for you? Independence may be
more difficult to achieve in another setting and another lifestyle.
If you relocate to a couple-oriented retirement community, you
may find that an independent life, if you are part of a couple, is
not the norm. Many of the women who live in retirement communities tell of twenty-four-hour togetherness lifestyles: food
shopping together, exercise together, and hobbies together,
even if the hobby is of more interest to either the wife or the
husband. Even though there are always single women or men
present at social functions, if you are married you are expected
to show up with your spouse. If you are used to having more
autonomy in your life, this may be something to consider when
you check out places to live. Perhaps you will be happier in a
city setting rather than a retirement community. Perhaps you do
not mind being a little different from the norm.

If you are single, a retirement community may be right for
you, since there is usually a built-in social life that makes finding
friends and activities easier than in a city setting. There are
usually discussion groups, craft groups, and evening activities,
with so many others looking to participate. If you are alone and
if your job is an important part of your social network, you may

want to consider relocating to a retirement community where you will have an easier chance to replace the social life of your working situation.

If you are moving from an urban area with public transportation to an area where buses and subways are not so accessible, you may have a problem getting around on your own. Do you drive? Perhaps this is the time to learn. It may be the time to become a two-car family.

Phoebe is contemplating relocation when she retires in the next two years. She has been a free-lance editor for most of her working life and was able to work in her home as she raised two children. She has been the editor for several successful authors, and she does editing for two prominent publishing houses. When her husband died five years ago she continued working from her home. She enjoys her career and does not expect to give it up altogether . . . ever. She just feels she wants more time to herself, to be able to think and perhaps write a book of her own.

Phoebe and her husband lived in San Francisco for most of their married life. They owned a small beach house off the southern coast of California in an isolated and still undeveloped area of Mexico. They spent many vacations there, and since his death she has spent four weeks each year enjoying the beach, the ocean, and the long quiet days. She enjoys passing the time of day with people in the nearby town. She has considered moving there permanently but is undecided about whether it's right for her. Her children and her brother are advising against it, telling her she will be lonely and bored spending her life there. Phoebe is not sure.

She has always known she is an independent person and has been autonomous, even within her marriage. She is able to motivate herself and impose a structure on her life, which is why she has been so successful as a free-lance editor. What she needs to determine before she makes her decision is the meaning of her relationships. She is one of those people who has always assumed that "works and plays well with others" is a significant measure of a person. She has always faulted herself to some extent because she has never been very active socially. Even when she was married, she and her husband did not have a large circle of friends. Although she has been content with the relationships she values and has fostered over the years, she can still hear the voice of her mother telling her to be more friendly. Even since the death of her husband she has not felt the need to reach out more. She is particularly close to her youngest daughter who has recently married, and this is probably the most important relationship in her life at this time.

She is beginning to understand why her friends' lives in retirement communities have never seemed attractive to her. It is not that she doesn't like to be with people, but she has a strong need for privacy and is not comfortable with organized activities, especially in large groups. She had never conceptualized this before, but she has discovered that she is a loner. She is starting to see that a life on the beach might be a viable choice for her, despite popular opinion. She is starting to weigh her options and will probably begin with a trial run of six months in Mexico by the end of next year. What is important to Phoebe is that she has a better understanding of herself and this knowledge is giving her power to make a thoughtful, realistic choice.

Many retirees, particularly those who retire before the age of sixty-five and who live in urban areas with cold winters, begin their retirement by spending a few winter months in a warmer climate. They usually remain for most of the year in their original home. Those who live in the East often pass the winter in Florida and those from the Midwest often go to Arizona or California. Many retirees own a small home or rent in the same area each year. Some arrange to travel during the winter months, and some spend the two or three months' time in a different area each year. They do not disrupt their everyday lives to any great extent and treat the few months away as vacation time.

If it is financially viable, this is an excellent compromise for couples who do not want to relocate. Whether you are single or married, spending just a few months in a place is a good way to find out if a particular area is compatible with your lifestyle. If relocation is what you are planning, take heed of the experience of many women we spoke with who had been retired for more than five years. Those who traveled found that travel became more arduous each year. After three to four years, they felt the need to rethink their options. Those who went to a different location every winter found it more difficult each year to settle comfortably into the new setting. This does not mean that they were sorry they had chosen to travel or to live part-time in another area; it means that most of them found themselves facing the issue of relocation without being aware that it was happening.

Those women who regularly went to the same area found that after several years, the few months away from the winter's cold did not seem to be enough. They gradually began to arrange their lives so that the time away from "home" became five or six months. Then things began to change. They were aware that they were suspending their lives "back home" for a longer period of time each year. Many of them were not comfortable about this. Cultural activities such as concerts, plays, and ballet; social activities; adult education courses—these and many other areas of interest developed over a lifetime had to be forgone or foreshortened when January and February in a warmer climate turned into November-through-April. What had been vacation time and a pleasant interlude in routine became a time of transition for many women. They had not seriously considered relocating, but that in fact was what they were doing. By the time they went back home it was almost summer and vacation time was beginning. Schools and colleges were on a summer schedule, and the cultural events and club activities were curtailed. Where friends and family were concerned, relationships of long duration changed in character as the time apart became greater.

When we met Alice she was just beginning to realize that she was going through this time of transition. She and her husband Steven had owned their small home in Naples, Florida, for eight years before they retired. They had spent summer vacations there each year and loved the area . . . even in the summer when the weather was too warm for many people. They lived year-round in a Long Island suburb of New York. Alice had worked for twenty-five years as a reading specialist in the public schools. She and Steven had retired at the same time, five years ago. He had been an executive for a large corporation and had retired with the understanding that his company would call on him for consultations on a fairly regular basis. Alice, too, after she retired worked on special projects and did some teacher training when called upon by her school district. The first year after they retired they left right after New Year's Day and drove to Naples. They returned the first week in March to a severe winter storm and several weeks of cold and rainy weather. (They had to be back because Alice had contracted to work on a project that began on March 15.) The second year they left shortly before Christmas and their children and grandchildren joined them for the holiday in Florida. That year they decided to stay away until the end of March and planned their consulting time so that it would not interfere. Steven particularly began to feel that there was no reason to stay so long in the chilly autumn and rush back to the cool and rainy season in April. Alice could only agree, since she shared Steven's enthusiasm for golf and liked being outdoors so much of the time. They had also developed a social network in Florida over the years.

By the fifth year of retirement, which is when we spoke with her, Alice was spending November through April in Florida. This time schedule severely limited her ability to work on her projects in the New York schools so she had decided to give up her consultants status. She had been aware that she would miss her work when she gave it up completely. She knew it was the part of her life that gave her a feeling of prestige and importance, and she had not counted on giving it up this early in her retirement. That is what triggered the realization that her life had changed more dramatically than she ever thought it would. Although she still considers Long Island her home, she is living half the year in Florida. She needs to assess her retirement situation within the framework of this reality.

As we spoke with her, she mentioned another aspect of her

situation that is a problem for her. She has two good friends in Long Island with whom she keeps in touch while she is in Florida, but she misses the almost daily contact with them when she is not nearby. This was not an issue when she first started coming to Florida, and she had not foreseen her need for close relationships with women in the new area. She is beginning to feel differently now that the time frame has changed. As she evaluated herself using the friendship questionnaire in Chapter IV, she realized she has a moderate need for intimacy and is able to reach out for it. She also realized that she uses structured situations to find new friends. She has used these insights to conceptualize the situation and attack her problem.

At this time Alice is planning to replace her work by volunteering in the local school, and she expects to join one of the women's organizations in her area. She is making plans to ensure that her partial relocation and her retirement years are as fulfilling as they can be.

Doris and Chet came from Ann Arbor, Michigan, in December 1979 to spend a week with friends in Mesa, Arizona. The friends live in a large retirement community and were enjoying the free and easy, good life. Chet and Doris spent an idyllic week playing golf, watching the sun set, and, best of all, never wearing more than a light sweater for warmth. Within the month they had bought a house in Mesa, returned to pack up their home in Michigan, and set up housekeeping a mile away from their friends. They lived happily ever after, or reasonably so. There are many stories such as this everywhere you go, particularly if you spend any time with real estate agents in the Sun Belt. Some of them are true.

Remember, "happily ever after" never just happens. Relocation and retirement issues are complicated and involved. Usually when people give up their roots, they have the feeling that they have moved for the last time in their lives. Many of the women who had relocated told us that the feeling of permanency about their move was difficult for them. Many said they felt better about relocating when they experienced it as just another transition, with other moves to follow if need be. Since there will be many seasons in a woman's life, because she has a future of twenty-five to thirty years after retiring, this thought can put relocation into another perspective.

The important factor to remember is that you take yourself with you. Making the necessary evaluations, preparing yourself as well as you can for the vagaries of the future, and looking at all your options and opportunities will help you make your relocation in retirement a successful adventure.

IX

The Caretaker

*There comes a time in a man's life when to get
where he has to go—if there are no doors or
windows he walks through a wall.*

BERNARD MALAMUD (B. 1914–1989)

Valerie was born in 1925 in Manchester, England. She was the
youngest child and the only daughter in her family. She recalls
the early comfortable and protected years of her life with great
pleasure. She also remembers the years immediately preceding
World War II, years of constant family concern, since her two
older brothers would certainly be called to serve in the army
should war break out. She remembers the "peace in our time"
statement of Prime Minister Chamberlain and the subsequent
invasion of Poland in the fall of 1939. She was and still is a great
admirer of Prime Minister Churchill.

She also remembers American soldiers coming to her country. Just as the war reorganized and refocused the world for all,
it changed Valerie's life dramatically. She fell in love and married
an American army major. He was nine years her senior and she
met him on a blind date. They were married in 1944, and in
1946, at the age of twenty-one, she left her home and family
and moved to the United States.

One of her brothers had been killed in the war. Her older

brother, his wife, their three children, and Valerie's mother and father were unhappy at her leaving, but they approved of Ben, her American husband, and wished her well. Valerie loved them dearly, but she adored her husband, who was a true take-charge person. He spoke of the idyllic life ahead of them in his hometown in Iowa where he had a law practice, political connections, and political ambitions.

Adjustment was difficult at first. There was no welcoming family to ease the way, as Ben was an only child and both of his parents had died before he left for England. His friends reached out, since Ben was a popular and active citizen. But in the beginning Valerie missed having her family around and often wished that her brother and his family could move to the United States. By 1952 she and Ben had their own family—two sons and one daughter. Valerie's life was busy and her time was full. Her brother was prospering and watching out for her parents, so, except for a yearly visit at Christmas, she did not think too often about Manchester.

Ben's needs and preferences comprised the main part of Valerie's days, and his career, both legal and political, was the main part of their social life outside the family. He was in charge of all phases of their life together except the cooking, housekeeping, and physical care of the children. Valerie was content with loving and being loved. The women's movement had little or no impact on her life. Ben had opted for a career in city politics and went on to become city council president and later mayor. He retired in 1986 when he was seventy and Valerie was sixty-one. Ben continued to maintain a part-time law practice and served as consultant to the city government. Several years before, all three children had moved to the East Coast and visits were infrequent, but Ben and Valerie were content with the way things were. They looked forward to a comfortable life in retirement, consisting of travel and time together at home enjoying gardening, golf, and each other.

In the late spring of 1987 Ben suffered a stroke. The stroke was not serious and he was home from the hospital in three weeks, recuperating slowly. On Thanksgiving Day, however, he had another stroke which was more serious and incapacitating. Not only was he unable to walk, but the parts of his brain that involved memory and speech were also affected. The doctor predicted a slow, uneven, and incomplete recovery.

Valerie functioned by rote while Ben was in the hospital. She drove back and forth, visited with him most of the day, and was cheerful in his presence. She thanked all of their friends for their concern. She ate her three meals a day. She fell into bed at night and slept dreamlessly.

She woke up to an unpleasant and unnerving reality the day before Ben was to be released from the hospital. The doctor and the social worker had been speaking with her for over a week about home care, nursing care, and doctor and hospital bills, and she had listened respectfully and had taken it all in. She had done nothing because she had not fully comprehended that it was her decision and her move. She had spoken with her children and they had all agreed that Daddy was to remain at home, and there was to be an arrangement for nursing and home health care. Valerie had thought that the hospital or the doctor or perhaps one of her sons would make the arrangements, and had not realized that she had to take charge. Neither had she thought about paying the hospital bill and filling out the medical forms. The last time Ben had been hospitalized he had made all the arrangements and had taken care of the necessary forms and bill payments.

Valerie called a former associate of Ben's, and he and his wife helped her make arrangements for home care and deal with the hospital red tape. This was only the beginning. Valerie went home to a situation that for her was a nightmare. Ben's physical condition was only a small part of her problem. He was making progress medically, was not a difficult patient, and responded well to the home health-care person.

Valerie, however, found herself faced daily with other decisions for which she had only limited experience. There were the regular monthly bills, which Ben had always paid; decisions awaited on their financial portfolio, of which she was largely ignorant. She had to deal with Medicare, the supplemental health insurance, and the medical personnel, who took advantage of her naiveté. She called on everyone she knew for advice and counsel. She felt helpless and confused most of the time and began feeling as though she were physically ill. Her children became concerned about the situation and started talking about moving Valerie and Ben to Massachusetts where their daughter lived. They would put Ben in a nursing home and Valerie could move in with her daughter and son-in-law. This was the shock she needed. She could not believe that her children actually thought she would consider being separated from Ben, or that she would move from her home where she had spent over forty years. For an instant she had a look at what they must be seeing if they even entertained this as a possibility. At the same instant she began to take charge of her life.

Human beings have no contract with the universe: Lives can be changed by catastrophic events that cannot be ignored or finessed; the world is random and bad things do happen to good people. A well-planned and well-executed retirement does not preclude the possibilities of the unexpected. The secret to coping is to maximize the control you have over your life.

Valerie had never thought about life in this way. She was indeed the product of the "little woman" era. As the only daughter and the youngest child, she had formed no expectation that she would or should grow up to become independent and self-sufficient. She had always expected men to take charge, and when they did she felt comfortable and loved. She had been sheltered in her traditional marriage and given no opportunity to develop her strengths. Now she had to do some work to find her inner resources.

Valerie had begun to do some self-assessment with us before her children descended upon her with *their* plan for the rest of *her* life. She had not been aware of the importance of self-evaluation but she had followed through on the suggestion of one of her friends who told her to seek outside help with her problems. She had been tentative and halfhearted at first, but now her certainty that she did not want to leave her home or be separated from Ben gave her the added motivation to discover options for herself. We began to explore them with her.

Valerie began to appreciate how her early experiences had prepared her for coping with what lay ahead. She remembered the years before and during World War II, and the courage of all of the members of her family as they dealt with the fact of war and the separation from loved ones. She had faced and dealt with the loss of her brother, and she had coped with the anguish of separation from Ben each time he went off into combat. With Ben's support she had left her country to begin a new life, but it was her own strength and will that had made her life successful. Valerie saw that these were her accomplishments, and that she had never taken credit for own inner strengths.

Valerie thought of herself as a passive woman, unable to cope and dependent on her husband for all decisions. It is true that most of her major adult decisions had been made at her husband's suggestion or in terms of what he thought she should do. She would never have left England if he had not believed it was so right for both of them. He decided where they would live and even when they would have children.

As we spoke, she remembered at least one time when she had made a major impact. Although she had never consciously made a career decision for herself (she had just assumed that she would always be a wife and mother), she had been instrumental in a career decision for Ben. Shortly after their third child was born he had to decide whether he should move into the national arena of political life and run for the congressional seat in his district. He had a lot of conflict because of the disruption this would mean for the family (if he won he would have to spend most of his time in Washington), but he was ambitious and knew that a seat in Congress might well mean that he could be a U.S. senator one day. He was very tempted.

Valerie felt very strongly about Ben's being away from home, since family life was very important to her. She knew that if Ben were to pursue a national political career, life as she knew it would be over. She told him that she did not want him to take this opportunity, that she was not prepared to make such a change in their lives. Ben made his decision to remain in city politics based on Valerie's wishes. As she talked to us about this, Valerie saw an effective woman at work. She had taken charge in a way she had not recognized or valued.

When Valerie reflected on her relationship with her daughter and on the life that her daughter was now leading, she again recognized her own effectiveness. Her daughter, Hayley, had always been independent; Valerie encouraged this but it made Ben uncomfortable. When the time came for college, Hayley had chosen one in Boston, although Ben had wanted her to attend his alma mater, the University of Iowa. Hayley wanted a career in communications and to be away from her family. Here again Valerie had interceded and won the point. She was very proud of Hayley, who was now working for a television station in Boston, on a solid career track in her chosen field; she was also a devoted wife and loving mother.

This was important assessment work for Valerie. She had never needed to look at her inner strengths and inner resources before, but they were there and she needed to know that now! She also needed to know that she was an effective person with impact on the lives of others. It was only a beginning, but it was the basis for the exploration of options.

Her first step was to make a plan of action for herself and Ben. She knew that if she could take charge of the home health-care situation and supervise it effectively, there would be no present need to move Ben to a nursing home. She had successfully nursed her children through their various childhood illnesses and she began to see this situation as more of the same. She took stock of the tasks required and the hours needed for his care. Then she evaluated this in light of what she could realistically handle alone.

She knew she had physical limitations and that she still needed to cope better emotionally. There were certain exercises Ben was required to do to gain back some of the mobility in his legs, and Valerie felt overwhelmed at the thought of dealing with this. She also felt disoriented with Ben, who was now unable to express his needs. She knew she had to gradually accept and deal with this. Fortunately, there was enough money and enough medical insurance to keep the help she already had, so that for the present her main task was to accept and take charge of the existing situation.

Valerie knows that she needs to become informed about the financial aspects of her life. She has resolved to search out one of the available courses on this subject, which will enable her to have a working knowledge of the financial world, but until she does, she has called upon one of Ben's associates to manage their finances. She will take care of the monthly bills, but she knows she doesn't have the expertise at this time to do more.

It was no surprise to Valerie that the most important relationship in her life was with Ben. They had always spent Ben's free time together. The short time they had of Ben's retirement before he became ill was more of the same; they had started to make plans to visit Valerie's family in England and to tour France and Italy. Valerie's emotional devastation at the loss of the relationship as she had known it was predictable. She now had to find support for herself from within, but also from outside sources.

When Valerie came to the United States in 1946 she had helped organize a group of "war brides," women who had married American servicemen and moved with their husbands to the United States. It was not a formal organization, but more like what we call today a "self-help group." The women gave each other support and helped each other adjust to a new country. The group had not stayed together after the first two years, but Valerie had formed a close friendship with Esther, another Englishwoman who belonged to the group. They lived only a few miles apart and had stayed in close touch throughout the years, although they did not see each other often. Ben and Esther's husband did not have much in common. The women spoke at least once a week and saw each other whenever they could. When Ben retired it had been more difficult for Valerie and Esther to get together; but when Ben became ill, Esther had made herself available and visited at least once a week. It was she who suggested that Valerie seek help, because she found it so painful to see her friend so emotionally distraught. Valerie realized her relationship with Esther was one she could count on and use in the weeks and months ahead. She also realized that her brother was available if she needed him. She began to evaluate the friendships she had developed with other women over the years, and remembered two women whom she felt she could call upon.

There is more emotional work ahead for Valerie. She may have to build a new life for herself without Ben's input or presence. She may have to make plans for a nursing home for him in the future. She may have to take on more of his caretaking as time goes on. The time ahead is uncertain but she can prepare to meet the unexpected with the self-knowledge she is beginning to acquire. She knows she needs to make plans for herself and for Ben's future, and she continues to grow and discover herself.

Becoming the caretaker for one's husband is one of the more difficult tasks a woman may be called upon to perform. It is difficult, whether the situation involves the final stages of a terminal illness or a condition that is long-term and incapacitating. It can be particularly painful if the illness diminishes the mental as well as the physical capacities, (as in Alzheimer's disease). We discovered the following reaction from the many women who shared their experiences with us: When their husband's illness struck, when they were called upon to face the situation, each felt it to be not only unexpected but unreasonable and unfair as well. Many couples had delayed pleasures in order to save money for their retirement. Many women had looked forward in retirement to finally having the companionship of their workaholic husbands. Many women had looked forward to the release from the routine of housework and meals. Most of them anticipated and planned their retirement as a time of relaxation and pleasure.

Life never continues in a straight line, and it is important to know who you are and where you have been so that you will be more prepared to cope with each curve. Vulnerability increases with age, and there is no way to bypass this fact except to know yourself and your own resources. Many of the women we spoke with told us of their anger at their husband's illness. Most of them were able to cope, but they did feel misused and abused by what was expected of them. They felt betrayed by their husbands, particularly if the husband had been the person in the marriage who was more in charge. All of them felt guilty because of these feelings, and several worked doubly hard at being cheerful because of this. Each woman had her own coping mechanisms and breaking point.

The only way to be prepared for this situation is to be financially aware. It is important that you make the decision to have or not to have nursing and home health-care insurance in light of your financial circumstances. For those who could not pay for this out of their own resources, insurance would be the only way to survive economically. It is important that you make this plan for yourself. Money was never the basic issue for the women we spoke with, although it was a factor for everyone no matter what their financial status. The issue was an emotional one. The more understanding each woman had of her feelings and her resources, the more power she had to deal effectively with the problems as they arose.

Iris had another issue when she moved into her life as a caretaker. She felt that she never had time for herself either in or out of her house, and this was a debilitating and depressing part of her caretaking. She was used to being active and not constantly accounting for her time. Her husband Eric was now confined to a wheelchair. He was often in pain, and she felt that he needed her to be by his side constantly. Her daughter, who lived nearby, and her neighbor did most of her shopping. Iris found that she rarely went out because Eric did not want to be alone. He particularly wanted *her* to be with him. She did not feel completely isolated, however, since she had their friends in for bridge once a week and Eric could still enjoy the game. They also rented movies to watch on the VCR, which was pleasant for both of them. Their daughter and grandchildren visited and

Iris found herself preparing family meals each Sunday, just as she did when the children were young. She felt she had made the best adjustment she could to a difficult situation, but she felt depressed and tearful when she awoke each morning. She knew she felt trapped, despite her efforts to resign herself to her new life situation. She was surprised at her strong feelings of regret and despair. She realized she would have to reassess her present situation if she was to continue successfully.

Four years earlier she had retired to accommodate Eric's time schedule. She had done this reluctantly, but without conscious conflict. She assumed that when Eric retired she had to do the same. She had been working as the executive secretary to the vice-president in a large manufacturing concern. It was a position of great importance in the company and she enjoyed the work and the prestige. She had not worked outside the home before this job, as she had liked being at home and caring for her house and her family. She had never considered working until her daughter and son left for college. She had been surprised at the pleasure she received from her job. The work and promotions had given her a sense of importance she had not felt since her senior year in high school when she helped edit her high school yearbook.

During our evaluations, Iris recognized that she was a typical product of her time. She had never seriously considered a career and had married right after high school. She had gone from compliant daughter to conventional wife and mother. This was how she experienced her life, but not unhappily. The job she had begun fifteen years before seemed to her to be an extra pleasure but of no real importance in the total scheme of her life —her true role was wife and mother. Because of this, she had never seen herself as the decisive, competent person she is, despite the many times in her life when she has been called upon to display these qualities. Women who view themselves as traditional wives and mothers often do not recognize these special attributes in themselves, despite life's events. Eric had traveled a lot during their marriage, and Iris had coped with the daily routines as well as the daily problems on her own. She had handled household catastrophes such as a leaky roof, a broken septic tank, an electrical fire in the middle of the night, all when Eric was away from home. She had been active in the parents' associations of her children's schools, and she had a reputation as one of the best hostesses in town.

Through her evaluation, Iris also discovered the degree of privacy and the autonomy she had within the structure of her marriage. She had never seen it so clearly and had never recognized its importance to her. Even before she began her job, her routine had allowed her to be independent during a good part of her week. She had been free to plan her time in terms of her needs rather than in terms of Eric.

Somehow during the four years of retirement privacy and independence had not been much of an issue for Iris, although she could remember having feelings of being intruded upon from time to time. She returned to her life as a housewife with apparent ease. These years had been very pleasant for Iris and Eric. They had traveled in a motor home and seen much of the United States, Canada, and parts of Mexico. They had friends who were also retired, and they had played golf and bridge and had learned to square-dance. Iris had begun reading novels and biographies again, something she had not done since she was at home with her children.

She and Eric had just sold their motor home and were planning a six-month tour of Europe when he had a heart attack. He had been diagnosed as diabetic when he was in his early fifties, and after the heart attack his diabetes worsened. He began to have circulatory problems that affected his ability to walk. Suddenly he needed Iris's care and attention full-time, and she felt obligated to build a life around this. She felt trapped, and then guilty for feeling this way.

When we spoke with Iris she began to realize that at the basis of her depression about being a caretaker was the feeling that she was furious most of the time. It was hard for her to acknowledge her anger. It was not easy to admit the rage she felt toward Eric for becoming ill. Not only had he spoiled their trip to Europe, he needed her to be there for him constantly.

Like many women in her age group, Iris had grown up to believe that women gave their time and energy freely and with cheer when it was needed. The women in most of the books she read faced this sort of situation with joy, as an opportunity to serve and be fulfilled. She was ashamed of herself.

Iris believed that a woman should put the needs of men, and certainly the needs of her husband, before her own. She had trapped herself in this myth for the second time in four years. She had not seen a choice for herself when she retired from a job she loved, because she lived within the framework of this outdated concept. She might never have experienced much conflict if this were the only sacrifice she was called upon to make, for she was enjoying the life that she and Eric were having in retirement. The angry feelings surfaced when she was forced to put her needs aside to a greater extent than she was emotionally prepared to do.

Although she was not consciously aware of it, Eric's need for caretaking tested her belief in the idea of female self-sacrifice. She believed that if Eric needed her presence constantly she had to care for him, yet she could not make the expected emotional peace with the idea.

She started to see her situation in a new perspective as she gained important knowledge about herself. She was an independent and autonomous woman with needs to fulfill, and she had limits to both her emotional and physical energies. She was still the loving wife and still the willing caretaker, but she could not function successfully unless she acknowledged the other parts of herself. Once she saw the emotional burden she had been placing on herself by her unrealistic expectations, she began to look for options to change her situation. She was quite willing to be the primary caretaker for Eric. She enjoyed much of the time they spent together, and she wanted to be the one who made him feel comfortable and loved. She wanted to be the one who relieved his pain and gave him solace. She needed time for herself, however, and she needed to plan. She knew that Eric did not want anyone else to stay with him, but she realized that if she was firm, and if she explained clearly why it was important, he would accept their daughter or a friend as a substitute caretaker on occasion. She planned for someone to help her with the chores in the house and with Eric's care. They were able to afford this care on a part-time basis, and although Eric did not want it to be this way, Iris realized it was imperative for her. Even as she planned, she felt her anger begin to dissolve. She was amazed at how much more loving she was able to feel toward Eric as she began to see that she had some options. She realized that she no longer wanted to be cooking Sunday family dinners, and she was surprised to see how agreeable her daughter was to sharing the burden.

Iris has begun to plan for a few college courses in the next year. She never had the opportunity to go to college and has always regretted it. She feels she can manage this, on a nonmatriculated basis at first, and still have the time to be with Eric. She finds that their relationship is back to where it was before he became so ill. No matter what life has in store for Iris, she is stronger than ever before in her knowledge of who she is and what she needs in order to survive.

With more people living into their eighties, nineties, and beyond, retirees are finding themselves increasingly involved with caretaking responsibilities for their aging parents. The burden of this situation falls mainly upon the women; statistics show that the daughter or the daughter-in-law most often becomes responsible for the physical care of an elderly parent. Often, siblings share the financial responsibilities, but the physical responsibilities are the province of the female, especially the unmarried woman in the family. Many of the women we spoke with who were the principal caretakers told us this had always been their family role, in one situation or another. If you are this person, married or single, do not expect that life will be different should your family present this situation at this time of your life. We met with one retired woman, aged seventy, who was caring for the ninety-three-year-old mother of her ex-husband. It seemed she had promised her then father-in-law on his deathbed that she would always provide for his wife's care, and she felt she had to honor this promise despite the fact that her ex-husband lived in another state and refused to be involved. Her ex-father-in-law obviously knew from whom he was extracting this promise, and he had chosen well! This is more extreme than most situations, but we find that everyone has experience of something similar. There are many dimensions to the caretaking of a parent, and often family matters, dormant for decades, unexpectedly surface. The stresses that can result make self-knowledge essential if one is to survive.

A year after we spoke with Robyn (see Chapter IV, Styles of Friendship), her husband Saul accepted his company's retirement offer. Robyn retired from her job and she and Saul planned for relocation. They were spending time exploring the Southwest and the California coast, and they even planned a trip to the west coast of Florida. Saul had conflict about relocation; he yearned to make a move to a warmer climate but was reluctant to do so because of his eighty-six-year-old widowed mother. She lived alone in the same city, in her own apartment in a housing complex built expressly for senior citizens. It had all the facilities necessary for elderly mobile adults, and she had been managing well with her friends and activities. Saul had a brother, Larry, eight years younger, who had never been too involved with his mother's care; he left the contact and concern to Saul, and Saul felt uncomfortable about leaving Minnesota permanently. Robyn had her own concerns about relocation, but she was coming to terms with them and was enjoying the traveling and the freedom she and Saul had.

Saul's mother fell and broke her hip ten months to the day that Robyn and Saul began their carefree retirement years. The hip fracture, the surgery, and the stay in the hospital changed Robyn's mother-in-law. She had always been active, alert, and feisty, but suddenly she lost her sense of humor and her sense of self-sufficiency. She remained in her home with full-time help for a while after she came out of the hospital, but she did not improve and had to be moved to a place where she could receive more care.

Saul and Robyn and Larry and his wife had a family conference. It was soon apparent to Robyn what was going to happen. Their family dynamics were going to repeat themselves once again, as they had for the thirty years of Robyn's marriage. Saul was the favored child, so the story went. He had been the family caretaker since he was an adolescent and his father lost his job. Saul felt called upon to fill in for his father when he was fifteen, and it had been his position in the family ever since. Larry never had the status in the family he would have liked. He was angry at his mother for preferring Saul, and was angry at Saul for being the favorite child. He was ambivalent toward Saul, both envying him his place of honor in the family and acknowledging and appreciating the fatherly help Saul had given him through the years. Larry had just remarried, to a woman ten years younger than he who was working on her own business career. She had no substantial history with the family and not much interest, although she did go with Larry once in a while when he visited his mother.

Robyn saw the family dynamics and she was correct. No one wanted Mom to go into a nursing home, so the only answer was for her to come to live with one of her sons. Larry would never accept that burden, although Saul pushed for some equitable sharing. Robyn and Saul had the large home and therefore the space to accommodate Saul's mother. They also now had the time, as neither of them was working. Robyn felt trapped and furious at the circumstances. She had always resented Larry for what she felt was his avoidance of responsibility. She had always felt some resentment toward Saul because he felt he needed to take care of everyone in his family, often at her expense. She was drowning in family matters in the midst of a carefree retirement.

We would like to tell you Robyn's story is atypical, but unfortunately it is common, with many variations. Many women had a similar situation with either or both of their own parents (usually the mother or mother-in-law, because statistically women live longer). How to prepare and cope for this possibility is an individual matter. The more you can recognize the real issues as separate from long-standing family patterns, the more clearly you can know your own feelings and needs, and the more you will recognize that you have options.

Robyn needed to see herself more clearly before she could examine her options constructively. Her feelings of helplessness and anger were not easy to accept. For a while all she could envision was herself and Saul stuck day after day in the house, waiting on her mother-in-law. Robyn had already evaluated herself in terms of the women's movement, and she knew that she was a fairly traditional woman despite her successful working life. Robyn had married Saul while she was in her senior year in college, and she had never worked until her children started school. She had been attracted to Saul because he was settled and mature, and she knew he was someone who would take care of her. She liked this. She does not envy her daughter, who has not married yet (she is twenty-five years old) and is pursuing a career in advertising; she cannot imagine that her daughter enjoys being out in the world unprotected. She would not have lived her life any differently and she is happy being the traditional woman, putting her husband's needs before her own, in return for his care of her.

When she had evaluated some of the other aspects of her life, she began to see another side of herself, a side she had not fully acknowledged. She is the decision-maker in the marriage. She decided on the two residential changes the family made. It was her decision to go to work, a decision that Saul had not wholeheartedly approved. Robyn had opted for an abortion when she was forty-three years old, much against Saul's wishes. She had felt strongly that she was finished with child-rearing when she was faced with this unexpected pregnancy, and since neither of them had religious convictions against abortion, Robyn made the decision for herself.

She felt herself to be on very different ground in the present situation, despite the fact that she had been able to consider her own needs within the marriage. She had a precarious relationship with her mother-in-law, although she did admire her independence and perseverance. The ambivalence came from the hold Saul's mother had on his time and energy, and from Robyn's response to this. Robyn always felt that Saul was too involved with his family and had always encouraged him to loosen the ties. One of the reasons she had so willingly agreed to relocate was to accomplish just this. She felt frustrated, confused, and angry.

The scenario proceeded as Robyn knew it would. Saul's mother moved in with them. Robyn knew she had no option here. They had not sold their original home, so the space was there, and Saul was there for his mother for companionship and love. Robyn found she was taking care of the physical needs of her mother-in-law as well as the daily household routine. She was soon aware of her constant anger at her situation. It became apparent to Robyn that if she were to handle her anger she would have to make some concrete plans. She arranged for daily home health care. This helped ease her anger, but she knew she needed more personal time.

Although she had never given herself credit for it, Robyn had always been extremely resourceful. Thus, she was able to plan for several other aspects of her mother-in-law's care. When Larry and his wife fix a date for their monthly visit, Robyn makes social plans for Saul and herself. She feels she does not have to entertain them since they are visiting their mother. She knows she and Saul will benefit from the time away. She also arranged with Saul to have a day, and sometimes two, each week when she can visit with her friends or shop on her own. She is preparing Saul to take a prolonged vacation of at least a month to continue searching for a place to relocate, and she is arranging with her daughter to live in the house and be with her grandmother while they are gone. Robyn is preparing herself for the possibility that if they do decide to relocate, they will buy a house with space enough for Saul's mother to move with them. Robyn is doing fairly well at this time, although she has her bad days. It's been a year since her mother-in-law came to live with them, and Robyn jokingly says it only seems like ten. Her mother-in-law's condition has not improved and she is only occasionally like her old self. Robyn finds this one of the most difficult aspects she had to cope with. She had always seen her mother-in-law as a role model for aging because of her ability to keep active and involved, both mentally and physically. Robyn had always expressed the hope she would grow old the way her mother-in-law did. She has now become too aware of her own vulnerability as she observes and lives with her mother-in-law's frail condition.

Robyn could easily have allowed old family issues and current anger at an unfair situation to immobilize her, but because she was able to see past this and recognize the resources she has available for coping, she was able to move on within the confines of a difficult and unexpected happening.

Caretaking is not always as clear-cut as it turned out to be for Robyn and Saul. Many of the retired women found money for home care to be a problem. Several were faced with a similar situation due to the limited space in their retirement residences. Many had relationships with the elderly patient that made it very difficult for them to assert their needs. Women who were used to being passive with either or both of their parents found it extremely difficult to tell the parent that they needed time for themselves and were turning over the parent's care to a third person. Sometimes the husband in the caretaking couple made things more difficult, particularly if his parent was the needy one. You may feel guilty in this situation if you resent having to care for a parent who lovingly cared for you. An even more difficult situation arises when you are required to care for a parent whom you felt never cared for you. Unresolved family issues frequently arise during this retirement time; feelings you had about the parenting you received resurface and may need to be resolved within a new context. Family matters like this complicate and confuse the self-image women have of themselves as the caretakers of family and society. How much do you owe to others? How much do you owe to yourself at this point in your life? You need to sort out many pieces of your life before you can make decisions on the way you want to be a caretaker.

Anne, like Robyn's husband Saul, was always a caretaker. She was married at nineteen to Jerry, just returned from the war in Korea. Together they began to operate a small photography studio in the suburb of New York City where they lived. The business grew very nicely because Jerry was an extremely personable salesman and a very talented photographer, and Anne had a strong business sense. In time they opened another studio in the next town, which also prospered. They had two children, a boy and a girl, and Anne was able to supervise their upbringing closely because work was so close to home. She never felt she needed household help despite her full schedule, and she juggled her time and her energy, serving a complete meal each evening, seeing that the laundry and cleaning were always done and her work at the store was attended to. Her children never considered her a working mother because she was always available, and Jerry often forgot that she was doing two jobs. In addition to her work at the studio and her work at home, when their daughter was ten and their son eight, Anne's mother-in-law came to live with them. She was terminally ill and Anne cared for her for two years until her death. Anne's step never faltered, she loved feeling needed, capable, and competent. She and her family thrived.

The children grew up and left home to attend college. The business had grown, so Anne and Jerry could begin to think of the time when college would be paid for and they could hire a manager for their business, take some trips, and have more time for each other. They made plans and even traveled to Europe for three weeks in 1985. By this time their daughter had married, and their son had gone into a business venture in computers. Anne was fifty, Jerry was fifty-five, they had been married thirty-one years, and it was their first vacation together alone (without children) ever—and they loved it! They went out west the following year and were looking forward to a new enjoyment of each other and their life together without encumbrances.

The roof caved in shortly after they returned from their western vacation. Their son's business venture had soured and he lost all his capital. He was looking for work and needed a place to live while he pulled himself together. He moved back home to his old room. Two months later, their daughter came home with her one-year-old son. She was divorcing her husband and needed a place to stay while she made plans. She and her son moved into her old room. There was, as well, the ongoing problem of Anne's own mother, who was becoming more infirm. Her mother lived alone in a retirement community in Florida. It was becoming more apparent that she could not be on her own much longer. Anne's response to all of this trauma was typical. She managed, she took care, she coped, and she loved. She became aware, however, that her enthusiasm was missing. She tired very easily. She became irritable with her children, her grandchild, and with Jerry. Why was she so resentful?

We talked with Anne as well as with a number of other women caught in her predicament. Their situation will become more typical as years go by. Statistics that show the elderly living longer and healthier lives also show the youth of our society staying in school longer, marrying later, and, because of high living costs, being dependent on their parents for a longer time. Couples now entering or already in their retirement years are finding themselves in the middle; they are the "sandwich generation." Women who spent their adult years caring for a family, often working outside of the home as well as in the home, are finding their retirement years to be more complicated than they had envisioned.

Anne had never imagined she could feel such resentment toward her family. She started by saying she felt so sorry for her two children who seemed to be having such a difficult time, but she ended by admitting she was feeling quite sorry for herself as well. She spoke about how disappointing it was for Jerry, who had been looking forward to more free time and more time alone with her, but she ended by admitting that she was angry with him as well. She did not feel his life had as many new problems as hers. She said it was her work load that had increased with the return of their son and daughter-plus-one. Jerry's retirement plans were still secure, even though they had to help the children financially for a time, but Anne felt she bore an unequal burden.

She believed she had no options. Growing up as she had in the 1940's, she had never questioned the many obligations of her daily married life of the 1950's and 1960's, despite the emerging women's movement. This was in part because she enjoyed her life and had plenty of physical and psychic energy for the long hours. She loved her children and did not mind doing housework and cooking, and the work she did for the business was always done on her own schedule, so she did not consider it an outside job. She was Supermom before anyone gave this phenomenon a name, and she did not know how to stop. We began guiding her to consider family obligations versus family commitment.

One morning, while we were still working on this issue with her, shortly after life had again settled into a busy routine, Anne received a phone call (which was half expected) from her mother's cousin who lived in Florida, a few doors down from Anne's mother. The cousin said she had made her usual morning visit and found Anne's mother unable to get out of bed. She had called an ambulance and rushed her to the hospital. Anne's mother had suffered a stroke and was unable to walk. Anne rushed to Florida to be with her and to arrange for her care. She had to spend almost a month there, which left her family to take care of their own meals and baby-sitting arrangements. Anne had plenty of time to herself while she was in Florida, and though she missed the company of her family at times, she found she enjoyed some of the solitude. Jerry came for two long weekends during the month she was away, and they realized how much they liked being alone together. At the end of the month, Anne saw that she could not leave her mother alone in the Florida apartment, even with full-time help and her cousin's supervision. She arranged to bring her mother home with them at least for the present and probably permanently.

Anne had already begun to recognize her feelings of resentment, and adding her mother to her caretaking chores did not reduce the extent of the problem. Her expectations of herself were blurring the subtle boundary between the obligation and commitment she felt toward her family, and were also confounding the possibility of her finding options for her situation. She came home from her month in Florida to discover the house was not as neat and clean as she would have liked, nor was she pleased with the baby-sitting arrangements her daughter had made. She felt that her daughter was going out too often and was was leaving her grandson unnecessarily with a baby-sitter. She was not happy with the way her son was progressing with his job hunting. She nevertheless had to admit that no one was falling apart, the house was still standing. Her son was twenty-five years old and her daughter twenty-eight. She could not completely accept that her children did not need all the care she lavished upon them, but she did see clearly how well they had coped without her. She began to get a glimmer of how she was holding on to an inoperative scenario, which involved the care of helpless and dependent children; she saw too how her children were accepting her perception, taking every advantage they could. Her daughter needed all the help she could get with child care, and both of Anne's children enjoyed having their physical needs cared for so competently.

Anne went on for a while distancing herself as much as possible from her daughter's social life and her son's job search while she digested some of this new information. Her mother became increasingly difficult because of her dependency and immobility. She was an autonomous and opinionated woman who was used to having her own way, and she did not take kindly to Anne's caretaking. Anne felt unsure how much help her mother really did need and unclear as to how to get it for her. She required physical care, and Anne hired a home health-care worker who came every day for several hours. This helped some, but did not improve her mother's disposition. When the suggestion was made that a social worker be brought in to evaluate her mother's emotional condition, and a physician to evaluate her physical condition, Anne found herself following through. She had begun to realize she did not have to take responsibility for it all. She was aware that an unbiased determination had to be made as to her mother's needs, and she could not do this herself. She had never recognized the possibility of having help from outside sources. Previously, Anne would have struggled along trying to please her mother, without thought to her own possible limitations and her own needs, but now she was feeling differently.

She does not feel that she wants to ask her children to leave the house and go out on their own, but she has begun to have expectations of them and their time. She has decided she does not have to do all the baby-sitting for her grandchild, since her daughter is working and living rent-free, and can afford help if she wants to go out. Anne has decided she does not have to prepare family meals every evening and weekends, and she and Jerry have begun to go out for dinner often, leaving her daughter and her son to make their own plans. She says eventually she will not feel called upon to do all the shopping, laundry, and cleaning.

The social worker–physician team recommended that Anne's mother should live in a residential facility where she would be able to have a social life on the premises. She needed and wanted more people contact than she was having at Anne and Jerry's house, and although she was not happy at first about leaving, after a few trial visits she became more amenable, and at this time is adjusted and content in her new home. Anne visits at least weekly and is in daily contact by phone.

This is not an easy time for Anne. Unlike Valerie, she has known how to cope and has done so all her life all too well. She is in a different situation entirely, since she is aware of her capabilities. She was brought up to serve, and she used all her natural intelligence and abilities to perform what she has seen as her function in life. Anne has to learn for herself in these preretirement years to look at and cater to her own needs as well as the needs of others. She had started this process of change when her family came back home and upset her new equilibrium. She needed to find a balance between the Anne she had always been, and the Anne who began to emerge two years ago when she and Jerry first experienced freedom from outside responsibilities. She began to reconcile the two parts of herself by agreeing to let an outsider evaluate her mother and then agreeing to have her mother live in an outside facility. She began as well by pulling back from some of the caretaking duties she was performing for her children. She and Jerry are now discussing setting financial limits on the help they are giving, so they can continue to go ahead with their retirement plans.

Anne is experiencing what many women have told us they experienced at this time of life, the yearning for more time and space to be themselves. It is an unfamiliar feeling for many women, particularly those who were products of a childhood in the 1940's and 1950's. The recognition of this need for self-fulfillment is probably, in part, a result of the general change in the attitudes of society toward women. Some of the women told us it came to them more directly from living side by side with younger women at work, from friendships with younger women, or in many cases from their daughters. It is a feeling that had been dormant or consciously put aside, while the tasks of raising a family or earning a living were the important parts of life. When retirement approached and these tasks had been success-fully completed, many of the women allowed these unusual thoughts of "What do I want?" to rise to the surface. Caretaking responsibilities for a child or parent can be a blow to dreams that have begun to take form. It is up to you to prevent the dreams from slipping away. Put them off if you must, but prepare to modify your responsibilities as well as your dreams.

X

Suddenly Single

When you come to the end of your rope tie a knot and hang on.

FRANKLIN D. ROOSEVELT (1882–1945)

The subject of death is still taboo in our culture, yet everyone who has lived to the age of forty has experienced the death of someone they knew. No woman likes to think about or plan for the death of the people she loves and certainly not for the death of her husband, but the average age of widowhood is fifty-six, and sixty-eight percent of all women are widowed by the age of seventy-five. If women who are planning retirement do not give thought to what statistically may be inevitable, they will not be adequately prepared for their future. We are not suggesting planning in the traditional sense, as there are far too many factors that are unpredictable, including the obvious one that a woman may die first, but becoming a widow is a universal as well as a personal transition, and it may be helpful to view it as such.

Bereavement is something for which no one is ever adequately prepared. It's true that living for a year or more with a terminally ill spouse may speed the mourning process. It's true that having a spouse ten or more years your senior may cause you to contemplate the possibility of widowhood. It's true that as you age, your seeming invulnerability, your own sense of your own immortality and the immortality of your loved ones becomes a thing of the past and you become far more connected with the fragility of life. All of this, however, never prepares you for the reality of loss. No woman can truly prepare for the death of her husband, but most of the widows we spoke with told us there were feelings and experiences they could share with others that would be helpful. Most of them wanted women to know that, although this was the single most stressful event of their whole life, they did survive. They did find solace, and went on with their lives and continued to enjoy their retirement.

How is that possible? Being a widow involves tremendous courage. It requires the mustering of all your coping skills to succeed in the overwhelming task of being a woman alone. Widowhood may be the ultimate challenge in your life, a challenge that tests the limits of your resources and capabilities. The death of a husband destroys thoughts of your immortality, and no longer lets you deny the inevitable. You have known for a long time that your parents are going to die, and you have lived with that fact. But life with your husband, for better or worse, is supposed to go on forever.

What follows is a broad outline of the inevitable steps each widow goes through, to get from where she is when her husband dies to where she must go in her life if she is to make a positive transition. There are many excellent books on the many facets of bereavement and grieving (see Appendix). It will be in your interest to refer to these if you need further details. The steps we have outlined on grieving have their own timetable, for each widow's circumstances are different.

There are three common stages of grief: *shock* and *numbness*, *disorganization*, and *reorganization*. These steps, at whatever pace and whatever time, will occur. They are part of the process of healing.

Recovery from your husband's death is possible. We cannot deny the possibility; we have seen too many women recover from the devastating blow. You will never forget your husband, but the intensity of your loss will recede. By having borne your pain and grief to this moment, so that you are able to read these pages, you have lived through some aspect of your bereavement and survived.

The women you will meet on the following pages are not the only women we spoke with who went through their grief and emerged from it, but we believe they most clearly illustrate the stages and the decision-making necessary for survival. Many used the assessment questionnaires from the previous chapters to help them view their lives, and each came away with new insights and fresh ideas for her future. We hope you will be able to do the same.

Muriel and Glenn had finally completely retired and relocated. They had spent seven years semi-retired and semi-relocated. Muriel was a social worker and Glenn an attorney. Both had managed to work on a part-time basis so they could remain in their home in Cleveland from April to October and spend November through March in a retirement community in New Mexico. They were active and interesting people and were able to be involved in both communities.

Glenn, however, had begun to feel the stress of two homes, two lives, and the accommodations necessary for both. After much discussion the couple agreed it was time to retire permanently. They sold their home in Cleveland and moved into the small house they owned in New Mexico. They were both content at the beginning, but after a year they decided they needed more space, and they purchased a larger, grander home with a studio for Muriel, for as part of her retirement she was pursuing an earlier love—painting. Several weeks before they were to move into their new home, Glenn had a heart attack. Fortunately, it was a mild one, and after a week in the hospital the doctors reassured them that with a change of diet and some exercise, Glenn could outlive them all. So they went back to the work of being retired. Life went along smoothly. It was restful, playful, a reward for their lifetime of work. Muriel continued to be active in her community and engrossed in her art. She sometimes felt she would like to spend more time painting, but Glenn loved to travel and she was willing to compromise her time to be with him. Their retirement continued along for four years until Glenn had another heart attack. He died on the way to the hospital.

When Muriel realized that Glenn had died she was in shock. She could not believe this had happened to her and for the first weeks she walked around unable to comprehend this episode in her life. She called Glenn's name as if he were in the other room and when she realized he was not, she cried inconsolably wih deep sorrow of a kind she had never known before. This intense pain lasted for what seemed an eternity. However, with an inner strength she didn't know she had, Muriel went about doing what was necessary. She let friends and family into her home, called her lawyer who told her to obtain death certificates as well as other information, and went to her bank to transact necessary, immediate business.

For the next few months Muriel showed unusual strength, and friends and neighbors in her community marveled at her ability to carry on. Muriel was going about her business in a mechanical way, still receiving the support given to a woman who has recently been widowed. Friends were calling her daily and her family rallied round. It was as if Muriel was being insulated from the reality of Glenn's death. Not until it came time for her family and friends to go back to their own lives was Muriel left to confront the pain of her loss.

Although Muriel was constantly aware that her life was not the same, she had an experience several months after Glenn died that gave her an emotional jolt. It occurred in a strange way. One evening after cooking one of her first suppers for herself she realized Glenn was not there to take out the garbage. This had been his job for thirty-four years and that night when Muriel performed this chore, she became disorganized, with feelings of desolation, despair, futility, and injustice. She also started to experience guilt that she hadn't taken better care of Glenn in the last years of his life. She even felt she may have caused his death. She felt guilty, angry, hurt, deserted, and overwhelmed. The intensity of these feelings was greater than anything she had ever felt, and the feelings wouldn't go away. When she finished with one of these feelings, another would come to take its place. The night seemed endless. When morning came, she became angry at Glenn for having abandoned her. She didn't want to be completely in charge of the affairs of her life. Glenn and she had shared all their decisions. They had bought their home together and it wasn't fair that now she had to live in it alone. If only she had known Glenn would die, maybe they never would have moved from Ohio. They shouldn't have considered moving from their smaller home. That home was fine. How could she have been so selfish to have wanted everything. Why hadn't Glenn told her she was selfish? Her selfishness probably killed him. Now she was stuck with a big house she didn't need or want. She would sell it immediately! Take the monetary loss and get away to some place where she would feel better. But she couldn't think of that place. She didn't want to go back to Ohio. She wanted to be alone and cry and stay in the house with her memories of Glenn. She needed this time to keep him close to her. She missed his conversation, his touch, and his companionship. The loneliness was especially intense when she was out with other people. If she saw a husband and wife laugh together, she would miss Glenn so badly she would think she shouldn't leave her house again. But the next day she would force herself to get up, get her coffee, do her exercises, and plan a day. Not that she wanted to, but she knew she had to.

It was at this point that Muriel met a woman in the supermarket who had become a widow several years before. They chatted and the woman mentioned to Muriel that she had been helped tremendously by a bereavement group that met at a local church. Muriel was not interested. Nobody could understand the loss she felt. What good would it do to listen to a lot of other women talking about themselves? It would just depress her more. No, she would get through this by herself. But the days and nights of despair did not go away as fast as Muriel thought they should. She couldn't get out of her grief. Glenn was not around to advise and comfort her; her children loved her but they had their own lives. She was on her own. What were her alternatives? She could wait this out, but she was doing that and tiring of the pain. She remembered the woman in the supermarket who looked pleased to be shopping for herself. Maybe she should consider giving the bereavement group a try. With great trepidation, Muriel called the church to find out when the group met, and that same week she went to her first meeting. She found it wasn't terrible to listen to other women. It was helpful. There were women in the group at different stages of their widowhood and grieving, and Muriel learned from them all. She discovered that what she was living through had happened to all of them in one way or another. Although she could not feel it emotionally, she learned from listening that the intensity of her pain was going to pass. At least she had that promise to hold on to. There would be a different kind of emotional work to do later, but she was not ready for that yet. She began to feel she might have a future. Muriel's grief continued even after she went to the bereavement group, and during the first year it reached such depths of despair she felt there would never be an end to the pain. But one day she discovered that a half-hour had gone by and she had not thought of Glenn. She thought she might be making progress. And she was. The normal grieving process was taking its course.

Although there was no clearly-marked demarcation, Muriel was starting the next phase of grieving: reorganization. She could see through the haze and she began to make plans for herself. Some of these plans were short-term, others had longer-term goals and dreams. The first thing Muriel decided was that she wanted to be retired and stay in New Mexico, at least for now. Glenn's death did not cancel that. She was not sure she wanted to be retired in the same way she had planned when Glenn was alive, but she wasn't sure in what way she might want it to be different. She decided to wait and see what came along before she made any major changes. The second decision Muriel made was to stay in the larger home she and Glenn had bought together. It involved their last planning and Muriel felt close to Glenn in the house, although not bound to him. She had no reason to give him up altogether. And how about continuing with her painting? Glenn's death had not made her love painting less; in fact, she could find time to take more art courses and immerse herself in her art. This had not seemed possible when Glenn was alive. Although Glenn had been supportive, art was not a particular interest of his. Muriel had sometimes felt she had to limit the time she worked on a painting so as to be with Glenn. Now she could go at her own pace and stay at her work as long as she liked. A subtle change, but an important one. Sometimes when she had thoughts about the difference between her time alone and her time with Glenn she felt disloyal to him, but then she remembered what she learned in the bereavement group. Her own well-being was most important now. So rather than dwell on thoughts of disloyalty, she dismissed them. It took Muriel at least two years to reach the point where she felt less confused, guilty, angry, and helpless, and more able to plan for her life as a single woman in retirement. She realized she was in transition to a future that held new possibilities. She began to see herself as a woman in charge of her life.

When we spoke with Muriel three years after she was widowed, she found it helpful to review those last three years. She felt she had made major inroads on building a new life for herself. She was still enjoying her home. She was doing more painting and had joined a group of local artists who met to discuss their work. She felt free now to pursue her interests. Looking back on her transition—for now she saw it as such—she realized she had gone through the phases of grieving. As a widow she was not exactly as she had been before. She realized that in the last year she was becoming increasingly reluctant to think of herself as a widow; more often she thought of herself as a single woman. What a tremendous change for her! When she looked back she knew she felt much less anger, guilt, and despair. She knew she was on the other side of the abyss.

Muriel had used all her emotional strengths to come to the place she had reached. She used our questionnaires for self-assessment and realized her life was strongly influenced by the woman's movement. She had lived a good deal of it feeling she should put Glenn's needs as well as other people's needs before her own, but she believed her successful career as a social worker was partly responsible for this feeling. She felt she had managed most of the time to feel independent and autonomous. She realized that when she retired from her work she felt she did not have as much power or control over her life as she did when she was employed. She felt this in an even stronger way when she was widowed. She evaluated these feelings of powerlessness, which still lingered. Was she actually as dependent, powerless, and helpless as she thought?

She remembered that while her children were growing up the women's movement moved into her life in a powerful and compelling manner, telling her she was entitled. She remembered the point at which she began to rethink her role as a wife and mother. With three children, a home in the suburbs, a dog and a cat who depended on her, Muriel—the clever, responsive wife of a young lawyer, a friend and confidant to many woman friends, feeling fulfilled and cared for—wondered how she might find something just for herself. Indeed, she believed she should have a life outside the home, a life that was as important as her husband's.

As a widow, Muriel found it difficult to remember when she had power and direction. She began to focus her thinking and realized that, although she had felt independent and emancipated at one time, she had been brought up to believe she would always belong to somebody. She realized that in addition to her altered life circumstances and her changed activities, she had lost part of her identity when Glenn died. She was no longer Glenn's wife and she needed to find a new identity. She had thought she would be a "we" all her life. Being widowed changed all that. She realized she needed to think of herself as an "I" rather than a "we," and she needed to feel strength in the "I."

She remembered what she had observed over the years about her daughters' lives. She had always known her daughters' lives were different from hers, strongly influenced by the women's movement. But when they spent time with her after Glenn's death, she noted again that they lived as if there were few limits to what their lives could be. Muriel was surprised to rediscover the ease with which her daughters considered taking risks, making changes, understanding alternatives. They had learned their lessons from their mother well! Muriel was now beginning to realize that as a widow she had options and alternatives, just as her daughters did. Perhaps in some ways she had even more. She had choices concerning many aspects of her life: where she might live, what she might do with her time, and what adventures she could have. For a brief moment she even considered joining the Peace Corps. She was not stuck! When Muriel reached that point in her grieving, she was ready to understand that her alternatives as a widow gave her power in her life. She realized she was not a helpless victim, as she sometimes felt. She had the power to make the decision to stay in New Mexico and keep the house she and Glenn had bought together. When she actually made these decisions—the first big decisions she had made alone since Glenn's death—they seemed momentous. She knew the uneasy feeling of being a woman alone and marveled at how strange it felt to be doing what she wanted, rather than considering what others would want her to do. She began to feel some control over her life. The acknowledgment that she had choices and options slowly seeped into other areas of her life. Although she was a widow, she was the same self-directing person she had always been. As a woman alone, she was now in charge of many aspects of her life and did not need permission, protection, or approval from anybody.

Muriel also examined the ways she had handled other transitions in her life. When faced with major decisions she had usually taken advice from her mother and, after she was married, from her husband. When she realized she was still looking for their input, she started thinking of how and when she had managed without them. She realized there were times when she had made decisions that seemed clear to her after examining the alternatives. One of the biggest transitions Muriel remembered was when she decided to get her degree in social work. Thinking back on her decision, she realized the choice was clear to her at the time, although she had consulted Glenn and her mother. She had felt strongly motivated to have a life outside of the home. She had not thought of it as a momentous decision, but as she looked back, she knew it had involved courage and commitment. She did the same thing when she made her decision to take a full-time job. Muriel knew that these early decisions, although made with help, were her own. They had helped her at the time to recognize herself as an independent and self-directing woman. She needed to rediscover these inherent strengths and the previous resourcefulness, so she could use these qualities to cope with the biggest transition of her life, becoming a widow.

Muriel had never realized the extent to which Glenn had protected her. Sometimes it was simply the knowledge of his presence that made her feel looked after. When she realized how angry she felt that he was no longer around to do this for her, she was able to muster more of her strength toward living and felt better able to give up trying to make her life what it had been before.

Muriel knew her women friends were important to her; she had always depended on her relationships with women, from the giggling days of junior high school to the consciousness-raising group she had joined in 1969. She had not realized the extent to which she had been able to make friends when she wanted, and she had not been aware of how much time she had spent with women friends throughout her marriage, particularly when she was at home with her children full-time. She was still involved with her best friend from her childhood. Margery had been part of her life for many years, with letters and phone calls when they could not meet. Margery was one of the first people who responded and supported her in the early days of her grief. Muriel knew she could count on her for emotional support and love, although she lived many miles away. She was the kind of friend who intuitively knew what Muriel needed. Muriel realized how much she had utilized this support of friends, new as well as old, during the three years of her widowhood. She had joined a bereavement group in response to a chance meeting but also because she instinctively knew she needed people.

When Muriel used the assessment questionnaire "for couples only," which you'll find in Chapter VI, she determined that many of the intricacies of her daily life with Glenn had been clouded over by time. She realized she tended to glorify and idealize their life together. She forgot the usual quarrels, arguments, and disagreements that are part of any marriage. But she knew from her bereavement group that this is what widows experience, so she was not surprised. In fact, she was faintly amused that it had happened to her too. She had always thought of herself as being realistic.

Muriel wonders if her life as a widow in retirement is different because she and Glenn had decided to relocate. From her vantage point as a widow of three years, Muriel told us she was glad she had been familiar with her new community when Glenn died. She said she could imagine greater desolation only if she'd been a stranger in a strange environment at the time of Glenn's death. She wanted women to know the importance of feeling comfortable and secure in the environment where they are relocating, for they may spend some time in it alone, often unexpectedly.

Women need to feel comfortable in their retirement situation, whether or not it includes relocation. Women must plan for the eventuality of being alone, and should feel comfortable, safe, and able to negotiate their lives, just in case.

Claire was married to Tom for twenty-eight years, most of them spent as the wife of an alcoholic. She did not know Tom was an alcoholic when she married him—he was just fun to be with, and he seemed to have a lot more fun when he was drinking. A year into their marriage Tom lost his job because of an argument with his boss. He quickly found another job but lost that one too. He got another job, but then began a pattern of staying out late and coming home drunk. Claire began to wonder if there was something wrong with Tom, but he was able to reassure her that everything was all right. He told her she worried too much, he was just having a series of bad breaks and needed time to talk with his friends after work.

When Tom worked he made enough money to support the family, which now included a daughter. Claire wanted Tom to be home more and pleaded with him, but his stop at the bar on the way home for "just a few beers" became the pattern. He often did not make it home for dinner sober. When he did come home, he usually had supper and then fell asleep on the couch. Claire was unhappy, but she was involved with bringing up her daughter, and her life with Tom really wasn't so bad. They still had good times together, there were many times when he was not drinking, and he did say he would stop. Besides, she loved Tom and she knew if he would stop drinking, everything would be fine. He was a good father and he loved their daughter. Every once in a while when Tom's drinking exasperated her Claire thought of leaving him, but these thoughts did not last very long. She knew she would have difficulty supporting herself and her daughter alone, and she knew she did not have the right to deprive Tom of his family. When she felt completely frustrated in her plight she tried to get help for Tom. She arranged appointments with their family doctor and the local priest, and she had even asked Tom's brother to speak with him. But Tom did not keep the appointments, and when he did speak with his brother, he told him he was turning over a new leaf and would cut down his drinking and spend more time at home.

Claire never realized she might be the one who needed help. Then she read an article in the newspaper about alcoholism and wondered if Tom was an alcoholic. The symptoms matched, but if it were so, why didn't she know this for so many years? The article explained alcoholism as a treatable disease and explained that Alcoholics Anonymous had groups for wives and families of alcoholics. With much trepidation she called AA and found out how she might attend an ALANON meeting. Could she really be the wife of an alcoholic? She thought she would need only one meeting to see what it was all about, but after the first meeting she realized she might need another one to understand a little more about her problem. This group ultimately changed her life. Claire realized she was the one who needed to change, in order for her life to change. As she listened and learned she began to understand that she had protected Tom for many years and in doing so had unknowingly enabled his alcoholism.

As their life went on, Tom's employment became sporadic. Claire realized that in order to have economic stability in their lives she needed to get a job. Her daughter would be starting junior high school, and Claire would be able to work from nine to five without feeling guilty about being away from home. She had worked briefly as a clerical worker before she was married. When she saw an ad in the local paper for a similar job at an insurance company she applied and joined the work force. Claire was an excellent worker and liked her job. At times she felt bored, but she knew she needed to work to support the family. After ten years she was offered the job of supervisor of her department and she accepted the position. After nineteen years with the insurance company, in a job which she now considered a dead end, she started to feel the need for a rest and change. She planned to retire after the completion of her twentieth year when she would be eligible for her pension.

Tom's alcoholism had advanced to where he was unable to hold a steady job, had many physical problems, and was dependent on Claire's money, care, and good will. Claire had, however, made her decision to retire and to stay with him. She knew she was attached to Tom in many ways. She had worked around Tom's disease for all of their marriage and knew she could continue to do so in her retirement. She still planned for the day when he would stop drinking, but thanks to ALANON she knew she needed to care for her own needs first. She wished Tom and she had been able to save more money for their retirement, but her pension and profit-sharing would see them through until their Social Security cut in. If they both took early Social Security they could manage pretty well.

Claire had a good deal of ambivalence about her retirement, because it meant that she would need to cope more often and directly with Tom's drinking. But she knew she was not going to let his alcoholism stand in the way of her retirement. She planned to work around Tom by spending time with friends from work who were also retiring, perhaps vacationing with them, and spending time with her daughter, son-in-law, and grandchild. Claire's first two years of retirement were full of conflict. She was able to travel with her friends, but she worried about Tom when she was away. She volunteered at the local hospital two days a week because she knew she needed to be away from home during the day. She wondered what she wanted to do with the rest of her life, and how Tom could fit into it. One day when Claire came home from her work at the hospital she discovered Tom lying on the floor, bleeding from his head. She dialed 911, the ambulance came, but Tom died on the way to the hospital. Claire was sixty-one years old.

Claire moved unexpectedly into widowhood, a word she hated to hear in association with herself. She began her time of grieving, but, unlike Muriel, she felt conflicted about what she was feeling. Although devastated by her loss, she felt relief and freedom that she was no longer burdened by Tom. But when she felt relieved, she felt guilty. The guilt was preying on her, depressing her so much that she often felt she could not get out of bed in the morning. These emotions resulted in many physical symptoms. She could not taste her food, lost her appetite, and roamed around the house at night unable to sleep for more than a few hours. She became forgetful about important matters and was generally irritable. She was at a loss to know what to do. She went to her doctor, who prescribed an antidepressant. This helped her feel a bit better, but she felt foggy and less functional. Many women find the pain of widowhood so unbearable that they start to take medication, but most of them find that although the medication takes away the immediate pain, mourning cannot be relieved by medication. Claire had that experience, and after several weeks she opted for the pain rather than the mental fog. She felt she had so much thinking to do that she wanted to do it with as clear a head as possible, even though the pain was at times unbearable. Her physical and emotional symptoms continued for many months and her depression appeared to be more than the usual. At one point, it became so severe her doctor suggested she talk to a psychotherapist. He referred her for short-term crisis-intervention therapy. The treatment focused on Claire's anger. She learned that in order to continue to grieve, she had to acknowledge her anger at herself for having stayed with Tom, and her anger at Tom for having deprived her of the life she wanted. Although she had difficulty acknowledging the full extent of her anger toward Tom when he was alive, his death made it even more difficult. If Claire was to mourn successfully, she could not allow misplaced loyalty to Tom to stand in the way of experiencing her anger. In the quiet of her time alone, Claire needed to acknowledge that it was all right to feel angry and relieved of the burden of her marriage. The feeling of relief, however, would not negate her feelings of being lonely and alone.

Claire began to understand that there were no correct feelings to have about Tom's death, and that she was not being disloyal to him by feeling relieved by his death. She learned that most people have trouble expressing feelings of relief when someone they love dies, for it seems like such an unacceptable, inappropriate reaction. Claire realized that her situation was similar to those widows whose husbands have had long illnesses and who, although they are bereaved, also feel relieved. Claire came to understand that each widow grieves in her own way and with her own feelings, and that there is anger in almost every widow's grief; only the kind and quality are different. There can be no right way to grieve, because only the individual widow knows exactly what she misses. Claire needed to accept this so she could move into the next stage of her bereavement.

As Claire began to understand her grieving process, she was able to minimize her time spent in self-hatred, and was able to gain back some self-esteem. She found it easier to get out of bed in the morning and had some vague inklings that she might have some things to look forward to. This enabled her to plan for her immediate future. Every once in a while, she began to feel that retirement as a widow could be more of an opportunity than a liability. She was justifiably frightened about how she would cope with her future as a woman alone, but she realized that in many ways she had really been alone throughout her marriage. She had not been conscious of just how alone she was because she was so frequently preoccupied with Tom and his problems. She became aware of how preoccupied she had been with him as she attempted to define the way she missed him. What she seemed to miss was the knowledge of Tom's presence. She began to realize she had organized much of her time around Tom because she had always had to think of his whereabouts and how he might be needing her. Now Claire felt the loss of this intangible structure that Tom's presence had provided.

Another unexpected realization came to Claire when she experienced difficulty making plans to be away from home. She found that she had trouble planning even a day's outing without feeling uncomfortable. When Tom was alive she'd traveled and had all sorts of adventures. Why had Tom's death made this so different? As Claire spoke with her therapist she began to realize that, like many women of her generation, she felt she needed a man in her life to make her feel whole. It didn't matter if the man was an alcoholic and unavailable; it just mattered that he was there. So even though Claire had not counted on Tom's accompanying her on her travels, the fact that he was alive gave her a feeling of belonging, strength, and well-being. Tom's presence in her life gave Claire permission and the credibility to be independent. She had never realized that Tom had protected her just by being alive.

Although Tom had never limited Claire's comings and goings on a daily basis, she was surprised to discover how much his presence had structured her life. Even though she had not necessarily listened to him, he was no longer there with input as to what to do and where to go. There was no one else to consider as she went about the routines of living. This felt like a tremendous amount of freedom, at first unwanted, but then interesting.

As Claire began the third stage of her bereavement—reorganization—she realized the independence she now had. The problem was how to become more comfortable with it. What did she want to do with the next months of her life, the next six months, the next year? It was helpful to break it down this way, for it made the future seem less formidable. Claire began to realize that she finally had the strength to think about the various aspects of her retirement. At about this time she met and spoke with us.

She had many questions about her future. Perhaps she should return to work. She realized she had gone back to work twenty years before not because she wanted a career but because she needed to earn a living. In many ways her life had been determined by economic need, but the situation was different now, since she did not have to work in order to do the things she planned. She had planned for the economics of her retirement, and with Tom's life insurance and his Social Security income she had a bit extra each month. This, strangely enough, put even more of a burden on Claire, as her future had more choices than she wanted or needed.

Claire evaluated her twenty years at the insurance company. She had started as a clerical worker, had been offered the position of supervisor, and took the opportunity. She realized she had some ambition, although she never acknowledged it in quite those words. She also had some skills and expertise. Claire had not identified herself by the work she did outside the home, since throughout her life her primary identity had been that of a wife and mother. As with other women of the 1950's, Claire did not see herself as having many identities and playing many roles. She needed to begin to conceptualize herself in this way and give herself credit for all the successes she had had in her life. Claire needed to acknowledge that she had been a successful wife, a good mother, a devoted daughter, a good sister, an interested friend, and a hell of a good Scrabble player. She had been a trustworthy, competent, and loyal employee, and she had been a very successful supervisor.

When she thought about what her work had meant to her, she realized that she had enjoyed having a place to go every day and had liked the camaraderie with her co-workers. She had never truly enjoyed the work itself, although she had enjoyed her supervisory work because she liked being in charge. Now that she was in retirement, why not try to find work she really would enjoy?

On the advice of others, she had made as few changes as possible in the year after she was widowed, but now Claire needed to explore all of life's opportunities. She felt our assessment questionnaires were helpful for this. She first needed to understand the way in which she had made other important decisions in her life. When Claire reviewed how she had handled the transitions in her life, she saw that she had either followed the path that was expected of her, or had done what everybody else did. She tended to minimize her efforts in her own behalf. When she evaluated further, she realized she had been the one who managed the family finances, paid the bills, called the plumber, and arranged for the contractor. She had been the one who had asked the contractor to come back when he had installed the storm windows incorrectly. She had been the one who held up payment, even though he threatened to sue. She put this in a new context and saw she had been assertive and self-directing when she had to be. She had gone to work when she needed to and had raised a daughter who had functioned well in her adult life, despite her father's alcoholism. She had never before put all of these facets of her life together. Just because she had been the wife of an alcoholic did not mean her life was a failure. As she became aware of these previously unrecognized aspects of herself, it became easier for her to examine her alternatives as a widow.

Claire needed to find resources in herself in a way she had not done before. Could she really make her retirement a time of personal growth? Her life needed a new emphasis and new definition and she was going to find it for herself. She decided to go to the library to find a list of jobs or careers, as though she were a young woman just starting working life. She could always weed out the impossible ones, but why not give herself all of the options? This was retirement, wasn't it? A time of leisure and opportunity?

As Claire went through all of the options available she remembered, and then researched, an early interest. She had at one time thought she might be interested in working as a dietician or nutritionist. She liked to plan meals and was always conscious of eating well. She had a large library of cookbooks and other books related to food and food preparation. Both occupations—nutritionist and dietician—required a college degree. Could she go to college? She decided to take the risk for her future.

As Claire pursued her plans she realized she was on the other side of her bereavement. She is discovering that being a woman alone has its up side. She is starting to restructure and redefine her life, slowly but surely. After all, she has many years ahead of her.

Toby is sixty-four years old. She had been a homemaker for all of her married life. She enjoyed being a wife to her husband Neil and a mother to her children, and Neil liked having Toby stay home to care for him. She has two married sons, both of whom lived at home until they were married. Toby and Neil had a good marriage.

Toby grew up in Oklahoma during the Depression, and she never forgot her family's poverty and concomitant despair. She remembered her mother serving the family watery potato soup night after night with apologies and sadness. These memories stayed with Toby, and she was grateful for the security she had, a security that was enhanced by her staying home and feeling cared for by Neil. Although he knew it was a bit old-fashioned, Neil loved feeling he was taking care of Toby. When many of her friends went back to school or to work when their children went to school, Toby was content to make a home for her family. She enjoyed her life, and the years passed with a good deal of satisfaction.

Shortly after both of her sons entered high school, Neil's parents became ill within months of each other. Toby's life at home made it possible for her to become the caretaker for Neil's parents. Although Neil's brother and his wife helped out financially, Toby was the major caretaker. She nursed Neil's father through a terminal illness and his mother through a slow decline before her death. Her own father died during these years and in his last years she was involved in helping her mother care for him. After he died, Toby visited her mother several times each week and arranged for a home health-care worker to be made available on a daily basis. Being a caretaker had taken a good deal of her time, but she was glad she had the patience and fortitude to do it well.

When her children grew up she continued to be involved in their lives. She was delighted when the weekly family get-togethers expanded to include grandchildren. Toby was pleased she never had to augment the family income, for she enjoyed her life. She was content to spend her days visiting her family and friends, taking care of her home, and watching soap operas. Toby did some volunteer work at her church, filling in when the secretary was unavailable, but she never wanted to commit herself to anything permanent. She really enjoyed keeping house.

Neil had worked for an automobile company for thirty-two years and the couple looked forward to his retirement. They planned to stay in their home although many of their friends had relocated. Toby did not want to leave her children and, besides, she still had to care for her mother. They wanted to travel, and they both had fun detailing their plans for a trip to Hawaii. They looked forward to being home together in their retirement and enjoying their lives as an older couple surrounded by their children and grandchildren.

When Neil first retired they had a wonderful time. Toby had to get used to his being home, telling her how to organize her kitchen, and trying to reorder her priorities. But they had a good relationship and she was able to steer him to other activities. They shopped together, visited friends together, planned together, and then took their long-dreamed-of trip to Hawaii. It was a wonderful trip and they enjoyed each other in the way they knew they would. Retirement was fun for both of them. They had started to consider relocation when one of their children took a job in the state of Washington. These plans were in the infant stage when Neil had a heart attack and died in his sleep. He was sixty-seven years old and had been retired for five years. Toby was sixty-five.

Toby was completely unprepared for what was to follow. She was not only in shock, she was too numb to do anything. Her children rushed to her aid and immediately took over. Toby did not have to worry about a thing. They made the funeral arrangements, went to the safety deposit box, called the lawyer, got the death certificates, and wept together. All of their friends flew in for the funeral, and Toby felt protected and cared for. Everybody promised to be in touch, and indeed they were as good as their word, for many months. But then Toby noticed she was starting to be alone a good deal of the time. Mornings turned into afternoons and nobody had called her. She picked up the phone a few times to see if it was still working. On the days she did not see her mother she was often alone. Neil's friends from work did not call, and their wives were not in touch either. Toby's friends from church, many of them widows themselves, rallied round, called and visited, but Toby felt it was not enough. Even though she had her children and grandchildren in her life and was continuing to care for her mother, Toby was unprepared for the depth of the feeling of being alone. Even more devastating was the unfamiliar feeling of being incomplete. When Neil died she lost not only her best friend, she lost the person who gave her a reason for being. The majority of her activities, indeed her life, both in and out of the home had been supported by Neil's participation, acknowledgment, acceptance, and interest. Without his support, her activities did not seem to matter. Feeling this, Toby began to think often of her own death, more then ever before. She began to feel very old and tired. Sometimes she wished she could join Neil, but these thoughts did not last very long. Primarily, Toby felt a tremendous amount of fear. She had never thought of what it might be like to be widowed and living alone. She had never planned for a life without Neil, and she was unprepared for the way she felt. She was at odds with the feeling that one day she was Neil's wife, needed and important, and the next day she was unnecessary and obsolete. There were other things troubling her, and she had many unaccountable unpleasant feelings. She noticed when she spent time with the couples she and Neil had always enjoyed she had the awful feeling they all missed Neil as much as she did. He had always been the life of the party. She didn't like to think of this, but it seemed that all these years they had liked him more than they did her. Another uncomfortable feeling concerned her children. Although she loved them very much and valued their input and presence, she began to feel stressed when they treated her as though she were inept. They seemed to have taken over Neil's role of caring for her and this made her feel inadequate. Toby felt strongly that she did not want her children to take care of her, but she didn't want to alienate them because she knew how much she needed them. Her children knew that the worst times during the first two years were around her birthday and her wedding anniversary, for they awakened painful emotions. These days were easier when she spent them with her children and grandchildren. On Neil's birthday, the second year after he died, when her children were going to be out of town, she arranged to spend the day with a friend. She felt good that she had arranged a plan for herself rather than sitting at home and crying.

We met with Toby shortly after this time. She had lost a part of her identity and needed to determine who she was and what she wanted to do with the rest of her life. She knew she had been a good, devoted, loving wife. She had taken good care of her husband, his parents, and her parents. She was a loving mother and grandmother. She had taken good care of her home. She was also a good loyal friend. How could she discover what was important to her? She had opinions and thoughts and she needed to give them credence and importance. Toby, like Muriel, was so used to being a "we" that she had never given much thought to the "I" in herself.

We suggested to Toby that she look over the assessment program we used in Chapter I. It was a somewhat neutral way to start and would prompt her to think. Toby determined that she had not been affected by the women's movement. She knew she had followed the traditional role set by her mother, and this had been fine for her. Toby was surprised, however, to discover that her friendships with women separate from her marriage were an indication of some independence. This was certainly a new way of looking at friendships in her life, and a small first step in experiencing herself in a different light.

As she began to listen to her inner voice, she realized how proud she was of one of her daughters-in-law who had started college when her second child began kindergarten. When she thought of her daughters-in-law, she noted that she kept going back to the word *options*. The young women of today had "so many options." Toby still did not know what she wanted to do but she was bolstered by the knowledge of so many choices, so many different opportunities. Did she perhaps have some as well? This was comforting for her.

The other question that interested Toby was about living her life differently. She would not have chosen to have lived it differently, but what about her fantasies? She'd always had fleeting ones about being a veterinarian. She had loved animals from the early days of her childhood but she'd never dwelt on this fantasy; it was just a dream. She certainly would have married Neil, but maybe, just maybe, she was starting to feel she might have had a little more say in the marriage. She remembered telling Neil, after he retired, to get out of her kitchen, and this started her thinking of how controlling Neil had been in the way they spent their free time. Perhaps she would have liked things to have been just a little different.

Toby began to evaluate the way she had handled some of the transitions in her life. It became clear to her that she usually followed the path she thought was expected of her. She did not remember making important decisions as if she had choices and options. She had usually given her decisions over to various authorities, first her mother and then her husband. She doesn't remember deciding to get married or have children, it just seemed to happen. The one decision she remembers making herself is that she did not want to go to work. She doesn't have any regrets, but she acknowledges that Neil had had a strong say in any decision affecting herself.

As Toby went along, the question of the way she had dealt with the serious illness of a loved one made her take notice. Becoming a caretaker for Neil's parents and then for her own parents seemed like the right and only thing to do. She never saw caretaking as an option or as anything special. But when put in a new context, Toby realized she had chosen to do it, and indeed she had done it all. She had rearranged her schedule to fit in all the caretaking tasks, continued to run her home so that Neil was not inconvenienced by his parents' illness, contacted the necessary agencies, and arranged personal time for herself. She even remembered with some pleasure telling Neil's brother and his wife that they needed to be involved in his parents' caretaking in some way, and being firm in a request that they spend at least one day every two months with his mother. She also had arranged for Neil's brother to send money as long as he or his wife could not give his parents more caretaking time. Toby remembered arranging for Neil's parents and then her father to go to the hospital. She remembered that she made the funeral arrangements. When Toby looked back on all of this, she realized she was a capable, resourceful take-charge person when she needed to be. She was not in reality the dependent little girl she had always imagined herself to be. Toby had confused wanting to be cared for by Neil, and the dependence that implies, with the actual independent, resourceful manner in which she had lived. As part of the reorganization aspect of her bereavement, Toby started to see her life in a different, more objective manner. All of these revelations were ego-strengthening for her. Each one inched her toward a day when she could put the loss of Neil in a less prominent place in her daily existence.

Toby was intrigued by the concept of independence. Was it possible she was an independent person? She had been a housewife and mother, as well as a caretaker, for many years. She never realized that the style of life she had arranged had given her a tremendous amount of freedom to come and go as she pleased. She had never interpreted this freedom as independence. For the past thirty years, nobody had told her how to spend her time during the day. She realized she never liked being tied down to anybody's schedule. She remembered how difficult it had been when Neil first retired, jeopardizing some of her autonomy in her sphere of influence. She had been much more independent and autonomous than she had ever given herself credit for. To her surprise she found she was a woman who knew how to care for herself. With the realization and acknowledgment of her achievements, she could now learn from them. When she thought how she was dealing with her bereavement she was amazed that she had done so well. She had no idea she could display so much resilience in the face of so much adversity.

She remembered that learning to drive had made her feel independent, although she never liked to drive. Neil had done most of the driving and she had been content with this. Toby still did not feel comfortable driving on highways. A new mall had opened up in the next town and she had never been there, though she wanted to go. On the suggestion of a friend, she decided to call the local driving school for some highway driving lessons. After the first lesson, Toby found highway driving easier than she had anticipated. When she got into the car to go to the shopping mall by herself, she had a feeling of major accomplishment. She felt too childish to tell anybody just how good she felt about herself, but she was very pleased. Toby was discovering many little things in her life that were important. Small accomplishments helped her feel more autonomous and raised her self-esteem.

Toby was starting to realize a goal, which was to feel independent and capable. The first step was to give herself credit, a good deal of credit, for those things she had done and continued to do independently. She no longer allowed herself to view her achievements as routine. She was building her confidence and figuring out what to do with the next years of her retirement.

In this context, she reviewed her financial situation. Toby

realized she was not happy with her children handling her finances. They were paying most of her bills and she was not aware of all her assets. She knew she had enough money to pay the mortgage and all her bills, but she was not at ease. She spoke to a few friends who were widows about the way they managed their finances. She went to the bank that held her home mortgage and the officers of the bank helped her open up new accounts in her own name. Toby was beginning to enjoy the feeling of being an independent person. She was becoming Toby, a woman alone, and not Toby, Neil's wife. It was not an identity she would have chosen, but with it this new Toby could now effectively live and prosper.

Toby was interested in going further with her explorations into self-knowledge and reassessment, because she had an idea she would like to do something productive outside of the home. While we were planning with her, she chanced on an article in the local newspaper. It featured a local couple who had been caring for various small animals who had been injured or abandoned. They were looking for someone to take care of one of their squirrels who had been hurt so badly it could never be returned to the outdoors. Toby remembered a squirrel she had nursed years before when the children were small. She became interested in the plight of this animal. She called the couple, told them she would care for the squirrel, and in so doing found a whole dimension to add to her life. Through the couple, she became involved in a wildlife organization that rehabilitates sick and injured wildlife. Recently she found herself caring for fourteen baby squirrels. She obtained the necessary licensing and has become involved in what she laughingly calls a "squirrel network." She works with the small local zoo and the county park association, which refer animals to her. The district schools invite her for school assemblies. She enjoys sharing her knowledge and concerns with the youngsters. She wishes Neil were here to share her new life with her though at the same time she is aware that it might never have happened if he were.

Emotional resiliency increases with age, and the older we get and the more we own of life's experiences, the more we learn how to cope with pain. Almost all of the women who were widows in retirement told us that through the days, months, and years of grieving they had learned how to go on with their lives. When they looked back they felt they had met a tremendous challenge and overcome overwhelming personal odds. We have spoken about a woman's retirement being a time of life with few guideposts. We discovered, however, as we spoke with many widows, that widowhood in retirement is different. It is the one area of retirement in which women have many role models; indeed, many women used widows who have survived this painful transition as a source of courage and strength to go on with their lives.

When we spoke with widows whose husbands had died just before they retired, right after retirement, or several years into retirement, we were struck by women's resiliency. We were impressed by the ways and means they had drawn upon to find the courage, strength, and alternatives to continue their lives. Many widows told us stories that showed it is possible to have many good, new, even sometimes liberating adventures after a husband's death. Once past the important and frequently arduous work of grieving, many widows discovered in their retirement that their opportunities could be limitless.

DIVORCE IN RETIREMENT

Beatrice was sixty-two years old and had been working for a large insurance company for twenty-three years. During that time she had been promoted to a responsible position as secretary to one of the vice presidents. She loved her job and felt extremely successful. When her boss told her that he was contemplating retirement, she realized that her circumstances would change drastically since the person replacing him was someone she never liked and never wanted to work for. She had been idly contemplating retirement and her changed situation at work caused her to consider it seriously.

Beatrice's job was an important part of her life. She had

been married to Jack for thirty-eight years, but the marriage had been emotionally empty for much of the past thirty years. They had initially stayed together because of their two sons—and then out of inertia and habit. Beatrice had filled her life with her children, her job, and then her grandchildren. She spoke about her possible retirement and plans for their future with Jack, who seemed disinterested and uncomfortable with the topic. Because she was conflicted and confused about retiring, she uncharacteristically pursued the subject. She is now sure that she precipitated a crisis by her persistence, for Jack finally told her that he had been involved with another woman for several years, and wanted a divorce.

They had moved so far from each other emotionally that Beatrice was truly shocked. She had had no idea that Jack had been having an affair or that divorce after all these years of marriage was even a possibility. She was also unprepared for the speed with which the divorce came about. Jack had obviously been giving this a lot of consideration and within a year the divorce was final.

Now, four years later, Beatrice describes herself during that period of time as "an emotional basket case." Her initial reaction when Jack had confronted her was to feel betrayed, bitter and furiously angry. She had continuous fantasies of revenge. She also had a strong feeling of failure. A woman who grew up in the 1940's and 1950's was supposed to know how to hold on to her man. This was part of the reason she had never initiated a divorce—to do so would have been to admit failure as a woman.

Despite the fact that her personal life had undergone such a change, Beatrice still had to cope with the probable change in her work situation. Because her financial settlement from the divorce was not what she would have chosen, Beatrice felt that she had to continue working. Jack had planned well for himself in the divorce.

Her boss retired and she discovered her new situation was not as bad as she had anticipated. Her new boss relies on her expertise, and she likes feeling needed on the job. She is still working at this time. As she looks back, she knows that her work has helped her keep her sanity during the past four years.

This was not, however, an easy task. She is aware that in many ways her situation was similar to being widowed. She needed to learn to cope as a single person after a lifetime of being part of a couple. Her social life after her divorce was different because the relationships with her couple friends had changed. She had to mourn the loss of her marriage much the way that widows mourn the loss of their mate. She went through many of the same steps of grieving. However, she pointed out several areas which are more difficult for the divorced woman. The support network for widows during the first several months is very strong. Family and friends rally 'round to give comfort. The divorced woman does not have similar sympathies from the general community. Beatrice found that her initial rage and subsequent tirades against Jack alienated all but her closest women friends. Beatrice also found that her children were very careful not to take sides in their parents' divorce, and therefore could not help her with her grief. She mourned alone.

Beatrice and Jack continued to live and work in the same community even though their house had been sold and the money divided. Beatrice did not want to be forced to leave her roots. She would hear about Jack and his new life or see him from time to time. She notes that the whole year before the divorce was final she was forced to deal with him either personally or through her lawyer at least once a week. She would not have experienced this if she were widowed.

Beatrice would like to say that she is better off today than when she was married to Jack. She knows that the marriage had not been fulfilling or happy for many years. She knows she had always been an independent woman and does not mind being alone as much as she thought she would. She actually likes being able to plan her time for herself and no one else. At this point in her life she has mourned her loss and is rebuilding her life as a single person.

Divorce is usually considered the province of the youth of our society, but without the taboo of earlier days, many marriages that were made in the 1950's and 1960's are being terminated in the 1980's and 1990's. When divorce occurs in one's later years, it is often as catastrophic for the woman as widowhood. Women who have been divorced in or near retirement usually have lived their lives with the expectation that they would be partnered forever. When faced with divorce, they feel the same sense of loss, depression, grief, and loneliness that newly widowed women feel. The ending of the marriage is mourned in the same way as a death would be. Particularly for those women like Beatrice who did not choose divorce, the enormity of this transition that has been thrust on them must be emotionally integrated. Divorce involves a change in roles, a change in status, and a change of relationships with family including children, friends, and the community. Aside from economic concerns, a divorced woman finds she is a woman alone, and she must cope with all of those changes. Divorced women and women who are widowed struggle alike with the diminished feelings of self-worth and the problems of developing a new identity. It is difficult to cope, but as with widowhood there is another side to the mountain. You can find the way with some hard work.

XI

Happily Ever After

In spite of illness, in spite even of the archenemy
sorrow, one can remain alive long past the usual
date of disintegration if one is unafraid of
change, insatiable in intellectual curiosity,
interested in big things, and happy in small
ways.

EDITH WHARTON (1862–1937)

So Larry and Susan retired! (Remember them from Chapter I?)
She was fifty-seven, he was sixty-two, and they both had left
their jobs and their home in the Midwest and relocated to New
Mexico. Larry is now sixty-nine, Susan is sixty-four, and they
are still healthy, still married, and reasonably content with their
lives in retirement. Neither of them can quite believe they have
been away from work and in New Mexico for seven years. They
both expressed how quickly the time has gone, but when they
look back, they are aware of how differently life has turned out,
and how many changes have occurred since the early days of
retirement seven years ago.

They left their old life with a fantasy in mind: days of
leisure in the sun with endless time to do as they wished. Larry
was a golfer, Susan liked to read and putter around the house,
and they looked forward to spending time together as they had

not been able to do over the previous years, when work and family were priorities. Neither of them was a traveler or sight-seer, and they agreed they would be content to limit their trips to visiting with friends and family. Susan cannot quite believe this, but other than financially, they had planned no more than this.

Within nine months, as the fantasy turned into reality, Susan realized she was unhappy, and she was pretty sure she knew why. She had always been introspective, and when she found herself impatient with Larry so much of the time, she put the pieces together. As we said in Chapter I, both she and Larry had tacitly assumed that in retirement she would resume the role of housewife. Susan found that this was impossible to do with any sense of comfort. She enjoyed being in her new house. She liked fixing it and shopping for new southwestern touches, but she was becoming increasingly annoyed with the daily routine of cooking and cleaning. As we told you, when Susan became aware of this, she explained to Larry her feelings about having "returned to the kitchen" and they negotiated a solution that left her free for lunch and had Larry doing some of the grocery shopping. She felt that this would make a difference in how she was coping with retirement. And it worked well for a while. Over time though, Susan told us, the effectiveness of this plan has eroded. Although Larry still sometimes does the grocery shopping, she still plans the meals and sets the housekeeping routine. The lunch arrangement, however, remains, and their discussions have made Larry aware of her feelings and needs. Although not thoroughly happy about their arrangement, Larry now complains less and expects less from Susan in regard to the household chores. She also has made peace with Larry's attitude and ascribes it to their mutual upbringing. Over the past seven years, as she worked out other aspects of their life together, it ceased to be an area of conflict.

Another factor that contributed to her unhappiness was the tacit assumption, common between husbands and wives who married in the 1950's and 1960's, that when the husband is ready to retire his wife will do so as well. When he retired from work,

Larry had been working at one job or another for over forty years. He had had a successful career in management as an chemical engineer, and had been with the company he retired from for over twenty years. He had a strong feeling of career accomplishment and success and was ready to leave the workplace and have some fun. Susan was anxious to have fun as well, but she neglected to consider how much of her life she had invested in her job. She had never earned the salary Larry did, and she always thought of herself as wife and mother rather than as a career woman. Therefore, she did not recognize and appreciate the feelings of accomplishment she received from her work. She had never evaluated her readiness to leave her job; she had simply followed Larry's lead. She quite clearly states that her choice to retire was the right choice. Still she feels that the early years of her retirement would have been happier if she had known more about herself in relationship to her working life.

We heard this comment often from the working women of Susan's generation. They said they would have remained on their jobs several years longer if it were not for the plans of their husbands. Most of them felt they either owed this time to their husbands, or they wanted to do what would make their husbands happy. Many women never questioned their own retirement decision. They felt that retiring with their husbands was the only thing to do. Some said they were aware at the time, and some realized in retrospect, that they had been premature in leaving the workplace. In many cases this contributed to uneasiness, restlessness, and sometimes resentment in the early days of retirement.

From the beginning of her retirement, Susan knew she would have to replace her work in some way; work was an important part of her life. As we told you, she didn't look for a job or do anything about employment for almost two years. It was only after she began her new life that she began to think of alternatives. She applied for a volunteer job as a docent in the city art museum, took the training course, and has been working two days a week for almost four years. She enjoys the intellectual stimulation and the contact with the public. She also likes having part of her life separate from Larry, for although they have a happy and loving marriage, Susan has always known that she needs some autonomy and independence. What she had never conceptualized was how much of this need was fulfilled by her work.

Susan told us there were many other issues that had to be negotiated in the early retirement years. Larry is a far less social person than she is, and he is content with his golf game and his projects in the house. She has always had friends and had never quite realized that she had conducted many of these relationships without Larry's involvement. She'd been part of a large social network that included her neighbors, the other mothers from her children's school, and her friends from work. In retirement and relocation, Larry's constant presence had limited her time and her ability to form new relationships, particularly any that did not include him. About nine months after their retirement she felt compelled to initiate a discussion with him about her needs. One thing they decided was that Susan would have her own car, providing her with more independence. Susan now belongs to several clubs and takes courses at the local community college, and these give her companionship with other women. Through her work as a docent she met one woman who is now a special friend. This relationship has broadened to include the husbands, who are compatible.

The couple have a routine to their lives which they both need and enjoy. Larry plays golf at least twice a week and for the rest of his time is engaged with his own projects. He is currently remodeling one of the bedrooms so they will have more closet space. Susan is taking a course in Spanish. She and Larry plan to learn bridge, as so many of their friends are bridge players. They do not entertain much except when they have out-of-town visitors, so their social life consists of dinner and movies with various friends. They are thinking about traveling to Italy, something they had never considered before. But, as they both say, "You are never too old to change."

Larry and Susan are not unusual. They typify a majority of

the married couples we interviewed who had been retired over five years. Each had adjustments to make, many very similar to those Susan and Larry made. Many women, like Susan, found volunteer work a substitute for a satisfying job. Even without a good deal of self-awareness the women had an instinct for what they needed. Each of these women wished she had begun sooner, however.

In retirement, women often have to adjust some difficult aspect of their husband's personality. When both were working, they could work around this aspect. In retirement and togetherness, it becomes an unavoidable irritant. Some women told us they never realized how critical their husbands were of everything, or how sloppy they could be on a daily basis. Some adjusted by talking about the problem and working it out to some degree with their husband. Some talked about it to friends, and some just bit their tongue. All of these women told us that somehow they had made peace with it, and felt it to be part of living together with a mate. Most women found themselves still doing the housework, but found it far less burdensome with only two people to pick up after and only two for dinner. Few of the women we spoke with were able to express and understand the dynamics involved as well as Susan did, but each woman knew she had made a successful transition.

THE SECOND CAREER

Anita's life five years into retirement has taken a 180-degree turn. Just a short five years ago, Anita, whom we met in Chapter I, was an elementary school teacher who retired after thirty years. She had never married and had not thought much about retirement until her married friends began to retire and she found herself one of the oldest teachers in her school. This was not a problem in itself, as she did not feel her age, but she no longer had the friendships she was accustomed to as part of her working life. She could not feel a part of the scene in the teachers' lunchroom when everyone was talking about weekend dates, shopping for new outfits, and musical events that were unfamiliar to her. She used to talk about these things with her friends twenty years ago, but they did not interest her much anymore. She had also begun to question her interest in teaching. It did not seem to excite her the way it had previously. She still enjoyed the children and still felt she was doing something important, but she no longer felt challenged. She knew she did not want to stop working because she had never had many leisure-time interests, but she was becoming increasingly uncomfortable when she thought about her life. She was fifty-five years old. Her mother had been eighty-five when she died, and her father eighty-six. The family genes gave her approximately thirty years more, almost as many years as she had been a teacher.

We began to talk with Anita when she was thinking about retirement. She was mildly depressed and concerned about her lack of energy and her early-morning wakefulness. She had spoken with her closest friend, a teacher in another school who had retired and relocated with her husband two years before. Anita was shocked to realize that she was actually beginning to contemplate retirement and perhaps relocation to an area near her friend. As we spoke it became obvious to Anita that this was not at all what she wanted or needed. As much as she loves her friend and as close as they are, her needs and her ambitions are completely different. She did, however, feel a strong pull to leave teaching, and she began to explore ideas. As we mentioned in Chapter I, Anita believed that if she were a young woman starting out today, she would be going to medical school, rather than teachers' college. She had no illusions about going to medical school at this advanced age, but she did decide to explore possible opportunities in the area of sciences. What she discovered was disappointing. It had been more years than she liked to count since she had been in a classroom as a student, and the advances in science were astounding. She would need to begin at an undergraduate level with chemistry, physics, and biology before she could even begin a graduate degree in any of the sciences. She would be involved in school for almost five years if she went full-time, and more if she tried to keep teaching while she went to school. She did not feel prepared to invest time and energy in this way, but she was not discouraged. The search had renewed Anita's energy and given her a new reason to get up each morning. She said the realization that she had options had given her a new outlook on her life. She discovered and pursued a determination to spend the future doing something different.

She had shared some of her thoughts with her niece Harriet, with whom she was close. Harriet was attending law school, partly with Anita's financial help, and was excited and encouraging about the possibility of a new career for her aunt. Anita had been a role model for her, and Harriet had always believed Anita was living below her potential as a school teacher. As a young woman of the 1980's, she had no real sense of how different women's lives were in the 1950's when Anita had gone to college. Anita's friends who had retired were less encouraging, although supportive, of Anita's quest. Anita read all the books on job-searching, went to the library and the colleges, and was thinking about going for aptitude testing and job counseling. The more she researched the more she knew she was finished with teaching school.

Anita and Harriet were planning a trip to Australia. Because of her two months' vacations and her unattached status, Anita had always been an extensive traveler. In the several years when she cared for her parents, and in the past five years since they died, she had not felt much like going anyplace, but she still read the travel magazines and the weekly newspaper travel section with great interest. This trip to Australia was a dream of Harriet's, and Anita for the first time in years felt she had the energy to join her. Harriet was busy with the final exams of her second year at law school and was preparing for her summer internship, so Anita did the planning. She became friendly with the woman who owned the travel agency and admired her expertise. Shortly after they returned from the trip, she went to speak with the travel agent. Anita knew that because of her familiarity with the many places she had been in the United States and Europe, she had a base from which to learn the travel business. She also knew that because of her contacts at school and with the teachers' union she could bring in a certain number of customers. (Teachers and their families travel during vacations.) She also had already discussed with her brother, Harriet's father, the possibility of booking trips for the executives of his consulting firm.

She was in the right place at the right time. The woman at the travel agency had enjoyed their contact. She was willing to train Anita so she could have more time to travel and explore some of the places for which she planned trips. It took more time and negotiating than is stated here, but by January of the following year, Anita had retired from teaching and had begun a new career.

Today, five years later, Anita is sixty-two years old and part owner of a successful travel agency. She enjoys the contact with the public and likes the scheduling and planning entailed in being a travel agent. She also enjoys working with the computer, something she had been fearful of at the beginning. She travels extensively, with an eye for hotels, transportation, and areas that would be convenient for older people who need a less strenuous itinerary. She is now specializing in trips such as those for retired people who want the convenience of a tour but need a more leisurely pace to their days. She looks back and cannot quite believe there was ever a time she did not do this work. She remembers her teaching days fondly, but has never regretted changing her life. Many of her old friends tell her they cannot understand why she wants to work so hard, when she could easily live on her pension and savings. They do not understand why, if she wanted to work, she didn't keep on teaching, where she would have her summers and holidays for herself. Anita cannot easily explain her move to them, but she knows, from the knowledge she has of herself and her needs, that she has chosen to do the right thing.

Anita's story is not as representative as Susan's, but it is not uncommon. Many women we interviewed, particularly women who had never married, or were widowed or divorced, found themselves ready to retire from the job or career they had spent most of their adult years with but were not yet ready to retire from the workplace. Many of these women found the answer in volunteer work since it was the easiest avenue by which to keep busy and involved. Many returned to school either for an education or to begin a new career. Some did extensive research after a few years of leisure and went on to new horizons. It is important for you to remember that the women's movement has helped to make life different for all women—single or married, of whatever age—and the opportunities are there if you have the time and the energy to find them.

REMARRIAGE

Hope, whom we met in Chapter IV, Styles of Friendship, was widowed three years after she and her husband Edgar had retired from their full-time work. She had maintained a small private practice in psychotherapy after her retirement from teaching. In this way she had not completely left the work force, although the time she works is limited to ten hours a week.

When we met Hope, a year after she had been widowed, she had already joined and left a bereavement group, and was beginning to put a life together for herself as a single woman. She liked the routine and structure of her life. She is a private person who does not feel she needs a lot of social interaction. She envisioned quiet and peace for the rest of her life. She visited with her children and grandchildren and her few close friends and so fulfilled her need for companionship. She also has a profession which allowed her to keep working part-time for as long as she wished.

She fulfilled her expectations of retirement for over a year and felt content most of the time. She felt strong in her new role as a single woman, so when she received the literature concerning her forty-fifth college reunion she decided she would attend for the weekend. She sent in her reservation and was surprised, several weeks later, to receive a phone call from the man she had dated during her junior year in college. He had seen her name on the list of people who were going to attend the reunion and called because he thought it would be nice to catch up a little (on the past forty years) before they saw each other at the reunion. Hope told us that this was the only other relationship in her life that had been meaningful, aside from her marriage, and she had often thought of Allen over the years. She knew he was married, lived in Silver Springs, Maryland, and was practicing law in Washington, D.C. She was not aware that his wife had died two years before. Hope planned carefully for the reunion. She bought new clothes and lost the five pounds she had recently gained. She was not exactly sure why, but she told herself it was because of the many people she would be seeing after so many years.

Allen and Hope met again and found that it was as easy for them to talk as it had been so many years ago. They spent the whole weekend together, and Hope found herself sexually attracted for the first time in well over five years.

They began a courtship that was not without its problems. They had separate lives which needed to be integrated if the relationship was to have a future. But they were close enough geographically (Hope lived in Philadelphia) to be able to see each other often, and each visit brought them closer. They are now both sixty-nine years old, have been married for almost three years, and live in a small retirement community in Florida. Allen retired from his law practice and Hope gave up her work as well. She cannot believe so much time has passed, as it seems only a short while since the wedding, which was attended and happily celebrated by both families and their friends. Hope's son gave her away, her daughter was her matron of honor, and Allen's son was best man.

Hope had many adjustments to make in her retirement. She had been caretaker for a terminally ill husband, had survived the transition to widowhood, and then made an unexpected transition into a second marriage. She looks back to the time after Edgar's death when she believed her life was right on track, and she almost cannot comprehend the changes. She likes being married again and she loves Allen very much and cannot imagine being happy in any other way. They both like to live a quiet life and neither of them is very social, but they play golf together and are friendly with another couple with whom they play bridge. Hope was quick to point out to us that she had not changed—she still prefers her own company to that of anyone except for Allen—but she is also quick to tell others that life is there to take advantage of, if you are ready to do so.

There are no statistics available on remarriages in retirement. It is known there are more available women than men in the age group from sixty to eight-five, as women generally outlive their spouses. It is known too that men who have been married, particularly widowers, tend to remarry; while those in their forties and fifties tend to remarry women who are ten or more years younger, those in their sixties and seventies usually marry women closer to their age. This accounts for the many retired couples we spoke with who were happily involved in a second or third marriage. Like Hope and Allen, many of them had married people they had known earlier in their lives. Many had known each other previously as half of another couple and had come together when one responded to the need of the other in his or her bereavement.

There are many problems inherent in remarriage in retirement, not the least of them financial. Some pensions cease upon a remarriage, and estates may have to be worked out equitably when there are children and grandchildren to be considered. There may be an emotional reaction in the children, who often feel they should have a say when an older parent considers remarriage. Many widows we spoke with who had been caretakers for husbands felt they did not want to risk a repetition of that experience and so would never remarry. Some women were involved with long-term relationships, with spoken or unspoken commitments, but had made the decision not to marry due to financial considerations. Dating and relationships among the single retired population are commonplace, and another confirmation that retirement can be a new beginning.

For Hope, as for Anita, and even for Susan, a new world opened in retirement. They each discovered, as you can, that life is not over until you decide it is over.

XII

Summing Up

We're all in this together—by ourselves

LILY TOMLIN (B. 1939)

Sooner or later retirement will be an issue in every woman's life, whether directly in relation to the workplace or indirectly in relation to marriage, family, or friends. For many women, however, retirement is viewed as an indistinct paradox, near and distant, probable yet impossible to imagine.* I know all this because I had always believed I would work forever. Other people would retire; I might cut back my work schedule after a time, but retiring in the traditional sense was something I was sure I would never have to consider. About five years ago, retirement suddenly became my issue to consider. There were several reasons, having to do with my career, my husband, and my sister.

First my career. After thirty years in the field of social work (including twenty years as an administrator in a mental health center) I discovered that my optimism of earlier years, when I had hoped to make changes and make a difference, had begun to erode, and my enthusiasm was waning. Like other women, I too had been passed over in the workplace. Up until now I had

* D.C.-V.A.

always decided to continue. I had negotiated trade-offs over the years because the satisfaction of the job out weighed my anger and frustration. At this time of my life the trade-offs seemed no longer in my favor. While I had been working as an administrator in a mental health clinic, I had maintained a small private practice in psychotherapy and I decided to devote myself to this rather than continue in the administrative position. Although leaving administration meant working as a psychotherapist and supporting myself without the certainty of a weekly paycheck, the salary had become less important, for I no longer had the same needs as when my children were young. Both of my children are now living away from home and have established their own lives. I enjoy doing psychotherapy, and the work with my patients has been one of the most rewarding aspects of my career. I knew I was not ready to leave the workplace.

My husband Leonard is a psychologist, more than ten years older than I, and he has been semiretired for several years. I knew he planned to stop working, or at least cut back even further on his work schedule, while I continued at my job. We had often discussed how this would be arranged. He wanted to be able to able to spend January and February in a warmer climate than New Jersey's, and I agreed to commute when possible and visit him on alternate weekends. We began living with this arrangement in the mid-eighties, and the first four years fit well into our lifestyle. We had both been married before, and when we married eleven years ago we opted to keep our separate residences. We have never lived together for a full week unless we have been on vacation, so to work out an arrangement whereby we lived in different areas for two months was not as unusual as it might seem for another couple with a more traditional marriage.

During the fifth year of this retirement arrangement, January and February seemed to be longer than in previous years. Leonard had decided to spend time on the West Coast in a climate he prefers, and to visit his children who live there. It was impossible for me to commute or to spend long weekends in California, and although I planned an extended vacation for that year it was not the same; I missed him. That was the same year my sister Phyllis began to make plans to retire and move to Arizona. I realized I would need to make some changes in my life. Neither Leonard nor I wanted to be separated for the winter months, and I realized that if Phyllis moved it would be more difficult for me when he was away, for I would not have her companionship. Phyllis and Stan had made their retirement decision, and I knew that it was now my turn.

I was not then, nor am I now, ready to leave New York and relocate. It is Phyllis's hope that Leonard and I will make the Southwest our home as she and Stan have done. I would like to live closer to her, but I do not feel ready to be more than a short bus ride from New York City. Leonard wants to spend winters in a warmer climate and the summers in the East. I have begun to rearrange my work schedule, and this may ultimately work for us. Leonard and I will probably spend part of the winter in the Southwest, so we will not be separated for so long a time and Phyllis and I will be able to have more time together.

I am surprised to see my retirement plans forming. I had thought that my winter arrangement with Leonard would last forever. I still consider myself an independent woman and I know I can be content with periods of aloneness. As I began to reevaluate my husband's and my retirement future, however, I was surprised to learn that I am considering a partial change in how I will spend my time. I know I have not changed, but as I get older the months and years become more precious, and my needs and desires have changed.

I am now being forced to consider retirement as a viable option, but not in the traditional sense. The research we have done for this book convinced me it is time to redefine not only my retirement but retirement for women. It is only with a new definition that we may see more clearly the priorities, options, and opportunities of this important phase of life. With this new definition, I have begun to view retirement as a beginning, not as an end. It is not necessarily a time to stop working, but a time of change, perhaps a time to add a new context to one's life, an opportunity for a new future. I know now, because it is happening to me, that it is a time to rethink the cultural legacy that views retirement as a backdrop to old age. I caution myself not to confuse retirement with aging. When I view the future this way, the thirty years that are statistically probable for me open up with possibilities.

Planning for my retirement seems to require a good deal of my emotional strength. When I see it as a problem to be solved, as just another one of life's problems, then I can view it as an opportunity and an adventure. What I need to remember as I struggle with these decisions is that until now in many ways I have always sculpted my world. It is not always easy for me to remember this, for I am a woman who was young in the 1950's. I am a woman who had to learn that I need not look to others to tell me who I am and how I'm doing, that I could do things for myself, that if things were going to happen I could make them happen. I may not be able to do anything I want in the whole world, but I can think of anything I want. In the past I have made many decisions as to the direction I wanted my life to take. I may not always have been as effective as I wanted, but as I matured, I took advantage of many opportunities and options. Although I never became as powerful as I wanted in the workplace, I cannot be confused about this lack of full power because I do have power over my life. I must remember that I define who I am and I am not at the mercy of others and their opinions.

Phyllis and I have learned much about women from researching and writing this book. We found that many women do not give enough value to their creativity, courage, and competence. Women are still uncomfortable when they see themselves as needing power and having ambition. They still tend to look to others rather than themselves for their definition. As result, they lose sight of their many strengths and their capabilities. They, as I, however, have not been powerless when it comes to making substantial, meaningful life decisions. Women can no longer devalue themselves and their life experiences. Women do have strengths and capabilities, and they have adapted those strengths to current possibilities. Women have a lifetime of exceptional experiences which they can use if they can conceptualize what they have lived through and give it value.

Retirement is a new chance, a new beginning. We have tried to give you the tools with which to reexamine your life at this time, so that the myths of the past do not inhibit the potentials for your future. Retirement is a time to put a true value on your life experiences and to become aware of your accomplishments and your uniqueness. It is a time to rediscover your self-worth and adapt it to current possibilities. If you can become aware of who you are and where you have been, you can go forth with assurance, feelings of power, and a sense of well-being.

Resource Guide

RELOCATION

No matter how carefully you explore the idea of relocating, nothing takes the place of being there! It is probably quite unnecessary to tell you not to rely on the written word without checking it out for yourself, but keep in mind that you should be checking on the recommendations and enthusiasms of relatives and friends as well. One man's or woman's Garden of Eden is another's internment camp.

The books listed below will help you to structure and to intelligently limit your search, as most of them spell out the facilities available as well as the climate, the resources, and the costs of the particular areas. Research well before you make a decision.

The American Association of Retired Persons will send you a free packet of literature about retirement housing. It is available by mail from HO7, Program Department Correspondence Unit, A.A.R.P., 1909 K Street NW, Washington, D.C. 20049.

Boyer, Richard and Savageau, David. *Places Rated Retirement Guide*. Rand McNally & Company, 1988.

This book is organized as to the factors you may be considering when you make your relocation decision. The authors list and rate the cities they have selected for each factor: Climate and Terrain, Housing and Its Affordability, Money Matters, Crime, Health and Health Care, and Leisure Living. The final section gives cumulative ratings. Be careful that the edition you use is an up-to-date one, as so many things change (housing and crime particularly) in a very short period of time.

Ford, Norman, Contributing Author. *Consumer Guide: Best Rated Retirement Cities and Towns.* Publications International, Ltd.

With the use of charts and tables as well as a clear and specific text this book rates and discusses 100 retirement locations in the United States.

If you are contemplating retirement out of the United States, there are several resources on the library shelves, but none of them are as current as we would like. Some of the information such as climate is probably constant, but much of it in terms of expenses, crime, available housing and facilities should be personally researched by you for a more up-to-date picture.

Dickinson, Peter A. *Travel and Retirement Edens Abroad.* A.A.R.P., 1988.

Howells, John. *Choose Latin America.* Gateway Books, 1986.

Choose Mexico. Gateway Books, 1988.

Other Resources

There are some travel groups which now offer retirement preview tours to retirement cities in the sunbelt states and abroad. These tours give the traveler an opportunity to ask pertinent questions of businessmen and government officials in the area, and to experience a brief taste of life in the area involved.

In the United States: National Retirement Concepts, 1454 North Wieland Court, Chicago, IL 60610; 1-800-888-2312.

For trips abroad: Lifestyle Explorations, P. O. Box 57-6487, Modesto, CA. 95355; (209) 577-4081.

Some pre-retired and retired people told us they stayed at elder hostels in cities or areas which were of interest to them. This gave them an opportunity to check out the area at the same time they took the courses which interested them.

CARETAKING

There is little to no literature on the emotional aspects of spousal caretaking by or for older persons, except for several very personal records by women who have cared for their husbands with Alzheimer's Disease. There are some books, such as *Heartsounds* by Martha Lear, that address many of the emotional issues which are of importance when this situation occurs, but these are written more for women who have young children and jobs or careers which need time and attention. There are also few books which deal with the particular problems of retired persons who are caring for elderly parents or other family members.

The books listed below address several different aspects of the caretaking situation. One book gives comprehensive information on a new approach to caretaking, the continuing care community, and two books deal specifically with the problems of caretaking a parent. The Resource Section that follows the bibliography will probably be of more help if you are caring for an ill spouse.

The New York City Department for the Aging and the Brookdale Foundation. *Agendas For Action: The Aging Network Responds to Alzheimer's Disease*, 1986.

Overall description of the services available to Alzheimer's patients and their families through the New York City Alzheimer's Resource Center. This program, funded by the Brookdale Foundation with matching funds from the City of New York, provides direct services: referrals to diagnostic centers, to support groups, in-home services, and adult day care centers. It provides counseling on financial and legal management, and family and individual therapeutic counseling. It provides guidance on residential placement.

This informative book also includes information on the available resources in other areas of the United States, on a state-by-state basis.

The information provides a model for other cities to follow, as there is discussion on how the program was implemented with the cooperation of city, state and national agencies.

If you live in or near New York City this program is invaluable. If you do not live in the area and you are dealing with this problem, it can be a good source with which to begin to search for support.

Maclean, Helene. *Caring for Your Parents. A Sourcebook of Options and Solutions for Both Generations.* Doubleday and Company, Inc., 1987

The appendix, which is the last 100 pages of this book, gives a comprehensive guide, state by state, of resources and services for the aging and their families. There is good information on nursing homes, on home health care, and adult day care centers. The text of the book is comprehensive and intelligently written and is a good sourcebook. It does not speak specifically of older people caring for their parents and is actually geared more for the younger adult caretaker, who is not knowledgeable about many of the facets of aging. It is nevertheless a useful tool.

Raper, Ann Trueblood and Kalicki, Anne C., Editors. American Association of Homes for the Aging: *National Continuing Care Directory.* Scott, Foresman and Company, 1988.

Continuing care retirement communities are an alternative living arrangement for retired persons, which provide a structure and personnel to handle a caregiving situation for couples or singles should it arise during the retirement years. The plan allows residents to be independent, knowing that should short-term or long-term illness occur the nursing care is available to them in the community. This directory gives general information as well as a check list to determine your needs in relationship to the particular community you might be considering. It gives specific information on the various communities available in the United States.

Should you be considering this arrangement now or at any point in your retirement this is an extremely handy and informative guide.

Shulman, Bernard H., M.D. and Berman, Raeann. *How to Survive Your Aging Parents.* Surrey Books, Inc., 1988.

This book assumes a younger adult caretaker and therefore gives information on aging more mature caretakers may know first hand. This book does, however, address specifically many psychological and emotional issues which will invariably come up when the caretaking of parents is involved, no matter what the ages of the generations. It deals with guilt and family patterns, as well as with the more practical issues of home care and how to deal with memory loss. The advice is both intelligent and sensible, and the text is interestingly written, with anecdotes which illuminate the many possible problem situations.

Community Resources

Alzheimer's Disease and Related Disorders Assn., Inc.
70 East Lake Street, Chicago, IL 60601

Agencies on Aging
330 Independence Avenue, SW, Washington, D.C. 20001

Foundation for Hospice and Home Care
519 C Street, NE, Washington, D.C. 20002

National Association for Home Care
519 C Street, NE, Washington, D.C. 20002

You may contact these agencies at the addresses above, or check your phone book, as they may have local services or chapters in your home community. If so, this is the best place to start to look for support. The quality of the support will of course vary from community to community, and you should search for what will best suit your needs.

Do not overlook the volunteer programs and religious organizations which provide day care facilities, respite help for the caregiver, and noon meals for the home-bound. Catholic Charities and The Federation of Jewish Philanthropies are good sources of information and practical help for the elderly. Information is usually available in your local library or your local phone book. Do not overlook support groups for caretakers of patients with Alzheimer's Disease or Parkinson's disease or other progressive illnesses. These groups are often found in local mental health agencies or community centers. Or think about starting one if none is available in your area.

BEREAVEMENT

As we read the literature on grief it became apparent that most of the literature was directed to women who were widowed at a younger age than retirement. We chose the following books because they are specifically applicable in helping older women cope with losses.

Deits, Bob. *Life After Loss.* Fisher Books, 1988.
This book is a straightforward guide to many aspects of grief, with an accent on specific things to do to ease your pain while you are grieving. Of special interest to women in pre-retirement and retirement is the chapter on preparing for loss. This chapter confronts the conspiracy of silence about preparing for the death of a spouse. For the more enterprising woman who is not able to join an existing bereavement group, there is an excellent twelve-session outline for forming and running your own support group.

Di-Giulio, Robert C. *Beyond Widowhood.* The Free Press, 1989.
This book has a great deal of factual information about coping with grief. It is intellectual in style as it charts the stages of widowhood. The woman nearing retirement will be helped to

gain insight into her available strengths during this time by the recognition of what she has accomplished in her life. Of particular interest is the comprehensive section "Sources of Organized Support Groups" which includes organizations all over the country which you can contact for further information.

James, John W. and Cherry, Frank, *The Grief Recovery Handbook.* Harper and Row, 1988.
This book is an excellent addition to grief literature. It gives specific advice about things to do to recover from loss. It addresses such varied topics as understanding the way you have lived with the many losses in your life to disposing of the belongings of the person who has died. It is truly a step by step program for moving beyond loss.

Porcino, Jane. *Growing Older, Getting Better.* Addison-Wesley Publishing Company, 1983.
This is a comprehensive handbook which contains important information on the many aspects of the needs of older women. The book as a whole is of interest to women of pre-retirement and retirement age, and we highly recommend it as a general resource. Chapter Two gives excellent information and support for women both divorced and widowed. There is a comprehensive checklist on what women need to know in order to plan realistically for the time they are alone.

Staudachef, Carol. *Beyond Grief.* New Harbinger Publications, 1987.
The first three sections of this book offer comprehensive material on understanding grief and specifically surviving the loss of a spouse. In an easy-to-read style, the author focuses on the specific problems of the older widow and a variety of plans she can make for her future as a woman alone. The book also addresses important but not often discussed issues such as a woman's vulnerability to schemes and scams during widowhood.

FINANCES

When we spoke to women in pre-retirement it became apparent that they were all concerned about financial matters. Retired women and men are concerned that the income they have projected be sufficient to last the rest of their lives. Major pre-retirement financial decisions must be based on as much knowledge as can be gathered.

There are an enormous number of books on finances, financial planning, and investment. We have learned a lot about finances from reading these books. The best advice we can give you is not to make any investment until you fully understand it. If you cannot explain the investment and the reason you are putting your money into that particular vehicle . . . wait to invest. Keep your money in bank Certificates of Deposit rather than under your mattress until you feel sure of your investment decisions. If a financial advisor or a friend offers you advice, get a second and even a third opinion. Nobody who has managed their own or other people's money has the perfect answer for you. There are many good ways to invest your money, not just one way. Take your time before you invest.

We have chosen the following books because they are thorough, clear and concise and specifically relate to retirement issues. Read any or all, part or parts. They will help you make informed decisions.

Dunnan, Nancy. *Your Year-Round Investment Planner*. Harper and Row, 1988.
This book is a short, simple, informative investment handbook and guide, with an easy-to-read format. Each investment is evaluated for its particular purpose, whether it be tax implications or future income. The risk level and fees of each investment are considered. The information as to where to buy the financial product is clearly referenced. This book will help people in pre-retirement set goals and find investments to fulfill these goals.

Klott, Gary L. *The New York Times Complete Guide to Personal Investing.* Times Books, 1987.
This book is a comprehensive encyclopedia of investment information. The information is clear and straightforward and carefully explains the array of investments that confronts the average investor. It is of special interest to the pre-retiree, as well as those people already retired, for it can be used as a resource to understand basic financial matters in order to make informed decisions.

The New York Institute of Finance, "Guide to Investing," The New York Institute (Division of Simon and Schuster), 1987.
This book will acquaint the pre-retiree with specific information about brokerage firms. If you are a first time investor, as many retiring women may be, this book offers techniques to establish a good relationship with a brokerage house to enable you to feel more confident in your transactions. There is sound advice to help you define your goals and determine which investments are best for you in planning for your retirement.

Weaver, Peter, and Buchanan, Annette. *What to do with What You've Got: The Practical Guide to Money Management in Retirement.* Scott, Foresman and Company, 1984.
This book is an educational and public service project of the American Association of Retired Persons and is specifically directed toward the pre-retiree and those in retirement. It will help you arrange long– and short–term goals which will give you more control over your finances. There are helpful check lists about future budget projections and lists to help you make decisions before buying, selling, or moving from your present residence. Whether you choose to seek professional financial advice or prefer to assume responsibility for your finances, this book will help you establish an overall financial retirement strategy to help you arrive at creative sensible goals.

Index

About the Authors

Diana Cort-Van Arsdale graduated from New York University and from Columbia University School of Social Work. For 20 years she was a Clinic Director and faculty member of a large mental health clinic in New York City. She is currently in private practice of psychotherapy, specializing in the issues of older women.

In 1983 she and her husband founded Seniors Options Service, an agency that services the elderly and their families. It was through this agency that she became interested in the problems involved with retirement. She counseled seniors who were concerned with their own retirement issues at the same time they were handling the stressful situation of aging parents. She speaks on women's issues in the NYC area and conducts theme centered groups on emotional factors in retirement.

Since 1983 she has been listed in Who's Who in American Women. She has written a chapter for "The Encyclopedia of Private Practice," a definitive handbook for mental health practitioners, published by Gardner Press.

Phyllis Newman graduated from Cornell University's School of Industrial Labor Relations. Her first work experiences were in corporate life, and she was a teacher and psychologist with the New York City Board of Education for 23 years. In 1976 she earned her Master's Degree in Education and a Professional Diploma in Psychology from St. John's University in New York City.

She has been specializing in women's issues since 1976, when she worked with the Nassau County Office of Women's Services counseling displaced homemakers and women who were returning to the labor force after many years at home. As a psychologist in Nassau County, New York and in New York City she taught numerous assertiveness training seminars for older women and counseled women on pre-retirement issues.

In 1988 she and her husband retired and relocated to Green Valley, Arizona. She is currently running workshops and teaching adult education classes at Pima Community College in Tucson, Arizona.

Diana Cort-Van Arsdale and Phyllis Newman are sisters who have first-hand knowledge of the experience about which they are writing. They began their research when Phyllis began to contemplate retirement and quickly discovered the lack of information and emotional support on the subject. In their book and workshops they use their experiences to illuminate the problems, pitfalls and pleasures of this special time of a woman's life.